LET'S TAKE
THE KIDS!

INCLUDING

The Catskills

The Capital Region

The Adirondacks

Lake George

The Berkshires

Cooperstown

LET'S TAKE THE KIDS!

Great Places to Go in
New York's Hudson Valley

3rd Edition

Joanne Michaels

St. Martin's Griffin

New York

To Erik, *my favorite traveling companion and fellow adventurer,*
both in life and on the road, and **To Bobby,** *who showed me*
the meaning of caring

www.stmartins.com

Maps by Alan McKnight

Book design by Michelle McMillian

Library of Congress Cataloging-in-Publication Data

Michaels, Joanne, 1950–
    Let's take the kids! : great places to go in New York's Hudson Valley (includ-
ing the Catskills, the Capital Region, the Adirondacks, Lake George, the Berkshires, and Cooperstown) / Joanne Michaels.— 3rd ed.
        p. cm.
    Rev. ed. of: Let's take the kids! / Mary Barile.
    Includes index (page 287).
    ISBN 0-312-33664-0
    EAN 978-0312-33664-6
    1. Hudson River Valley (N.Y. and N.J.)—Guidebooks. 2. Children—
Travel—Hudson River Valley (N.Y. and N.J.)—Guidebooks. 3. Family
recreation—Hudson River Valley (N.Y. and N.J.)—Guidebooks. I. Barile,
Mary. Let's take the kids! II. Title.

F127.H8M534 2005
917.47'30444—dc22   2004060163

Third Edition: May 2005

10 9 8 7 6 5 4 3 2 1

Contents

Contents

Acknowledgments

It is impossible to thank everyone who helps in creating a travel book; for every tourism department head who answers a question, there are scores of office and administrative people who provide additional assistance, source material, and suggestions. So, a heartfelt thanks to everyone I spoke to throughout the region on my travels, and an extra-special thanks to the county tourism directors for their enthusiasm during my research and writing.

This book would have taken a lot longer to produce and would have been a lot less fun to write without the suggestions and patience of Tom Mercer, my editor.

I would like to acknowledge Michelle McMillian, without whom this book would not look as interesting as it does.

Jillian Laks, my research assistant, spent hours on the telephone obtaining information for this edition of the book, as well as helping to organize the voluminous material.

Dr. Joseph Appel's advice regarding the medical emergencies parents might encounter on a trip and how best to handle such situations is greatly appreciated.

And, of course, Erik Michaels-Ober was always willing to travel with me throughout the region, acting as the final arbiter of taste for this project in its first two editions. Now a college student, his excursions on research trips for this new edition have been limited, but his thoughtful suggestions have been invaluable.

Introduction

Traveling with children is an art: no matter how many trips you have taken on your own, once you put a car and a kid together, there is a whole new world to take into account. Food, travel time, boredom, rest stops must now all be considered and planned for, especially when you are heading for unfamiliar territory outside of your hometown. Since the first edition of this book appeared in 1990, I have answered literally thousands of questions about what to do with the kids outside the New York metropolitan area. Children will be enchanted by the variety of experiences to be found upstate. Rich with culture, history, and even some magic, the region has captured the imagination of writers, artists, and visitors alike for over three centuries. This is the land of Rip Van Winkle, and what child wouldn't want to stop by the bridge where Ichabod Crane outran the Headless Horseman? (You can visit the bridge in Tarrytown, Westchester County.) Wild animals still roam the land at the Catskill Game Farm, and Revolutionary War battles are still fought at the Old Stone Fort in Schoharie.

This book is not meant to be comprehensive. The attractions and activities selected for inclusion were chosen for their appeal to young travelers. The places featuring outdoor activities are those that are appropriate to people traveling with children: hiking and biking areas are flatter and geared toward the beginner or novice. Historic sites included are those that contain exhibits of interest to most youngsters. Occasionally, a resort is listed; just about all of these places have children's programs. Additionally, they offer an alternative way to explore a large area for travelers who want to stay in one place for a few days or a week at a time.

Let's Take the Kids! is organized by county and provides travelers with a tourism "loop" around the region. The counties follow the Hudson River northward, then west through the Catskills, north again to the capital district and Saratoga, and, finally, reaching the lower Adirondacks. For the Massachusetts section, the Berkshires have been given their own chapter. It would take at least a week to ten days to follow the New York loop in its physical entirety; and you couldn't possibly see all of the sights in this time. But you can use the book to plan day and weekend trips, as well as longer vacations, a fact that should appeal to teachers and scout leaders as well as parents.

For each of the sixteen geographical sections covered in the book, the county tourism Web site is provided. You can go online to check out accommodations and restaurants before you depart, as well as search listings of seasonal special events. Major annual celebrations and parades are noted in the entries for each site, but details about a variety of workshops, talks, and "happenings," and their exact dates are best found on Web site calendars.

When planning any excursion, be mindful that winter may be over in your neck of the woods, but often the snow doesn't melt until well into April in parts of northern New York State. Pack accordingly and remember to dress in layers.

This book was written from a car traveler's point of view, but you can get around certain areas by bus and train. If you want to plan a trip by train, call Amtrak, (800) USA-RAIL, for information; for bus transportation to the Catskills and Adirondacks, call Adirondack Trailways, (800) 858-8555. Both train and bus lines offer children's fares.

I have spent most of my life in the region covered by this book, and I remember many wonderful years exploring the area with my family and friends. Of course, things have changed since I was a kid—for the better, in many cases—and I hope that a new generation of travelers will enjoy discovering the wonder and magic of this diverse region as much as I have loved rediscovering it year after year.

BEFORE YOU HIT THE ROAD . . . A TO-DO LIST

The following thoughts evolved out of my experiences during trips throughout Upstate New York and the Berkshires, and while these tips may not solve all your travel concerns, I wish I had thought about most of them before I set out on my excursions away from home!

• **Map out your route ahead of time.** I traveled thousands of miles during my research trips, and much of the area is rural. One of the easiest things to do before you leave is to *call ahead*. Although I try to keep the material in this book up to date, activity times and locations do change on occasion, especially annual events and festivals. The telephone numbers provided here will put you in touch with someone at the business or site.

While the views are beautiful in this part of the world, you will find that sometimes, especially in the off-season, there are not many places to stop for restrooms or snacks. I advise making certain that there are several larger villages and towns on your itinerary; they nearly always have a restaurant or diner with public bathrooms. Finding such an oasis in a tiny hamlet on a Sunday evening can often be difficult and uncomfortable for everyone in the car.

I heartily recommend that you think about taking some of the older side roads, instead of the newer thruways and interstates. It is easier to stop if the kids see something of moving interest—like cows or sheep—and there are often clean, quiet picnic stops along such routes, as well.

- **Take along a good supply of snacks for the drive.** Unless you and the kids are thrilled with fast-food chains, bringing snacks will do three things: allow you to cut down on travel time (especially during summer lunch hours, which can be busy); help you stay within a travel budget (most food is overpriced at special events); and let you pack nutritious items for the kids. Don't forget to add a damp washcloth, a roll of paper towels, or towelettes to make cleanup easier.

- **Keep a collection of small toys and coloring books in the car.** This will keep even the youngest child happy for some of the time on a long drive, especially in areas where there is not much to watch for out the windows. I found that kids enjoy drawing pictures of what it is they are going to see: horses, houses, trains, boats.

- **Dress the kids in layers of clothing.** Much of the upstate region is mountainous, and wide temperature ranges can be expected year-round. Summer temperatures can go from the 90s or higher in the afternoon to the low 50s at night; spring and fall may range from the 70s to the 30s. Winter can bring below-zero temperatures and windy conditions. Don't forget hats and boots (sneakers are fine for dry, warm days, but not for mud and ice). If you are planning to spend time out in the fields picking fruits and vegetables at one of the many farms, bring hats, long-sleeved shirts, comfortable shoes, and sunscreen. River trips are always very windy, so bring along sweaters and scarves or hats, even on a balmy spring day.

• **Make sure each activity is appropriate for your child's age.** Because many places in this book are historic, there are some things you have to consider before you go, especially with very young children. Some sites are geared for all ages, and they allow kids to explore and participate in special hands-on areas; other sites are for looking only, and while kids are welcome, they are not allowed to touch anything. While I have tried to make this clear in each of the entries, if you are unsure about the appropriateness of a site for your children, call before you go and ask before you pay.

• **Find out about a tour before plunging ahead.** You know your child best, and while one five-year-old might enjoy a thirty-minute tour, another one may be tired after ten minutes. Most sites will allow adults who are not taking a tour to wait outside with children without charging them admission or will charge a reduced admission; if this fee isn't displayed at the ticket office, ask about it. Even if your child is well behaved and takes a tour, you may want to schedule a stop afterward at an amusement park or a nature center where kids are encouraged to participate in the activities. This prevents associating history with boredom, and lets parents see some adult-oriented sites on the outing.

• **If you are taking a group of children, bring along enough adults to keep the group supervised properly.** Many smaller sites are understaffed, and it is more pleasant for other visitors if your group is well behaved and stays together with the guide. If you are bringing more than six children to a site, it is wise to call before you go; some limit the number of visitors who can be accommodated and require special group reservations and fees.

- **During the winter months, always call before you go.** Outside of ski areas, many sites close down in the winter season (usually November through March) or offer limited hours at this time of year. The flip side is that many smaller sites will make special arrangements for a group in the off-season if they have enough advance notice. Parks and recreation areas are notorious for not listing winter hours in their brochures; if you like to spend time outdoors in the winter, call the park and ask about their hours before you set out.
- **Protect yourself and your family against Lyme disease.** Lyme disease is a critically important consideration when you are traveling with kids in a rural, wooded area. This tick-borne infection has spread throughout the Upstate New York and Berkshire regions (it is particularly a problem in Dutchess and Columbia Counties). If you are planning to hike or camp in wooded areas, check with your doctor or the local health department for information about this disease. Make sure you and your children wear long sleeves, tuck pants into socks, and check exposed areas of the skin for ticks at the end of the day. Dogs and cats can carry the ticks as well. Deer ticks are smaller than others and it is often difficult to see them on the skin.
- **Prepare for emergencies.** Dr. Joseph Appel, a pediatrician with Pine Street Pediatrics in Kingston, New York, suggests that parents create their own first-aid kit rather than purchase one that is prepackaged. Those that are ready-made are often more expensive and contain items most people probably wouldn't use. "When our family goes on a trip, we take acetaminophen (Tylenol), simple cold remedies, antibacterial ointment, adhesive bandages, and syrup of ipecac for infants."

In an emergency medical situation miles away from home, most people might not think of calling their primary care doctor.

Dr. Appel emphasizes that this is exactly what parents should do. "In almost all situations," he says, "there is time to wait for a call back from your doctor or pediatrician." In this way, you can explain the problem to your family doctor before making any medical decisions. "Use your primary doctor as a broker for the system," explains Dr. Appel. "I have had phone calls from Paris, Los Angeles, and other remote places." In his experience, there are many medical conditions perceived as emergencies that can be taken care of over the telephone.

If you are unable to reach your primary care doctor, Dr. Appel believes it is best to contact a local physician rather than relying on emergency room personnel. (Emergency rooms are often staffed by nonprimary-care physicans or specialists who are not always comfortable with children.) Dr. Appel suggests locating such a doctor by talking to locals whose judgment you trust, or by calling the emergency room and obtaining the names of local pediatricians. If there is a group practice, you may have luck reaching one of the physicians fairly quickly, since groups tend to have more extensive office hours than individuals.

Now that you have thought about what could go wrong on your trip, and have prepared for the possibility of such an event, as well as the inevitable minor inconveniences, you are ready to get in the car and start your journey. Don't forget to take this book with you . . . and enjoy!

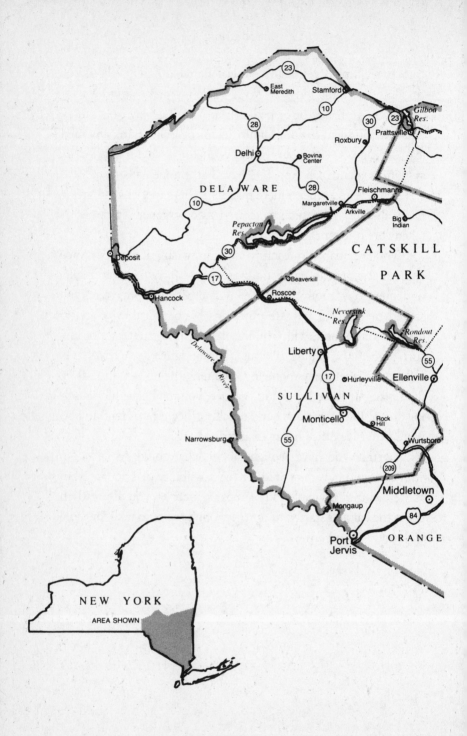

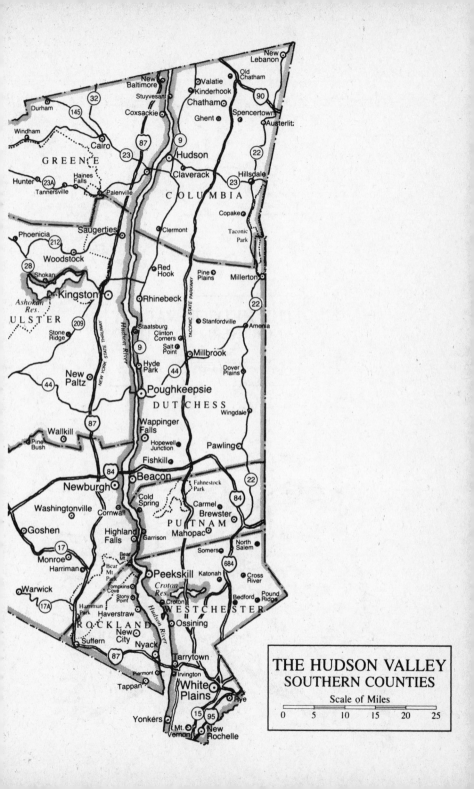

THE HUDSON VALLEY
SOUTHERN COUNTIES

Scale of Miles

0   5   10   15   20   25

AREA SHOWN

NEW YORK

THE HUDSON VALLEY
NORTHERN COUNTIES
Scale of Miles

0   5   10   15   20   25

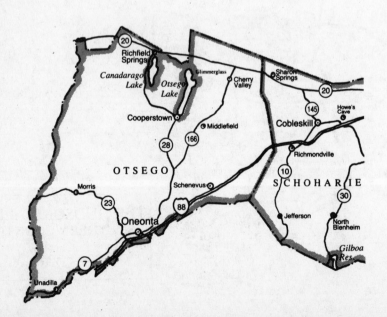

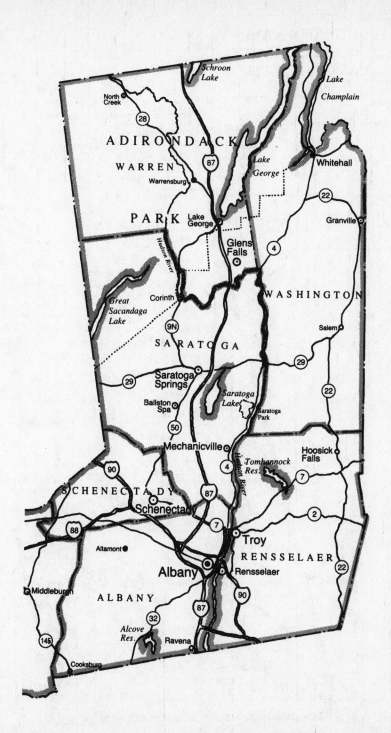

THE HUDSON VALLEY
BERKSHIRE COUNTY
MASSACHUSETTS
Scale of Miles
0   5   10

NEW YORK
AREA SHOWN

Williamstown   North Adams
New Ashford   Adams
Cheshire
Windsor
Dalton
Hancock Shaker Village   Pittsfield
BERKSHIRE
Lenox
Becket
Lee
Stockbridge
Great Barrington   Otis
South Egremont
Mt. Washington
Sheffield

Westchester County

Although Westchester borders New York City, the county is proud of its sixteen thousand acres of parkland and dozens of family-friendly facilities, including historic sites, nature preserves, and bicycle trails. Throughout the year there is an array of children's activities and special events just about everywhere—from sheepshearing at a seventeenth-century Dutch mill to a toy show at the busy County Center.

The following attractions are just a few highlights not to be missed on a visit to the county. **Rye Playland,** one of Westchester's most popular attractions and America's first planned amusement park, has been a family entertainment center since 1928. Three of the original rides are still in operation—the Ship, the Derby, and the Carousel, with its hand-carved horses. Washington Irving described the enchantment of Westchester in his short stories, immortalizing Tarrytown and the Headless Horseman. A visit to his home, **Sunnyside,** is well worthwhile to see the cozy "snuggery" where Irving wrote *The Legend of Sleepy Hollow.* Another special place to stop when traveling with children is the **Greenburgh Nature Center,** in Scarsdale. The youngest travelers may explore a hands-on discovery room containing more than one hundred exotic and local animals, along with a huge greenhouse containing many plants of the region. And don't leave without taking a self-guided nature tour.

Make sure to check for special events on the county's Web site before leaving on a trip to Westchester. Some of the best annual family events include: the White Plains Cherry Blossom Festival in Tibbits Park in May; the Great Hudson River Revival at Croton Point Park, and the Pinkster Festival at **Philipsburg Manor** (a cross-cultural celebration welcoming spring), both in June. **Van Cortlandt Manor** hosts eighteenth-century dinners on weekends throughout the month of August using historic recipes served by waiters in period costume, and November brings the Family Turkey Scavenger Hunt at the **Greenburgh Nature Center**. December's candlelight tours of the county's historic sites add a festive dimension to the holiday season for visitors of all ages.

For further information, contact: **Westchester County Office of Tourism,** 222 Mamaroneck Avenue, Suite 100, White Plains 10605; (914) 995-8500, (800) 833-WCVB; www.westchesterny.com.

What to See

MUSEUMS AND HISTORIC SITES

Hudson River Museum and Andrus Planetarium. 511 Warburton Avenue, Yonkers 10701; (914) 963-4550. The museum is open year-round Wednesday through Sunday noon to 5 P.M.; until 8 P.M. on Fridays. The planetarium is open year-round with one-hour public shows on Saturday and Sunday at 12:30, 1:30, 2:30, and 3:30 P.M. There is a free Friday night showing at 7 P.M. Call for information on group rates. Admission.

The museum, housed in an old mansion, offers an array of science exhibits and programs; most are family-oriented. Hudson Riverama, a permanent teaching gallery about the Hudson River, simulates the river's habitats and geographic areas with realistic scenic designs, interactive experiences, multimedia technology, aquariums, and a scale model of the river. Teachers should note that special tours and workshops are available, but reservations are required. There is also the unique **Red Grooms Bookstore,** a colorful shop where art, magic, and books come together for people of all ages.

The **Andrus Planetarium,** which adjoins the museum, is home to a state-of-the-art Zeiss M1015 Star Machine, a powerful scientific tool that can project thousands of stars and planets onto the planetarium's forty-foot dome ceiling. A quadrophonic sound system makes the planetarium the perfect setting for multimedia programs, which provide the chance to see stars, comets, constellations, and galaxies up close. The shows are accompanied by explanatory narratives that fit the season of the year and the age of the audience, from kindergarten to college. The planetarium also sponsors a series of free night observations in the summer in conjunction with local astronomy clubs and even birthday parties.

Facilities: *Restrooms. Gift shop is wheelchair and stroller accessible.*

Katonah Museum of Art. Route 22 at Jay Street, Katonah 10536; (914) 232-9555. Open Tuesday through Saturday 10 A.M. to 5 P.M., Wednesday until 8 P.M. (free after 5), Sunday noon to 5 P.M. Admission.

This lively teaching museum was founded in 1953 to display art of the past and present, and to foster arts education. There are exhibits by museum members, annual local studio tours, and changing displays, which may range from fashion designers to

Navajo rugs to modern art. Special events, shows, and children's programs are held year-round, and the museum is well worth a stop. There is also an outdoor sculpture garden.

Facilities: *Restrooms, gift shop. Strollers are easy to maneuver here.*

Lyndhurst. 635 South Broadway (Route 9), Tarrytown 10591; (914) 631-4481. Open mid-April through October, Tuesday through Sunday 10 A.M. to 5 P.M.; November through mid-April, weekends 10 A.M. to 3:30 P.M. Admission.

The term *Gothic revival* may bring to mind castles, turrets, and crenellations, but it won't prepare a visitor for the wealth and magnificence of Lyndhurst. Built in 1838 for William Paulding, a former New York City mayor, the house and grounds were enlarged by the Merritt family and were later owned by the notoriously wealthy Jay Gould. Much of the furniture, paintings, and decorative accessories are original to the mansion, which was owned by the Goulds until 1961 when it was given to the National Trust. The rooms are sumptuous—each is filled with rare furniture, artwork, and decorative pieces: Tiffany glass and windows are outstanding highlights. Youngsters will enjoy the gardens, a children's playhouse, a conservatory with intricate brick paths, and nature trails that meander among the dozens of different trees (many on the grounds are centuries old), ferns, and plantings. Call ahead to check on scheduled children's programs; the Halloween celebration is a wonderful fun-filled family event.

Facilities: *Restrooms, gift shop. Strollers are difficult to maneuver outside of the paved paths.*

Neuberger Museum of Art. Purchase College Campus, 735 Anderson Hill Road, Purchase 10577; (914) 251-6100. Open Tuesday through Friday 10 A.M. to 4 P.M., Saturday and Sunday 11 A.M. to 5 P.M., except national holidays.

This is a great place to introduce children to modern art and sculpture. Masterpieces by Avery, Hopper, O'Keeffe, Pollock, and others are displayed in several spacious galleries at this extraordinary teaching museum. There is also an impressive amount of African art, and selections from Nelson Rockefeller's collection of ancient art. An outdoor sculpture area with works by Henry Moore, Andy Goldsworthy, and Alexander Liberman should not be missed. This is one of the county's finest cultural resources, with sixteen rotating exhibits every year. The museum offers lectures, workshops, tours, performances, and concerts throughout the year.

Facilities: *Restrooms, gift shop, and café on the premises. Wheelchair and stroller accessible.*

St. Paul's Church National Historic Site. 897 South Columbus Avenue, Mt. Vernon 10550; (914) 667-4116. Open year-round Monday through Friday, 9 A.M. to 5 P.M., except for holidays. Free. Special weekend programs are held five to six times each year; call in advance. Groups and school tours are available by reservation. Church tours, leading to the historic 1758 bronze bell and a magnificent view, are offered Fridays at 3 P.M., from mid-April through early October.

Construction of the church (which was deconsecrated in 1978) was begun in 1763 and the interior has been restored to its 1787 appearance, with interesting high-walled box pews, and other decidedly historic features. During the Revolutionary War, it was used as a field hospital, and an exhibition preserves the appearance of the building during the war. The cemetery is one of New York's oldest, with legible headstones dating from 1704. Guided tours explore the historic church, the burial yard, the museum, and the remnant of the town common. Allow about an hour and a half for a tour. The museum features various exhibi-

tions on American and local history, and it includes special scavenger hunts, interactive activities, and historic toys for children.

Facilities: *Restrooms and water cooler. The museum is fully wheelchair and stroller accessible.*

Philipsburg Manor. Route 9, Sleepy Hollow 10591; (914) 631-
8200. Open March (weekends only) and April through December.
Closed Tuesdays, Thanksgiving, and Christmas. Open April through
October 10 A.M. to 5 P.M.; March, November, December 10 A.M. to
4 P.M. Admission (free for children under the age of five). Tours
available for students from March to December.

Philipsburg Manor was once a late seventeenth- early eighteenth-
century milling, farming, and trading complex owned by an
Anglo-Dutch family of merchants, tenanted by farmers of diverse
European backgrounds, and operated by enslaved Africans. The
site is of particular historical interest because of the size of the
enslaved community and the highly developed nature of this
eighteenth-century commercial property. Featuring a stone manor
house, the site also includes a working water-powered gristmill
and millpond, an eighteenth-century barn, a slave garden, and
a reconstructed tenant farmhouse. The grounds are home to cattle,
sheep, and chickens. Children are greeted by costumed interpreters after they cross the mill bridge. The mill is a crowded,
creaky place, full of noise and motion. Children delight as the
miller lets in the water to run the great grinding stones that transform wheat and corn into flour and meal (which can be purchased
on the spot). The manor house features a number of rooms with
touchable reproductions such as beaver pelts, milk buckets, and
iron pots. On the farm (depending on the time of day) children
can participate in farm chores, thresh wheat, watch a cow being
milked, and marvel at the team of oxen as they are hitched to their

cart. Colonial food preparation and textile production are explored in the Activity Center. Special events occur throughout the year. In April, Sheep to Shawl features border collie demonstrations, sheepshearing, wool dyeing, and hands-on activities for children. In May, drummers, dancers, and storytellers contribute to the festive atmosphere of Pinkster, an African-American celebration of the spring. The Green Corn Festival (Labor Day weekend) brings together Native American storytellers, dancing, and many activities for children, including cornhusk doll making, apple cider pressing, and colonial games. During Legend Weekend (late October), Philipsburg Manor is transformed into a haunted landscape that is "spooktacular" fun for children and adults of all ages.

Facilities: *Restrooms, picnic tables, small café, and gift shop.*

Sunnyside. 89 W. Sunnyside Lane, Tarrytown 10591; (914) 591-8763. Open weekends only in March from 10 A.M. to 4 P.M. (last tour at 3 P.M.). From April through October the site is open daily except Tuesday from 10 A.M. to 5 P.M. (last tour at 4 P.M.); in November and December, daily except Tuesday, from 10 A.M. to 4 P.M. (last tour at 3 P.M.). Closed January and February, Thanksgiving, Christmas, New Year's Day. Admission (free for children under the age of five). Children receive creativity totes free with admission. Tours available for students March through December. A reduced-fee, grounds-only pass is available.

Sunnyside was home to author Washington Irving, who described his charming house as being as "full of angles and corners as an old cocked hat." The creator of Ichabod Crane lived and worked at Sunnyside in the 1840s, and this is a fine place to introduce children to American literature. The house stands much as it did in Irving's time, with a graceful carriage drive and wisteria draped over the front door. Inside, costumed guides take visitors through this "cottage," which still has many of Irving's personal belongings, including his writing desk and piano. Although Irving never had children of his own, he did have nieces and nephews living with him, and several of the bedrooms reflect the children who stayed at Sunnyside. Younger visitors who are familiar with *The Legend of Sleepy Hollow* and *Rip Van Winkle* will be fascinated to learn that Ichabod Crane did, indeed, live in the neighborhood (Irving based the character on a neighbor) and that the ghostly hoofbeats are still heard on windy nights along the local roads. Outside the cottage, many walking paths offer lovely views of the Hudson, and there are several outbuildings to visit: the woodshed, the root cellar and milk room, the outhouses, and the icehouse among them. A graceful swan pond, which Irving dubbed the "Little Mediterranean," has picnic tables alongside and is a perfect spot for lunch in the summer. For kids who love trains, there are railroad tracks running next to the Hudson, and Amtrak trains can be seen (and heard) shooting by several times a day (earlier trains used to stop and pick up Mr. Irving for his trips to New York). Special events are held throughout the year, and many are especially for children. Past celebrations have included a Strawberry Fest, Independence Day, an ice-cream-making workshop, Apple Time, a nineteenth-century Thanksgiving dinner, and candlelight tours at Christmas. Teachers should note that there are many workshops for classes, but they have to call ahead.

Facilities: *Restrooms, picnic tables, gift shop with many lovely children's items. Parents with strollers will be fine on the grounds, but the house has some steep staircases; not recommended for wheelchairs. If accessibility is a problem, call ahead.*

Van Cortlandt Manor. South Riverside Avenue, Croton-on-Hudson 10520; (914) 271-8981. Open April through October, daily, except Tuesday 10 A.M. to 5 P.M.; November and December, weekends only 10 A.M. to 4 P.M. Closed January through March. Admission.

This manor originally consisted of 86,000 acres of land. The main floors of the present manor house were built in 1748; the

---

TARRYTOWN

After you finish touring Sunnyside, there are a few other places to see in the area. Make a stop at the **village park** on Route 9 in the center of Tarrytown. Markers show where Major André was captured during the Revolutionary War (he was Benedict Arnold's British contact), and a bridge over the stream where, according to legend, Ichabod Crane was carried away by the Headless Horseman.

The kids will also enjoy stopping at the **Old Dutch Church,** which was built in the late seventeenth century and still is used for services. Route 9, north of Tarrytown near Philipsburg Manor, on the right; watch for the parking area signs. Call (914) 631-1123 for church hours and guided tours of the cemetery. The cemetery, a national historic landmark, contains fascinating old tombstones (many in Dutch), which were decorated in the seventeenth century. Washington Irving's grave is here, and an old belief holds that the ghost of a headless Hessian soldier haunts the site.

You may want to call ahead for a tour of the **Tarrytown Lighthouse** (follow the signs from the center of town to Kingsland Point Park on the Hudson River, (914) 864-7177), which offers displays of logbooks, photos, and furnishings that illustrate what life was like in a lighthouse over the past hundred years. Even if you don't take a tour, the lighthouse and the Hudson River traffic are wonderful attractions for kids. The lighthouse is also the focus of several school- and group-centered tours and workshops; call for schedules and reservations.

house remained in the Van Cortlandt family until the middle of the twentieth century. The house reflects life in an eighteenth-century Dutch home. As supporters of the American Revolution, the Van Cortlandts were hosts to such luminaries as George Washington, Benjamin Franklin, and Marquis de Lafayette. Inside the house there is a blend of decorative styles and periods reflecting the history of the family. One impressive item is the fowling gun, a huge firearm that was fired into a flock of birds and reduced hunting time considerably. Outside, the gardens beckon flower lovers, and the Long Walk—a brick path that leads to the Ferry House, a nearby inn and tavern—wanders by well-maintained flower beds and herb gardens. Special events are held throughout the year. Animals and Acrobats, over the Memorial Day weekend, examines the birth of the American circus with a number of traditional performers such as jugglers, magicians, fortune-tellers, slack-rope walkers, and musicians. The July Fourth Celebration is complete with military re-enactors and a parade through the manor. There is Heritage Crafts over Columbus Day weekend, when children can try their hand at almost twenty-five vanishing skills like candle making and coopering. The Twelfth Night celebration on the weekends before and after Christmas in December, is a great time for candlelight tours, and here, the kids get to participate in them. A visit on weekends during the summer months includes several hands-on opportunities for all family members. There is brick making, blacksmithing, and a variety of children's games. At the Ferry House (also open for tours), kids will notice the familiar white-clay pipes—they were rented out once, with the ends broken off for each new smoker.

Facilities: *Restrooms, picnic tables, and gift shop.*

Yorktown Museum. 1974 Commerce Street, YCCC Building, Yorktown Heights 10598; (914) 962-2970. Open year-round

Tuesday noon to 4 P.M., Thursday 10 A.M. to 1 P.M., Sunday 1 to 4 P.M., other times by appointment. Admission is by donation for individuals; there is a small charge for prearranged group tours.

The Yorktown Museum, which contains five exhibit rooms, offers children a chance to look at daily life a century ago through a re-created Colonial two-room house filled with furniture from homes and settlements of northern Westchester's past. One of the best-known rooms is the Small World, where miniature houses and rooms enchant the viewer. The main attraction here is the Marjorie Johnson Victorian dollhouse, which is filled with tiny re-creations of furniture and furnishings. It is seven feet tall, has eight thousand hand-cut clapboards, a stonework base, and a resident ghost! The Railroad Room contains an operational scale model of the "Old Put" line as it came through Yorktown. Also included are many photographs and artifacts of the Old Put Railroad. In the Woodlands Room you can sit in a replica of a Mohegan village longhouse, see how corn was ground and what life was like for the Native Americans of the area. The Tool Room displays tools used during everyday activities from the eighteenth century. The museum also boasts a library/research room filled with local history and genealogical records. The three annually changing exhibits are displayed in Memory Lane. The museum is small and cozy. A gift shop has a large selection of miniatures, assorted items for the home and garden, and small toys for children.

Facilities: *Restrooms, changing area, gift shop. The building has an elevator and is wheelchair accessible.*

OTHER ATTRACTIONS

Greenburgh Nature Center. 99 Dromore Road, off Central Avenue, Scarsdale 10583; (914) 723-3470. The grounds are open every day from dawn until dusk; Nature Museum is open weekdays 9:30 A.M. to noon and 1 to 4:30 P.M.; Saturday and Sunday, 10 A.M. to 4:30 P.M., year-round. Admission. Groups welcome.

   The Greenburgh Nature Center, a thirty-three-acre oasis in the center of bustling Westchester's greenbelt system, offers a unique opportunity for families to discover nature together. Younger visitors will enjoy the Nature Museum, housed in a former mansion, which contains more than one hundred twenty exotic and local animals that can be handled by the children, along with a five-hundred-square-foot greenhouse that contains fascinating plants from around the world. It's a good place to introduce very young children to the natural world, which at the GNC includes short, marked walking nature trails, a pond, brook, rock outcroppings and glacial boulders, maple sugaring sites, an old apple orchard, and lots of different trees and ferns. Fifty-eight species of flowering plants are found here, which makes a spring or summer walk a nice outing for youngsters. Because the property is located along bird migration routes, you might see any of several dozen different songbirds in the woods. Over thirty species, including woodpeckers and nuthatches, can be seen year-round. The center also sponsors children-oriented special events on weekends and has hands-on exhibits and computer games. Seasonal holiday camps will keep kids busy with games, walks, and crafts that are nature related. There are chocolate egg hunts in the woods, mushroom walks, grape-picking parties, maple sugaring in March, Halloween day and night events for younger and older children, and seasonal fairs with live music on the lawn. Some classes are one session; others are scheduled on a once-a-week basis from month to month. Teachers and other group leaders should ask about the center's special programs geared to preschool, elementary, and upper-level age groups. Nature-related arts exhibits, which appeal to adults and older children, are also held throughout the year.

Facilities: *The restrooms, first-floor classrooms, and gift shop are wheelchair accessible. The main trail and walkways around the museum are stroller accessible.*

Muscoot Farm. Route 100, Somers 10589; (914) 864-7282. (From I-684, exit at the Cross River/Katonah exit, follow Route 35 west to the intersection with Route 100. Turn left and drive one mile to park entrance.) Open daily year-round, 10 A.M. to 4 P.M. Free admission. Group rates and tours available.

Now run by Westchester County, Muscoot Farm is a seven-hundred-acre farm built in 1885. This is a unique chance to visit a model farm of the late nineteenth century, when technical advances like electricity and indoor plumbing were just being introduced into the area. Younger children will be especially impressed with the multitude of farm life to be seen here. This is a working farm, with horses, cows, chickens, pigs, goats, sheep, and ducklings on the grounds. The farm is complete with outbuildings, such as corn cribs, an outhouse hidden by a grape arbor, a wagon shed with a fine transportation collection of antique wagons and sleighs, and a huge dairy barn. Throughout the farm, interpretive exhibits include farm tools, housewares, and hardware that was created in the farm's blacksmith shop. In the summer, the herb garden blooms with plants that were used in cooking and medications, and corn and other crops are still grown and harvested here, so what you see will depend upon the season in which you visit. The emphasis at Muscoot Farm is on "working," so visitors will see farm life in action: special programs may show the skills needed to be a blacksmith or a beekeeper on a farm, and often, there are hayrides to be enjoyed as well. Along with the farm, many acres of park can be explored along marked trails, which are home to beaver, raccoons, birds, and many wildflowers.

Facilities: *Restrooms, picnic area. Strollers can be maneuvered on the paths, but the farm can be muddy and slippery.*

Playland. Playland Parkway, off I-95, Rye 10580; (914) 925-2701. Different sections of the park are open year-round, although hours vary widely during the season, so call ahead. Open daily mid-May through Labor Day; weekends only in the month of September.

A true old-fashioned amusement park and National Historic Site, Rye's Playland is an architectural gem. Built in 1928, this was the first amusement park constructed according to a plan where recreational family fun was the focus. Fortunately, the park's family atmosphere and art-deco style are still here to be enjoyed. Set on the beaches of Long Island Sound, Playland offers a famous twelve-hundred-foot boardwalk, a swimming pool, gardens, a saltwater boating pond (paddleboats can be rented), a beach, and, of course, fifty rides and an amusement area. Seven original rides are still in use; among them are the carousel (with a rare carousel

If you are in Somers at Muscoot Farm on a Friday (2 to 4 P.M.), you may want to plan a stop at the **Historic Elephant Hotel,** now a town office building, located at the junction of Routes 100 and 202 in Somers; (914) 277-4977, free. The hotel itself was built by showman Hackaliah Bailey, who imported the first elephant, called Old Bet, to America circa 1805. Today, the third floor of the building houses a delightful circus exhibit arranged in five rooms. You will be treated to displays of circus memorabilia, posters, and a miniature big top. This is a stop for those interested in the history of circuses in America, which suits just about everyone. There is no wheelchair accessibility.

organ and painted horses), the Dragon Coaster (a rare wooden roller coaster), and the Derby Racer (horses zip around a track). Fireworks and special entertainment, including free musical revues, go on all summer; in winter, the three ice-skating rinks at Playland are open to the public.

What to Do

BICYCLING

Bicycle and Skate Sundays. (914) 185-PARK. From County Center in White Plains to Scarsdale Road in Yonkers, fourteen miles round-trip on the Bronx River Parkway; if your family loves bicycling, plan to take part in this activity, May through September, except holiday weekends, from 10 A.M. to 2 P.M., when the Bronx River Parkway is closed to vehicular traffic.

If you are a bicycle buff and would like to spend a Sunday teaching the kids to ride safely, Westchester sponsors this comfortable and convenient bike path. The parkway is well paved and relatively flat. You bring your own equipment for this ride, but hundreds of people take advantage of the program and all ages participate. The parkway is lined with flowering shrubs and trees in spring and summer. During the autumn months, the rides are a wonderful way to see the foliage while getting some exercise.

Briarcliff Peekskill Trailway. (914) 864-PARK. This county-owned linear park runs twelve miles from the town of Ossining to the Blue Mountain Reservation in Peekskill. **North County Trailway.** (914) 864-PARK. There are twenty-two miles of county-owned trail, running from Mount Pleasant north to the Putnam County Line in Yorktown. **South County Trailway.** (914) 864-

PARK. This 5.2-mile county-owned trail runs from Hastings to Elmsford. Call and request trail maps for the Bronx River Pathway, North County Trailway, South County Trailway, Briarcliff-Peekskill Trailway, and Old Croton Aqueduct State Historic Park, which have free bike paths that are open year-round. In-line skating is also welcome in these areas.

BOAT CRUISES

Hudson Highlands Cruises. (845) 534-7245. On the last Saturday of the month from May through October, the excursion boat *Commander* offers a three-hour narrated cruise to the Hudson Highlands, leaving Peekskill at 12:30 P.M. from Riverfront Park, passing West Point, Fort Montgomery, Garrison, Constitution Island, and the Bear Mountain Bridge. Advance reservations are required.

Hudson Valley Riverboat Tours. (914) 788-4000. Open May through October for Saturday afternoon (2 to 5 P.M.) and Sunday evening (5 to 8 P.M.) cruises plus Wednesdays in July and August. This historic refurbished paddle wheeler, *The River Queen*, sails on the Hudson from the Sixth Street dock in Verplanck. Northbound cruises pass Bear Mountain and West Point, while southbound cruises pass Croton Point Park. Advance reservations are required.

New York Waterway. (800) 53-FERRY. Enjoy special-theme sightseeing cruises up the Hudson River from New York City to Sleepy Hollow to visit Lyndhurst, Kykuit, Sunnyside, and Philipsburg Manor. A two-hour northbound Hudson River tour departs from and returns to Tarrytown on weekends and holidays, mid-May through October. Weekend getaway cruises leaving Saturday and returning Sunday are also available. Call for schedule and reservations.

HORSEBACK RIDING

River Ride Equestrian Center. 960A California Road, Eastchester 10707; (914) 633-0303. Open Wednesday through Sunday for both English and Western riding lessons. What makes this a nice stop is that there is a petting zoo on the premises that will enchant the youngest travelers.

ICE-SKATING

Edward J. Murray Memorial Skating Center. 348 Tuckahoe Road, Yonkers 10701; (914) 377-6469. The center is open Wednesday through Sunday for figure skating, speed skating, and ice hockey.

Hommocks Ice Arena. 140 Hommocks Road, Larchmont 10538; (914) 834-1069. The arena is open daily and offers both figure skating and ice hockey sessions. Call for the schedule.

New Roc City. LeCount Place, New Rochelle 10801; (914) 235-6200. This 500,000-square-foot entertainment complex has two ice rinks, a nineteen-screen megaplex theater, a giant-screen IMAX theater, restaurants, and the Sports Plus entertainment center with video, motion simulator, and virtual-reality games for all ages, as well as the Space Shot, a rooftop slingshot thrill ride.

Playland Ice Casino. Playland Parkway, Rye 10580; (914) 813-7059. There are three ice rinks open August through May; call for schedule of public sessions. The temperature here is always set at a comfortable level so that the youngest skaters will not feel too cold!

Westchester Skating Academy. 91 Fairview Park Drive, Elmsford 10523; (914) 347-8232. The academy has two NHL-size rinks with figure skating, ice hockey, and clinics. Daily public skating sessions.

PARKS

Blue Mountain Reservation. Welcher Avenue, Peekskill 10566; (914) 862-5275. Open year-round, 8 A.M. until dusk.

This lovely county park in northeastern Westchester offers a full range of year-round outdoor activities for youngsters. Summer brings lots of action, and groups who want to stay overnight can make arrangements to camp in the rustic lodge (available for rental year-round). There are also trails for hiking, a new playground, extensive picnic areas, and fishing ponds. In winter, the park has excellent cross-country ski trails and fine sledding hills.

Facilities: *Restrooms (wheelchair accessible), picnic tables. Strollers are difficult to maneuver off the paved paths.*

Cranberry Lake Preserve. Old Orchard Street off Route 22, North White Plains 10601; (914) 428-1005. Open year-round, 8 A.M. until dusk.

This beautiful preserve consists of 135 acres of unspoiled wetlands and hardwood forests. The park has a 10-acre pond with trails and boardwalks, so visitors can observe life in an aquatic habitat. You will also find fishing, cross-country ski trails, and hiking. A small lodge offers interpretive programs and seasonal exhibits that the kids will enjoy.

Facilities: *Restrooms, picnic tables. Strollers are difficult to maneuver off the paved areas.*

Croton Point Park. Croton Avenue (off Route 9), Croton-on-Hudson 10520; (914) 271-3293. Open year-round, 8 A.M. to dusk.

This park is located along the banks of the Hudson River and features a pool, canoe-launching area, recreation hall, and ball fields. The location is ideal for fishing, hiking, and picnicking. Cabins, lean-tos, and facilities for tents and trailers are also available. In mid-June the park is the site of the annual Hudson River Revival Festival, a lively celebration that includes a weekend of live music, an array of food vendors, and family entertainment.

Facilities: *Restrooms (wheelchair accessible), picnic areas.*

Rye Nature Center. 873 Boston Post Road, Rye 10580; (914) 967-5150. Open daily year-round, 9 A.M. to 5 P.M. A small nature center (under fifty acres), this is a nice stop for those traveling with very young children. The museum has exhibits of local plants and animals, and there are some mini-exhibits about nature. You can take the 2.5-mile walk, described in a guide available at the museum.

Facilities: *Restrooms, picnic area with tables.*

Teatown Lake Reservation. Spring Valley Road, Ossining 10562; (914) 762-2912. Take exit 134 off the Taconic, and then follow Grant's Lane to Spring Valley Road. Open daily year-round; museum open Tuesday through Saturday 9 A.M. to 5 P.M. Free.

This four-hundred-acre reservation has marked nature walks and hiking trails, a museum, and outdoor exhibits. Wildflowers are abundant in the spring, and there is an unusual selection of fences. Kids will enjoy watching the waterfowl and other animals at the large lake. Inside the museum are live exhibits of local plants and animals.

Facilities: *Restrooms, picnic area with tables.*

Ward Pound Ridge Reservation. Box 461, Cross River 10518; (914) 864-7317. From Interstate 684, take Cross River-Katonah exit 6, go east on Route 35 for four miles to Route 121 south; turn right and drive to entrance on your left. Open year-round, daily, 9 A.M. to dusk; Trailside Museum open Wednesday through Sunday, 9 A.M. to 5 P.M. Small park use charge. Group rates available; school visits to museum by appointment. Camping is on a first-come, first-served basis or by advance reservation (two-night minimum), and is allowed in the park's rustic shelters and tent sites.

A 4,700-acre park, Ward Pound Ridge Reservation is both a wildlife sanctuary and education center. It has thirty-five miles of hiking trails and was designated an Important Birding Area by the Audubon Society and was also named a Biodiversity Preserve by the Westchester County Parks Department. There are a variety of outdoor activities to be enjoyed here, including hiking, fishing in Cross River, camping, cross-country skiing on marked trails, and sledding in the Pell Hill area. In addition, the excellent **Trailside Nature Museum** features wildlife, nature and fossil exhibits (including the molar of a mastodon). A honeybee hive vibrates behind glass. Even the youngest children will enjoy participating in the special workshops and events that are often held at the park and museum. From late February to mid-March, activities include maple tapping programs, in which participants learn the mysteries of sap boiling, and bird walks to see hawks and other wild birds; in other seasons, there are dog shows and Revolutionary War battle reenactments. Just outside the museum is a half-acre wildflower garden, with more than one hundred kinds of wildflowers, all labeled; note that children must be accompanied by adults in this area. There is also a replica of an Algonquin wigwam.

Facilities: *Restrooms, picnic areas with tables and grills. Strollers* *can manage on the paths and in the museum; if wheelchair accessibility is a concern, call ahead.*

Westmoreland Sanctuary. Chestnut Ridge Road, Mount Kisco 10549; (914) 666-8448. Open year-round, Monday through Saturday 9 A.M. to 5 P.M., Sunday 10:30 A.M. to 5 P.M. Free, but fees are charged for some workshops and special events.

While the sanctuary is an active site with more than fifteen miles of walking and hiking trails, the special programs at the museum here are the biggest attractions for the younger visitor. A varied offering of classes, hikes, and workshops are held throughout the year, and include Building Bat Houses, birdsong identification walks, Earth Day celebrations, and even a search for the first ferns of spring. The bird-feeder-making workshop will intrigue preschoolers, as will the Sounds Around gatherings in the woods—you listen to the woods sounds with a naturalist who explains what it is you are hearing. A Halloween night hike and party enliven the fall, as does the Fall Festival (third Sunday in October), complete with sheepshearing, blacksmithing, spinning demonstrations, and petting zoo.

Inside the museum are displays of local animals and plants, along with descriptive exhibits about the area's history. It is best to call in advance and find out what is scheduled each weekend.

Facilities: *Restrooms, picnic area. Not recommended for strollers; if wheelchair accessibility is a concern, please call ahead and make special arrangements.*

PICK-YOUR-OWN FARMS

Outhouse Orchards. Hardscrabble Road, Croton Falls 10519; (914) 277-3188. This is a wonderful place to pick apples in the autumn or shop at the farm-stand store where there are fresh vegetables, jams, and other treats.

Wilkens Fruit and Fir Farm. 1335 White Hill Road, Yorktown 10598; (914) 245-5111. Open daily. Pick your own apples and peaches in season on weekends from 10 A.M. to 4:30 P.M. Choose and cut Christmas trees after Thanksgiving through mid-December, 10 A.M. to 4 P.M.

THEATER

Emelin Theater. 153 Library Lane, Mamaroneck 10543; (914) 698-0098. This performing arts center was an unusual gift to Westchester County from a local businessman; the money for the theater's construction was donated to the Mamaroneck Library. The Emelin, in operation for over thirty years, offers exceptional entertainment in eleven different series including drama, extensive family programs, folk, jazz, holiday performances, klezmer, bluegrass, and films. A children's series runs throughout the year, with most shows offered on weekends. Call for a schedule.

Northern Westchester Center for the Arts. 272 North Bedford Road, Mount Kisco 10549; (914) 241-6922. Open Monday through Friday 9 A.M. to 9 P.M.; Saturday and Sunday hours vary, so call ahead. There are changing art exhibits, concerts, recitals, and a poetry series. Art, dance, music, theater, and creative writing classes are offered year-round. Call in advance to get a schedule of activities for children.

Paramount Center for the Arts. 1008 Brown Street, Peekskill 10566; (914) 739-2333. This restored one-thousand-seat movie palace of the 1930s offers quality arts and entertainment, ranging from classical to pop music, comedy to drama, art exhibits and excellent children's programs. The theater's facade contains its original two-thousand-bulb marquee with running chase lights. Call for a schedule.

Westchester Broadway Theater. One Broadway Plaza, Elmsford 10523; (914) 592-2222. This is a terrific place to enjoy Broadway-caliber musical revivals in an intimate theater setting where every seat offers good views of the stage. There is a children's theater series; call in advance for the schedule.

UNUSUAL AND GREAT FOR A RAINY DAY

Come Out and Clay. 253 Mamaroneck Avenue, Mamaroneck 10543; (914) 777-3761. Open daily, except Monday, year-round, 11 A.M. to 7 P.M. For a small hourly fee, both children and adults can work together on a variety of projects that include painting, jewelry making, and mosaics. A pleasant, fun place for parents and children to connect creatively.

Westchester County Center. 198 Central Avenue, White Plains, 10606; (914) 995-1050. Take exit 5 off Interstate 287. If eastbound, follow Route 119, half mile to County Center on the left. If westbound, turn left at the end of the ramp and follow to the intersection with Route 119. There are several terrific shows all year at this multipurpose facility with forty thousand square feet of space. Make sure to check out the annual Toy & Train Show in February. Call for a schedule of events.

Rockland County

The incomparable beauty and charm of Rockland County offers pastoral countryside sprinkled with quaint villages, historic sites, and one of the world's most scenic river valleys chock-full of parks with fine recreational activities. One of the most popular family destinations in the county is **Bear Mountain State Park,** part of the Palisades Interstate Park System. This four-season outdoor wonderland offers visitors a multitude of outdoor recreation opportunities. There is also a wonderful zoo in the park, as well as a carousel housed in a stone-and-timber Adirondack-style building. **Rockland State Park,** another jewel in the crown of the Palisades Interstate Parks System, is a popular recreation area located at the base of Hook Mountain. In addition to hiking on lovely trails, families may enjoy swimming, fishing, and boating in the park, as well as special events throughout the summer season at the Nature Center. Don't miss **Stony Point Battlefield,** the mountaintop meadow where American troops defeated the British Redcoats; it's still very much as it was more than two hundred years ago. Kids will enjoy seeing the Stony Point Lighthouse and special events including dramatic military encampments held in the warm weather months.

Try to make time for a relaxing stop at **Dr. Davies Farm,** founded in 1881 by Dr. Lucy Meriweather Davies, a general practitioner who in her time delivered a significant part of Rockland's population, seven thousand babies. She was also a farmer with acreage in Congers and her descendants operate the farm there today. This family orchard is a wonderful place to pick apples in season or enjoy a picnic.

While touring Rockland, you will hear again and again the names of those who made history here and are still remembered in ceremonies and festivals throughout the county: George Washington, Benedict Arnold, John André, and even Captain Kidd! Make sure to take in a couple of the special events unique to the county. One of my favorites is the Nyack Springfest, an April weekend when the town becomes a huge street fair filled with family fun activities. The Family Music Festival, held every August in New City, will delight just about anyone. October brings the Halloween Parade in Nyack. And in December families will enjoy a visit to Piermont for its festive holiday open house, with tasty treats for the kids offered at the town's shops.

For further information, contact **Rockland County Tourism,** 18 New Hempstead Road, New City 10956; (845) 353-5533; (800) 295-5723; www.rockland.org.

What to See

MUSEUMS AND HISTORIC SITES

Haverstraw Brick Museum. 12 Main Street, Haverstraw 10927; (845) 947-3505. Open Wednesday and Sunday, 1 to 4 P.M. and by appointment. Small admission. The exhibits in this museum explain the century-old history of brick making in Haverstraw, once known as the brick-making capital of the world. Children who are interested in local history will particularly enjoy a stop here after exploring the town and waterfront.

Historical Society of Rockland County & Annual Dollhouse Show. 20 Zukor Road, New City 10956; (845) 634-9629. Open year-round, Tuesday through Friday, 9:30 A.M. to 5 P.M.; Saturday and Sunday, 1 to 5 P.M. Small admission. A modern museum featuring changing exhibits and children's programs throughout the year. The annual dollhouse exhibit will delight children who have an interest in that area; call ahead to find out dates. The Blauvelt House and Barn, built in 1832, are located on the museum grounds. Both structures have been restored and include period furnishings.

Stony Point Battlefield. Park Road off Route 9W, Stony Point 10980; (845) 786-2521. Admission. There are charges for some special events, and advance reservations are often required. Group tours are available with park rangers, but call ahead to make reservations. Open mid-April through October, Wednesday through Saturday 10 A.M. to 5 P.M.; closed Monday and Tuesday, except Memorial Day, Independence Day, and Labor Day.

General Anthony Wayne led his troops on a midnight raid here in 1779, and their victory over the British forces turned out to be one of the turning points of the American revolution. A walking tour of this beautiful but wild park allows visitors to see the remnants of the battlefield and its fortifications. If you don't take a guided tour, many trail and battlefield markers explain the movements of the troops during that fateful night. Costumed guides and staff members are often on hand to demonstrate cooking, camp life, and artillery skills. At the orientation center, a series of exhibits describe the history of the site. Popular with children is the Stony Point Lighthouse, the oldest lighthouse on the Hudson River, restored and open to the public. I recommend this site for older children who are fascinated by the American Revolution, although younger children will enjoy the military displays and musters that are offered on holidays throughout the summer and fall. One treat is the Fall Lantern Walk, in which children meet some of the officers who fought in the battle; the kids also have a chance to serve as judges at a court-martial.

Facilities: *Restrooms, picnic tables. Pets are not allowed. Strollers may be taken onto the battlefield.*

What to Do

BICYCLING

Both **Bear Mountain State Park** and **Harriman State Park** offer a number of excellent biking routes. However, both of these areas can become very congested on weekends. You will be better off at **Rockland Lake** or **Tallman State Park,** which both have paved bike paths. Another option is **Nyack Beach State Park,** located off Route 9W with access from Broadway in upper Nyack. This park runs along the river, and the paths are flat with fine views of the Hudson River. **Hook Mountain State Park** also has biking paths with scenic views of the Hudson. To get there, go east on North Broadway in Nyack; the park is located at the end of the road.

BOAT CRUISES

Hudson Highland Cruises. Haverstraw Marina, Haverstraw 10927; (845) 534-7245. The season runs from late May through October with Hudson River excursions aboard the *Commander*. Call for a schedule or wander down to the marina.

ICE-SKATING

Sport-o-Rama Ice Rinks. 18 College Road, Monsey 10952; (845) 356-3919. There are two indoor rinks here that have scheduled public sessions as well as full hockey and recreational figure skating programs year-round. Call for a schedule.

Palisades Center Mall. Route 59, West Nyack 10994; (845) 353-4855. The ice rink here will delight the kids year-round. There are both figure skating and hockey sessions, but the public sessions on weekend afternoons are a particularly "cool" spot to take the kids on a hot summer day.

PARKS

For a complete list of hiking spots call NY-NJ Trail Conference, (201) 512-9348 or www.nynjtc.org.

Bear Mountain State Park. Route 9W off the Palisades Interstate Parkway, Bear Mountain 10911; (845) 786-2701. Open year-round; call ahead for swimming schedules. Free, but there is a parking charge. Group tours accommodated by special reservation.

This huge park contains enough activities to fill a week of vacation time. Lovers of the outdoors will enjoy the hiking trails and views that are found around almost every turn. There are bike trails of varying lenghts suitable for all ages, a swimming pool, and lakes; paddleboats and rowboats may be rented during the summer. Even the youngest children will love the zoo, the beaver lodge, and the reptile house. Colorful birds, and fuzzy mammals in the forms of bears, fox, coyotes, and raccoons cavort in their zoo homes, while outside, the beavers busily chip away at trees and gambol in the waters near their winter lodge/log home. In the reptile house, face-to-face encounters with snakes and lizards will thrill adventurers of all ages. Note, however, that there is a lot of walking involved and it may take up to an hour to see the whole zoo complex; it's a good idea to bring a stroller for very young children. At the **Trailside Museum,** special exhibits explain the natural and human history of the park and surrounding areas. Ice-skating is offered from mid-October to early March (skates may be rented at the rink), and in December, don't forget to stop by the Holiday Festival, which offers a resident Santa Claus, a talking bear, carolers, and gingerbread house contests.

Facilities: *Restrooms, picnic tables, and gift shop. Diaper-changing facilities available. Strollers and wheelchairs can be used on the paved paths throughout the zoo and museum area. Pets are allowed (if leashed) in all areas except the zoo. The Bear Mountain Inn offers lunch and dinner, as well as overnight accomodations.*

Hook Mountain State Park and Nyack Beach Park. (845) 268-3020. Open year-round daily, dawn to dusk. Free. To reach Hook Mountain State Park, take North Broadway in Nyack east to the end and and follow the the signs. To reach Nyack Beach Park, take Route 9W from Broadway.

Hook Mountain was once referred to by the Dutch as Verdrietige ("Tedious") Hook because the winds could change rapidly and leave a boat adrift in the river. The area was also a favorite campground of Native Americans because of its wealth of oysters. For visitors today, the park provides a place to picnic, hike, bike, and enjoy scenic views of the Hudson. A hawk watch is held every spring and fall, and the park is said to be haunted by the ghost of the Guardian of the Mountain, a Native American medicine man who appears during the full moon each September and chants at the ancient harvest festival. Nyack Beach is open for swimming, hiking, fishing, and cross-country skiing in the winter; the views of the river are outstanding.

Facilities: *Restrooms and picnic tables.*

Rockland Lake State Park. Route 9W, Congers, 10920; (845) 268-3020. Open year-round. The Nature Center is closed November through April.

A park packed with lots of activities and open spaces, this is a great place to stop no matter what time of year it is. In the spring and summer, fishing, boating and swimming are popular, and a picnic is always suitable. The paved 3.2-mile loop along the lakeshore is great for walking, in-line skating, or biking. For fall and winter, pull on your hiking boots or grab your sled and head for the trails and hills. Also when the green flag is flying at parking field number six you can ice fish or ice-skate (no equipment rentals or bait available in the winter). The Nature Center offers many displays including two videos, "The Wild and Wonderful at Rockland Lake" and a film on the ice industry at Rockland Lake with actual ice-industry artifacts. Special nature-oriented events and guided tours begin here (call ahead for tour topics and hours: (845) 786-2701 ext. 293) during the warmer seasons. All the nature trails are easy to walk, even for young adventurers.

Facilities: *Restrooms, picnic tables; in the summers two adult and two child pools, snack stand, boat rentals, and bait shop.*

PICK-YOUR-OWN FARMS

Dr. Davies Farm. Route 304, Congers 10920; (845) 268-7020. One of the oldest pick-your-own farms in the county, open May through November, you can pick berries in the spring or apples and pumpkins in the fall, and select from a wide variety of produce and other goodies at the farm stand.

The Orchards at Concklin. South Mountain Road, Pomona 10970; (845) 354-0369. Open March through December. This farm has been in business since 1712. You can harvest your own fruits on weekends from 10 A.M. to 5 P.M., and pick a pumpkin at Halloween.

Van Ripers Farm. 121 College Road, Suffern 10901; (845) 352-0770. Open from May through Thanksgiving. You can pick raspberries in season, or select from a wide variety of fruits, vegetables, and bedding plants at the farm store.

THEATER

Helen Hayes Performing Arts Center. Playhouse Plaza, Main Street, Nyack 10960; (845) 358-6333. The Children's Theater here is first-rate, so it's worth calling or stopping by to get a schedule of events.

Palisades Center Mall IMAX Theater. 4270 Palisades Center Drive, West Nyack 10994; (845) 353-5555. A great place to go for indoor activities on a rainy day (or a beastly hot summer afternoon) is the IMAX Theater at this mall. The offerings continually change and you will find excellent family entertainment year-round.

Putnam County

From the magnificent views of the Hudson River in the west to the rolling hills of the east, Putnam County is a recreational wonderland. The county may be a small one, but it boasts two excellent state parks—Fahnestock and Hudson Highlands—as well as a ski area, Thunder Ridge. There are acres of wetlands, lakes, forests, and meadows here, a virtual paradise for families who love the outdoors. And after exploring the natural wonders of the region, a visit to the charming village of Cold Spring is a must. Kids will enjoy watching the trains go by at the depot in town, while enjoying an ice cream cone or chocolate chip cookie from one of the many eateries on Main Street.

A highlight of any trip to the county includes a stop at **Boscobel,** a Federal-style mansion in Garrison dating back to 1805, which has been restored to its former elegance. A spring walk through the gardens showcases thousands of flowers in full bloom, permeating the air with their lovely scent. Overlooking the Hudson River, this is a wonderful place to enjoy an outdoor concert, summer theater production, or a nature program.

In the town of Cold Spring, **Fahnestock State Park,** with nearly twelve thousand acres, has a lovely sandy beach area, boat rentals, and camping in the summer. There are wonderful places to picnic in the park, and special programs for children are offered throughout the year. This is an excellent destination for a day trip: the park offers a variety of activites that are sure to keep everyone in the family happy.

Try to coordinate a visit to Putnam with one of the county's outstanding annual events. In June kids will love the Circle of 1,000 Drums Festival at **Veterans Memorial Park** in Carmel; this multicultural event is geared to youngsters with drum making, games, music, and live entertainment. Also in Carmel is the county 4-H Fair with animals, exhibits, and lots of activites for children, held every July. And October ushers in spectacular fall foliage and a storytelling festival at Fahnestock State Park.

For further information, contact the **Putnam County Visitors Bureau,** 110 Old Route 6, Building 3, Carmel 10512; (845) 225-0381, (800) 470-4854; www.visitputnam.org.

What to See

MUSEUMS, HISTORIC SITES, AND OTHER PLACES OF INTEREST

Boscobel Restoration. Route 9D, Garrison-on-Hudson 10524; (914) 265-3638. Open April through December, daily except Tuesdays; closed Thanksgiving and Christmas Day; April through October, 9:30 A.M. to 5 P.M. (last tour is at 4:15 P.M.); November through December and March, 9:30 A.M. to 4 P.M. (last tour is at 3 P.M.). Admission. Group rates and school tours are available by advance reservation.

This magnificent New York Federal-style mansion on a bluff

high above the Hudson River was once sold for $35 to a demolition contractor, but local interest saved the house and restored it to its new magnificence, complete with Federal-style furniture and decoration. There are also breathtaking flower gardens. Older children who enjoy seeing "mansions" will appreciate the sweeping staircases and elegant interior, but we don't recommend the house tour for the younger set. Outside, however, everyone will want to walk through the rose and tulip plantings, watch the boats on the Hudson, visit the Orangerie (really a greenhouse) and the Gate House, a smaller, less pretentious nineteenth-century servants' home. There are seasonal programs and exhibitions of interest to both adults and children, including concerts, nature and gardening programs, and Christmas holiday candlelight tours. The Hudson Valley Shakespeare Festival is in residence during July and August each year, with regular performances. Discounts ranging from 10 to 25 percent are offered for groups of ten or more. Anyone can form a group. Call the festival office for more information at (845) 265-7858. There is also a summer Arts on the Hudson theater program for young people ages six to fifteen.

And after Boscobel, you may want to stop in the village of **Garrison Landing** and walk down to the bandstand on the Hudson River, where children's events are held throughout the summer. Children like seeing the river up close, and you can tell them that the bandstand was once a movie location: it was used in *Hello Dolly!*

Facilities: *Restrooms, picnic area, gift shop.*

Mahopac Farm. Route 6, Baldwin Place, Mahopac 10541; (845) 628-9298. Open daily April through October, 10 A.M. to 5 P.M. Small admission fee per family. This is a fun stop for kids of any age. There is a petting zoo, pony rides, and hayrides (in the autumn), as well as a variety of farm animals.

Facilities: *Restrooms, picnic area, gift shop.*

Manitoga/The Russel Wright Design Center. Route 9D, P.O. Box 249, Garrison 10524; (845) 424-3812. Open year-round; self-guided hikes are available on weekdays from 9 A.M. to 4 P.M.; April through October, on weekends from 10 A.M. to 6 P.M. Admission.

The name Manitoga is taken from the Algonquian word for "place of the spirit," and the philosophy of Manitoga lives up to its name. Here people and nature are meant to interact and visitors are encouraged to experience the harmony of their environment. Russel Wright, who designed the center, created a five-mile system of trails that focus on specific aspects of nature. The Morning Trail is especially beautiful early in the day; the Spring Trail introduces walkers to wildflowers; and the Blue Trail wanders over a brook and through a dramatic evergreen forest. (The trail system even hooks up with the Appalachian Trail.) This is a great stop for kids who like to walk and explore. You will find a full-sized reproduction of a Native American wigwam, which was constructed with traditional methods and tools. There are a variety of programs at the environmental learning center, so call before you go. Workshops are offered in art, photography, and botany, along with guided nature walks and music and dance concerts. Everyone will enjoy visiting Dragon Rock, the glass-walled cliff house built by Wright. Manitoga is a place where design and nature reflect and enhance each other, and it's a good place to demonstrate this to children.

Facilities: *Restrooms, gift shop.*

Southeast Museum. 67 Main Street, Brewster 10509; (845) 279-7500. Open April through December, Tuesday, Wednesday, Friday, and Saturday 10 A.M. to 4 P.M. Suggested donation.

This Victorian-style building houses a small museum with an eclectic local collection. There are permanent exhibits on the Borden Dairy Condensory (condensed milk was developed by a Putnam County resident), the construction of the Croton Water System (a project remarkable for its engineering innovations), the American circus, Harlem Line Railroad, and a large collection of minerals from area mines. The focus of this museum is local history, and kids who have a curiosity about their surroundings will enjoy the exhibits.

Facilities: *Restrooms.*

What to Do

KAYAKING AND HIKING

Hudson Valley Outfitters. 63 Main Street, Cold Spring 10516; (845) 265-0221. Open year-round daily from 11 A.M. to 6 P.M.; open at 9 A.M. on weekends. Complete packages are available to families from April through October for both kayaking and hiking. There are guided tours with certified guides, from beginner to advanced levels, with daily rentals of all equipment for both sports. This is an excellent place to go if you are thinking about organizing an active family outing but are unsure exactly where to go.

PARKS

Clarence Fahnestock Memorial State Park. 75 Mountain Laurel Lane, Cold Spring 10516; (845) 225-7207. Located off the Taconic Parkway at the Route 301 West exit. This park is open year-round and offers visitors seasonal camping, swimming, boating, fishing, hiking, cross-country skiing, snowshoeing, and sledding. The concentration of activities make it a great locale for a family outing. Several public programs are offered each year. Naturally Nocturnal, on a Saturday night in October, features astronomy presentations, night hikes, demonstrations of nocturnal adaptations and crafts for youngsters. WinterFest, on the first Sunday in February, celebrates winter sports such as snowshoeing, tubing, and ice fishing, and also offers bird walks and demonstrations of outdoor survival skills. Sap to Syrup in March is completely dedicated to maple sugaring and includes a pancake breakfast, demonstrations of methods used to make syrup and sugar, a country band, a blacksmith, and local craftspeople carding and spinning wool. A small donation is suggested to defray the cost of the programs, and food is available for purchase at all events.

Facilities: *Restrooms, swimming area, boat rental, and hiking trails.*

Taconic Outdoor Education Center (TOEC). Clarence Fahnestock Memorial State Park, 75 Mountain Laurel Lane, Cold Spring 10516; (845) 265-3773. The center is open year-round and is a place where schools, clubs, retreats, and scout groups immerse themselves in the outdoors. Day or residential trips are available by reservation, but not open for drop-in activities, except for certain public programs. Taconic Outdoor Education Center offers programs for groups of all ages.

The center is located on a large pond with varied terrain and habitats including mixed deciduous forest and wetlands. Wildlife is plentiful, and program participants may see or hear deer, owls, coyotes, small mammals, wild turkeys, many species of birds, and even bobcats. A wide range of environmental programs is available, including aquatic ecology (study of streams and wetlands), forest ecology (relationships between components of a forest), map and compass skills, mammal- and bird-watching, and outdoor skills. Night programs include stargazing and night walks in the woods.

Facilities: *Cabins, lodge, lake trails, and Project Adventure course.*

PICK-YOUR-OWN FARMS

Ryder Farm. Starr Ridge Road, Brewster 10509; (845) 279-3984, has 125 acres of organically grown raspberries on its pick-your-own family farm, in operation for over two hundred years. The farm is open August and September, but call for hours since the season is weather dependent.

SKIING

Thunder Ridge. Route 22 & 137 Birch Hill Road, Patterson 12563; (845) 878-4100. Open December through March, Monday through Thursday, 10 A.M. to 9 P.M.; Friday until 10 P.M.; Saturday from 9 A.M. to 10 P.M.; Sunday from 10 A.M. to 5 P.M.

This ski center is so close to the metropolitan area that those heading north won't hear the kids ask, "Are we there yet?" Located in the rolling hills of eastern Putnam County, the owners pride themselves on running a family-oriented mountain. Skiing at all levels and ages is welcome, from beginner to expert. There are thirty trails, three chairlifts, and one T-bar, and several slow, gentle slopes to meet the needs of the newest skiers and snowboarders. However, there are also advanced trails for the more adventurous. The ski school is dedicated to teaching the fundamentals; daily group lessons or six-week programs are offered for all levels of ability. Ski packages are available that include lessons, rentals, and lift tickets. There is snowmaking capability throughout the entire mountain, which makes for good conditions throughout the winter season.

Facilities: *Restrooms, cafeteria, full-service nursery, and baby-sitting services.*

Orange County

When Henry Hudson sailed his ship *Half Moon* up the Hudson River and into Cornwall Bay in 1609 he was the first explorer to arrive in Orange County, a place with a rich and interesting history. Today, museums, restorations, and educational exhibits are everywhere, from Native American displays in the **Goshen Courthouse** to the collection of military equipment at **West Point**. Moreover, children can watch a costumed group of interpreters reenact a battle that turned the tide of the revolution at the **New Windsor Cantonment**.

The county is rich in family attractions and the following are a few highlights. The **Museum of the Hudson Highlands** is a must for children who love wildlife. The indoor mini-zoo houses small animals and plants native to the Hudson Valley. **Museum Village** is restored like a typical midnineteenth-century village with over thirty-five buildings populated with costumed guides. Kids will enjoy watching the blacksmith hammer hot metal into a door latch, a weaver at her loom, housewives churning butter, and a potter making mugs at the wheel. The paved walkway to the Hudson River at **Newburgh Landing Waterfront** offers spectacular views of Bannerman Island, Storm King Mountain, Mount Beacon, and Newburgh Bay. There are several shops and places to enjoy a snack al fresco in the warm weather months.

Orange County is also a place where the agricultural heritage of New York State is still strong, where vegetable farming is a way of life for families and has been for generations. Make sure to visit one of the many farms and take home some fresh fruit and vegetables. Half the onions grown in the state come from the Black Dirt area in the southern part of the county. A drive through this unique farming district in early summer will show the kids what a bountiful harvest is all about.

When you plan a visit to Orange County, make sure to take in a couple of special events. The annual Riverfest in Cornwall-on-Hudson is held in June and features live entertainment, crafts, and children's activities. The **Harness Racing Museum** in Goshen sponsors a series of children's programs offering hands-on crafts projects on Saturday mornings. A popular annual tradition at **Sterling Forest** in **Tuxedo Park** on weekends in August and early September is the Renaissance Faire. Experience sixteenth-century England brought to life with hundreds of costumed characters, strolling minstrels, and storytellers in a Tudor-style marketplace with a living chessboard and horseback joust. Relax and watch the Renaissance world pass by, or walk through the site, which is filled with beautiful gardens and ponds.

For further information, contact **Orange County Tourism**, 30 Matthews Street, Suite 111, Goshen 10924; (845) 786-5003; www.orangetourism.org.

What to See

MUSEUMS AND HISTORIC SITES

Fort Montgomery Historic Site. Route 9W, just south of the USMA, Highland Falls 10928; (845) 786-2701, ext. 226. Open year-round from dawn until dusk. Free. This spot offers magnificent views of the Hudson River, interpretive signs describing the turning-point battle that occurred here centuries ago, and a pedestrian suspension bridge permitting access to nearby Fort Clinton and the Bear Mountain Zoo. It's a nice place to stop for an interesting walk that will appeal to the kids and yet also weave in some history.

Harness Racing Museum and Hall of Fame and Historic Track. 240 Main Street, Goshen 10924; (845) 294-6330/7542. Open year-round 10 A.M. to 6 P.M.; closed Thanksgiving, Christmas, and New Year's Day. Admission. Group tours by advance reservation.

Messenger and Hambletonian, pacers, trotters, and standard-breds—all call to mind the speed and grace to be found on a trotting track, and the history and color of the sport can be discovered at this unique museum established in 1951. Trotters and pacers (trotters move their right front and left rear legs at the same time; pacers move both legs on one side at the same time) have long been a part of American history. George Washington, Abraham Lincoln, and Ulysses S. Grant spent time breeding and racing these swift horses. At the museum, the history of the sport can be traced through a world of interactive exhibits. They can call and judge their own race. Three theaters also take you behind the scenes of this great sport. There are also several dioramas, prints, exhibits, and statues displayed throughout the former Good Time Stables building. Galleries include permanent displays of Currier and Ives prints, famous racing silks, and the amazing Hall of the Immortals, where dozens of small lifelike statues recall the greatest participants (both human and four-legged) in the sport. There are films and shows in the auditorium, changing gallery exhibits, and the world's only three-dimensional harness-racing simulator that makes you feel you are the driver in a race (the kids will enjoy feeling the wind blow through their hair!).

The Historic Track. (845) 294-5333, located directly behind the Harness Racing Museum and Hall of Fame (see above). This is the only sports facility in the country that is a National Historic Landmark; it has been hosting meets since the 1830s. Although the Grand Circuit races visit here only the first three Saturdays in June and over July Fourth weekend, the track is used as a training facility, so you may be able to see pacers, trotters, and a local blacksmith at work, no matter when you visit. The track is such a local institution that some of the private boxes have been passed down in families for generations.

    Facilities: *Restrooms, picnic facilities at the track. The gift shop is particularly worthwhile, especially for those who love horse memorabilia and souvenirs. The museum is completely wheelchair accessible.*

Karpeles Manuscript Library Museum. 94 Broadway, Newburgh 12550; (845) 569-4997. Open year-round Monday through Saturday, 10 A.M. to 4 P.M.; Sunday, noon to 4 P.M. Free. School groups from elementary to university level are welcome with advance notice.

    What were the first thoughts of our forefathers as they decided what freedoms and rights should be guaranteed in the Constitution? How many people are aware of the existence of a final Indian Peace Treaty signed by every tribe in the country and the president? An unusual museum, Karpeles Manuscript Library Museum contains original handwritten drafts, letters, and documents of historical significance in many fields. These works enable visitors to learn about historical events and people through primary sources. The manuscripts are classified by subject and exhibits travel between the nine other Karpeles Manuscript Museums in the United States. Exhibits relate to subjects like atomic energy, children's literature, history of flight, early baseball history, and a millennium retrospective featuring a collection of notable events over the last thousand years.

In addition to historical documents, there is a sizable display area that features an array of rotating art exhibits. Make sure to call about the schedule of children's workshops, which offer firsthand experience in the development and creation of historic manuscripts.

Facilities: *Restrooms; stroller and handicapped accessible.*

When you are in Newburgh exploring this museum and **Washington's Headquarters,** you may want to visit the retail establishment, **Commodore Chocolatier,** 482 Broadway, (845) 561-3960, where homemade ice cream and gourmet hand-dipped chocolate candies tempt hungry travelers of any age.

Museum of the Hudson Highlands. There are two locations, one in Cornwall and one in Cornwall-on-Hudson; (845) 534-5506. To find the **Museum at the Boulevard** where the live animals are, take Route 9W north or south to the Angola Road exit. Make a right to a rotary, then take the first right onto Hasbrouck Avenue. Follow to the end where it runs into "the Boulevard." Go straight for about one mile and the museum will be on the right. To find the **Museum at Kenridge Farm,** take Route 9W south and Kenridge Farm is the first right after the Angola Road exit. From 9W north, take the Angola Road exit, go to the left, back across Route 9W, and get onto 9W going south. Both facilities are open year-round. **The Museum at the Boulevard** is open Thursday through Saturday, 10 A.M. to 4 P.M. and Sunday noon to 4 P.M. The trails of the **Museum at Kenridge Farm** are open from dawn to dusk; the gallery is open on Saturday and Sunday from noon to 4 P.M. There are often special programs here so you may want to call in advance. Small admission.

The Museum at the Boulevard is an excellent site to visit with children who love wildlife and want to learn more about the lives and habitats of various animals. Often the changing exhibits in the smaller exhibit hall are also geared to children and nature. Upon entering the Hall of Animals, you will find an indoor mini-zoo that houses small animals native to the Hudson River region. Lots of amphibians, reptiles, small mammals, and birds crawl, creep and in the case of Edgar Allen Crow, talk, to the education and delight of the younger children. Outside this site and at the museum's other site at Kenridge Farm, you can take year-round nature walks over 250 acres of woodlands, meadows, and wetlands where old stone walls, ponds, and streams offer information about the natural world. The museum is also known for its summer camps which require preregistration, and weekend programs for families, which are open on a drop-in basis. Teachers will appreciate the environmental education classes offered to school groups ranging from preschoolers through middle school.

Facilities: *Restrooms, gift shop (featuring lots of nature items for adults and children; books as well as many nature guides), picnic tables. Strollers can navigate the Museum at the Boulevard and some of the trails at Kenridge Farm.*

Museum Village of Orange County. Museum Village Road, Monroe 10950; (845) 782-8247. (Exit 129, Route 17 west; watch for signs.) Open May through the first week in December, Wednesday through Sunday. Hours vary, although in general, they are 10 A.M. to 5 P.M. during the summer and until 2 P.M. in spring and late fall. Admission. Special rates for groups of twenty or more (advance reservations required).

Though we sometimes forget, America was once a rural nation, without electricity and modern conveniences. At the Museum Village, children can visit a re-creation of a typical crossroads village of the midnineteenth century. Many of the buildings were rescued from other parts of Orange County and moved to the village, where they now serve as working shops and houses. Children often enjoy visiting the wagon maker, the blacksmith (with a working forge), the schoolhouse, a log cabin homestead, and even the barbershop. The Natural History Museum houses a mastodon skeleton, and you can buy penny candy at the General Store. Craftspeople are at work throughout the site, and children are welcome to watch the costumed weaver, printer, and broom maker go about their businesses. Some are entranced by the taste of open-hearth cooking. This is a wonderful place to spend a day with kids, and teachers should note that the village has an extensive variety of special workshops.

Facilities: *Restrooms, picnic tables, snack stand, gift shop. The site is stroller friendly.*

New Windsor Cantonment. Box 207, Vails Gate 12584; (845) 561-1765. (From NYS Thruway exit 17, or I-84 exit 7S, take Route 300 south one and a half miles to Temple Hill Road; turn left, proceed approximately two miles.) Open mid-April through the last week in October, Wednesday through Saturday, 10 A.M. to

5 P.M.; Sundays 1 to 5 P.M. Open Memorial Day, Independence Day, and Labor Day. Admission. (A combination ticket provides admission to Knox's Headquarters in Vails Gate and Washington's Headquarters in Newburgh.) Groups welcome by advance reservation only.

This site portrays the everyday life of the soldiers in George Washington's army. The northern Continental Army spent the last days of the American Revolution at the Cantonment, where log huts housed the soldiers, officers, tradesmen, and camp followers. The tour starts at the visitors center, where there are exhibits on the life of the eighteenth-century soldier and the use of cannons during the Revolutionary War. (There is also a fascinating exhibit, for adults, of the history of the Purple Heart, which Washington established as the Badge of Military Merit.) Then it's down a wooden walkway to the site itself, where buildings have been reconstructed from old military plans. In fact, one of the buildings might be the only surviving structure from a Revolutionary War encampment. On any given day, costumed interpreters may be drilling on the parade ground, cooking food over an open fire, forging army equipment in the blacksmith shop, or playing a fife. Special events are held throughout the season, including concerts, a Kids Day with period games, a candlelight evening, and the annual encampment of the Brigade of the American Revolution.

Facilities: *Restrooms, picnic tables. Paths have gravel and are appropriate for strollers. An upper parking lot provides easier access for visitors in wheelchairs.*

Storm King Art Center. Old Pleasant Hill Road (just off Route 32 north; watch for signs), Mountainville 10953; (845) 534-3115. Open daily April through October, 11 A.M. to 5:30 P.M.; November 1 to 15, 11 A.M. to 5 P.M. Admission. Group tours available by advance reservation.

Situated in a five hundred-acre expanse, Storm King is an outdoor sculpture park. Within the small indoor museum and the outdoor area, more than ninety artists are represented, including David Smith, Alexander Calder, Louise Nevelson, Mark di Suvero, Andy Goldsworthy, Richard Serra, and Isamu Noguchi. Over one hundred twenty outdoor sculptures are situated along field and woodland walks. Older children will appreciate viewing modern art up close since there are few places where large sculptures are displayed in a natural environment. Unlike more conventional museums, Storm King's open landscape is liberating and provides a good way to introduce children of all ages to modern art. The views are magnificent, and kids enjoy exploring the grounds. Free self-guided tram tours. Family events.

Facilities: *Restrooms, picnic tables. This is a comfortable place for wheelchairs and strollers. Plan to bring a lunch and spend an hour or two.*

Washington's Headquarters. 84 Liberty Street, Newburgh 12550; (845) 562-1195. Open April through October, Wednesday through Saturday, 10 A.M. to 5 P.M.; Sunday 1 to 5 P.M. Limited winter hours; call in the off-season to make arrangements for group tours.

The end of the American Revolution was announced on the grounds of Jonathan Hasbrouck's stone mansion set on a bluff overlooking the Hudson River. Construction began in 1750 but was not finished until 1782, when Washington's troops added a gunpowder laboratory, a barracks, a privy, and a larger kitchen. Washington remained here for nearly a year and a half, waiting for the British to leave New York under the terms of surrender. The house and grounds were acquired by the government in 1848, and on opening day, July 4, 1850, Washington's headquarters became America's first National Historic Site.

In the adjacent museum, opened in 1910, is an exhibit called

"First in the Nation," which highlights the site's history of over one hundred and fifty years. The galleries here recall the events of 1882–83, including the establishment of the Badge of Military Merit, forerunner of the Purple Heart. A section of the chain and boom that was stretched across the Hudson at West Point, a life-size portrait of George Washington, and even a lock of his hair are just a few of the many fascinating items on display that will intrigue visitors of all ages.

The story of the Revolution comes alive inside Hasbrouck House, where visitors are guided through eight rooms in which Washington and his staff lived and worked. The dining room where George and Martha ate their meals still contains the original Dutch fireplace, open on three sides. The plain bedrooms and offices are sparsely furnished, and a field bed with its tentlike covering speaks clearly of the winter cold, while bedrooms show that not everyone was fortunate enough to have a room. The grounds are well kept and offer wide views up and down the Hudson. Special events are held throughout the year and include kite-flying days, Martha Washington's birthday celebration, and, of course, George Washington's birthday festivities.

Facilities: *Restrooms. Picnic area. Strollers can be used around the grounds, but you will have to carry them upstairs in the museum, and you may have problems with them in the Hasbrouck House. For vision-impaired and blind visitors, a Braille tour is available.*

West Point (United States Military Academy). Visitors Center, Pershing Center, West Point 10996; (845) 938-2638. Take Route 9W and follow signs. Open daily year-round 9 A.M. to 4:30 P.M.; closed Thanksgiving, Christmas, and New Year's Day. Free. Access to the grounds is by guided tour only, except for special events. Photographic identification is required for every visitor over the age of sixteen. Daily tours are on a first-come, first-served basis. Call the

visitors center for tour times. Group tours may be provided by
West Point Tours, (845) 446-4724. During certain times, such as
graduation week and home football games, tours are unavailable.

While most people know a little of West Point's history, a tour
of this historic military site is unlike any other you will take. West
Point has been a continuously operating military post since 1778
and a military academy since 1802. The tour of West Point, which
overlooks the Hudson River, will take you past historic buildings,
athletic facilities, monuments, and chapels. As you step on a bus
at the visitors center, you will be met by a knowldgeable tour
guide. Your first stop is the Cadet Chapel, a Gothic cathedral con-
secrated in 1910, with impressive stained-glass windows and the
largest church organ in the United States. Depending on the tour
you take, you will then either visit the West Point Cemetery—the
final resting place of over five thousand men and women who
have served their country and the home of the Old Cadet Chapel,
built in 1837—or go directly to the historic Trophy Point and
Plain areas. Trophy Point is home to Battle Monument, which
commemorates the Union Army's Civil War dead and is ringed by
large cannons. Also in the area are links of the chain that was
stretched across the river in order to stop the British from bringing their warships up the Hudson. You can enjoy the famous "million-dollar view" looking north up the river. Crossing the street,
from your seats alongside the historic Plain, the drilling field of
the *Long Gray Line,* you will learn about cadet life, see the super-
intendent's and dean's quarters, and view monuments commemorating Washington, Eisenhower, MacArthur, and Sylvanus Thayer,
father of the military academy.

Another must-see is the **West Point Museum**. Open daily
10:30 A.M. to 4:15 P.M., year-round. The museum is organized by
wars (Revolutionary, Civil War, etc.) and displays thousands of
items that appeal to younger viewers. Of particular interest are

the colorful uniforms, guns, cannons, tanks, and the display of an atomic bomb. The museum covers all of America's military history and it's a relatively painless way for children to learn about part of their heritage.

In the fall, you may wish to purchase tickets for a football game at Michie Stadium, (877) TIX-ARMY. Preceding the game, hundreds of cadets parade on the Plain in their dress uniforms, with music and military panoply. There is time for a tailgate picnic in the parking lot, and view of Fort Putnam, a partially restored Revolutionary War fortress. The football games are colorful with lots of excitement. This is one of the best football series in the Northeast.

Facilities: *Restrooms, gift shops. A restaurant in the Thayer Hotel on the grounds. Strollers are usable on the site, but you may have to deal with some hilly areas and graveled walkways. All buildings are wheelchair accessible.*

What to Do

BICYCLING

Orange County Bike Club. P.O. Box 122, Warwick 10990; (845) 457-6027. This club offers weekend rides (road biking with some mountain biking) year-round, as well as warm-weather weekday rides. The trips will appeal to all levels of riders and all ages. This is an excellent resource to check out before going on a family bike excursion in the county.

BOAT CRUISES

Hudson Highlands Cruises. P.O. Box 355, Cornwall-on-Hudson 12520; (845) 534-SAIL. Departing from West Point weekdays at

12:30 P.M. and the first Sunday of the month, a cruise on the *Commander* (on the National Register of Historic Places) with its narrated tour, offers a relaxing way to introduce youngsters to the scenic beauty of the river. There are floating classroom programs for schools by advance reservation.

Facilities: *Restrooms, snack bar.*

Hudson River Adventures. Newburgh Landing, Newburgh 12550; (845) 782-0685. Daily two-hour narrated cruises operate from May through October (call for schedule) aboard the *Pride of the Hudson*. On Friday, Saturday, and Sunday explore Bannerman's Island, which opened to the public in 2004. Customized cruises for school groups and camps can be made by advance reservation.

Facilities: *Restrooms, snack bar.*

River Rose Tours and Cruises. Newburgh Landing, Newburgh 12550; (845) 562-1067. Cruises available from mid-April through October aboard a New Orleans paddle boat with upper and lower decks.

Facilities: *Restrooms, snack bar.*

HIKING

Kenridge Farm. (See Museum of the Hudson Highlands, p. 43.)

Schunnemunk Mountain. Route 32, Mountainville 10953. There are six marked trails here ranging from 1.6 to 8 miles in length, and just about every trail affords spectacular views. This area is recommended for older children.

HORSE FARMS AND HORSE-DRAWN SLEIGH RIDES

Denman Farm. 219 Red Mills Road, Pine Bush 12566; (845) 744-7791. During the winter months, an excursion to this farm makes for a wonderful outing. Antique horse-drawn equipment is on display and in use. Enjoy an old-fashioned horse-drawn sleigh ride through the countryside. Group discounts available for schools and youth groups; all visits by advance reservation.

ICE-SKATING

Bear Mountain. Route 9W, Bear Mountain 10911; (845) 786-2701. Open mid-October to early March for public skating sessions. Admission (kids under five free). This outdoor rink is an excellent place for beginner and novice skaters. Rentals are available.

Ice Time Sports Complex. 21 Lakeside Road, Newburgh 12550; (845) 567-0005. Open year-round, but call for schedule of public sessions. The two Olympic-sized indoor ice rinks here offer a great place for family fun. Lessons, rentals and skating camp in the summer. There are lockers, a snack bar, a pro shop and a spacious seating area for spectators.

Fancher-Davidge Park. Lake Avenue, Middletown 10940; (845) 346-4180. Open to the public, weather permitting; free. This large lake with lots of room for hockey and family skating is located at the end of Lake Avenue. Call in advance to check conditions.

Mill Pond. Route 17M, Monroe 10950; (845) 782-8341. Open to the public, weather permitting; free. This small pond offers skating when a green flag is visible on the ice. When a red flag is up, the ice is unsafe. You can call in advance to check. This is a nice place to skate for those who prefer an outdoor venue.

PARKS

Algonquin Park. Powder Mill Road & Route 52, Newburgh 12550; (845) 561-1880. Open May through October during daylight hours. The twenty-seven acres of parkland include three ponds, a stream, picnic areas, and a children's playground. During the 1800s, this was the site of the only black gun powder manufacturing facility in the region, and there are many stone structures remaining from that time that may intrigue older children.

Kowawese Unique Area at Plum Point. Route 9W (across from Anthony's Pier 9), New Windsor 12551; (845) 457-4900. Open daily April through November, 8 A.M. to dusk. This one-hundred-two-acre park that runs along the Hudson River offers magnificent vistas and two thousand feet of sandy beach front.

Newburgh Landing. Front Street, Newburgh 12550; (845) 569-7300. Open daily year-round. This city park abuts the Hudson River and is the site of an array of annual festivals and events. It's a lovely place to hang out with the kids; and there are several restaurants along the waterfront offering a variety of fare. The landing area is completely paved, which makes it easy for strollers to negotiate. Scenic boat cruises leave from this area in the warm weather months, if you decide to take an excursion on the Hudson.

Orange County Park. 211 Route 416, Montgomery 12549; (845) 457-4949. Open 9 A.M. to dusk weekdays and holidays; 8:30 A.M.

to dusk on weekends. This park offers tennis, pedal and rowboat rentals on the lake, picnicking, fishing, playing fields and even an arboretum with lovely paths to stroll through. And there is snow tubing and cross-country skiing in the winter. A wonderful stop for a family picnic any time of year.

PICK-YOUR-OWN FARMS

Applewood Orchards. 82 Four Corners Road, Warwick 10990; (845) 986-1684. Open September and October for a combination of pick-your-own apples and pumpkins. There are also free wagon rides, puppet shows, an animal petting area, and a short nature walk.

Hodgson's Farm. 2290 Albany Post Road, Walden 12586; (845) 778-1432. Open May to Christmas, Friday through Sunday 10 A.M. to 5 P.M. Children will enjoy picking a variety of seasonal crops, as well as exploring the petting zoo. There are farm and greenhouse tours available. In the autumn there are hayrides and a haunted house.

Pine View Farm. 575 Jackson Avenue, New Windsor 12553; (845) 564-4111. Open weekends in December 9 A.M. to 4 P.M. Here you can cut your own balsam, Canaan, or Fraser fir; there are also blue, white, and Norway spruce trees. Candy canes, coloring books, and live animals will delight the kids.

SKIING

Mount Peter. Route 17A & Old Mt. Peter Road, Warwick 10990; (845) 986-4940. Open daily from about December through

March. This mountain has a vertical drop of four hundred feet, two double chairlifts, and eight downhill slopes for skiing and snowboarding. A good portion of the mountain is geared toward the beginner and novice skiier so it's a good place for families to enjoy the sport.

Facilities: *Restrooms, snack bar/cafeteria, ski school.*

Sterling Forest. Route 17A west, Tuxedo 10987; (800) 843-4414. Open daily, mid-December through mid-March with night skiing every day of the season. There is a vertical drop here of four hundred feet seviced by four double chairlifts on seven slopes. A relatively small ski area, Sterling Forest is an excellent choice for those with small children.

Facilities: *Restrooms, snack bar/cafeteria, ski school.*

SNOW TUBING

Thomas Bull Memorial Park. 211 Route 416, Montgomery 12549; (845) 457-4949. Open Friday, Saturday, and Sunday in season; call for hours. This is a wonderful spot if you want to try snow tubing. There are five groomed lanes with a rope tow. You can rent the specially designed tubes and there are stadium lights for the evening session. It's a beautiful spot, as well, with scenic views of the Shawangunk Mountains.

Facilities: *Restrooms in lodge with restaurant, bar, stone fireplace; adjacent area for cross-country skiing, sledding, and ice-skating.*

SWIMMING

Bear Mountain Pool & Harriman Beaches. Route 9W, Bear Mountain 10911; (845) 786-2701. Open from Memorial Day weekend through Labor Day. Admission. These swimming areas are ideal for those traveling with young children. A family-friendly atmosphere prevails, and all the services parents might need are at their fingertips. (Bear Mountain is located in both Rockland and Orange counties.)

Facilities: *Restrooms, lockers, restaurant, snack bar.*

Redwood Tennis and Swim Club. 620 Van Burenville Road, Middletown 10940; (845) 343-9478. Open daily, June through Labor Day weekend. Admission. The pool here is huge and it is located in a nine-acre recreation area with picnic tables as well as outdoor and indoor clay tennis courts.

THEATER

Eisenhower Hall Theater. 655 Ruger Road, USMA, West Point 10996; (845) 938-4159. There is an array of programs featured here including drama, dance, Broadway musicals, comedy, and children's theater. Call for a schedule of events if you will be in the area.

Paramount Theater. 17 South Street, Middletown 10940; (845) 346-4195. The theater offers several programs throughout the year in dance, drama, comedy, and children's productions. Call for a schedule of events.

Orange County Community College. 115 South Street, Middletown 10940; (845) 344-6222. There are music and dance performances, as well as films and plays, that would be of interest to young people, year-round. Call for a schedule of events.

UNUSUAL ATTRACTIONS

New York Renaissance Faire. Route 17A, Sterling Forest, Tuxedo 10987; (845) 351-5171, after June 1). Open late July through mid-September, weekends only. Call for exact dates and hours. Admission.

Knights and ladies, sorcerers and their apprentices, fools and varlets, bumpkins and wantons all gather on the glorious grounds of Sterling Forest to re-create the lusty days of a merry olde English fair. The festival runs for eight consecutive weekends and presents a colorful, noisy look at a distant period of time somewhere between King Arthur and Shakespeare. Falconers show off the skills of their birds; opera and Shakespeare are presented at the Globe Theater; Maid Marian flirts with Robin Hood; ladies dance beneath a maypole; and the extensive rose gardens are open for strolling. Craftspeople display and sell their wares (many belong to the Society for Anachronisms and stock things like chainmail shirts), and the aromas of "steak on a stake," mead, and cheese pie flavor the air. There are jugglers, knife throwers, mud fights, and a living chess game in which the "pieces" wander the gardens to their squares. The actors play their roles throughout the entire festival, so authenticity combines with the personal touch. Kids adore the noise and action and there is lots to see and do for everyone.

Sugar Loaf Village. Sugar Loaf 10981; (845) 469-9181. The village is reached from Route 17 west, exit 127; follow signs. Open year-round. Most shops are open Tuesday through Sunday from 11 A.M. to 5 P.M. Free.

Named for the local mountain that is shaped the way sugar was during Colonial times, Sugar Loaf has been the subject of unusual speculation. Originally the mountain was a Native American burial ground, and over the years various relics and bones have been uncovered there. Over thirty years ago, Sugar Loaf established itself as a leading craft village, and it now offers many shops and demonstrations by craftspeople at work. This is really a site for parents who want to shop but also would like their children to be amused. Most of the shops offer something for kids. Throughout the year, special events include concerts in the Lycian Center, a fall festival, and a Christmas caroling and candlelighting service (held the weekend before Christmas), when Santa visits and the village glows with an old-fashioned, small-town atmosphere. This is a fun holiday stop!

Facilities: *Public restroom in the Barnsider Tavern is wheelchair accessible. Parents with strollers should keep in mind that this is a small one-street town with sidewalks, and that you will have to fold and carry strollers in and out of many shops. Parking is at either end of the village in well-marked lots.*

Sullivan County

The unspoiled beauty and mystique of the Catskill Mountains of Sullivan County has made this area a popular family vacation destination for decades. Bordered on the west by the Delaware River, one of the best places in the state to canoe or kayak, the county is also chock-full of hundreds of pristine lakes and ponds for swimming. The rugged, untamed countryside here is home to the largest population of bald eagles in the eastern U.S. Renowned for excellent trout fishing by anglers throughout the world, the county is truly one thousand square miles of outdoor recreational opportunities.

There are a few musts for families traveling through Sullivan County. At the top of the list should be **Apple Pond Farming and Renewable Energy Center** in Callicoon. Kids will see horse-powered machinery, the bounty of organic farming, and a variety of renewable energy sources, including windmills. They can try their hand at activities like milking goats, and cheese and bread making. Another fun-filled, educational stop is the **Eagle Institute** in Barryville. On weekends from mid-December through March, when eagles migrate to Sullivan County from Canada, they can usually be found perching and flying to and from the ice and tree-line surrounding the lake here. Kids have an easy time spotting them. So don't forget the binoculars! **Fort Delaware** in Narrowsburg offers children a fascinating journey through the early American history of the upper Delaware River and the lives of the pioneers from the French and Indian War through the Revolution.

After sightseeing, Sullivan County's combination of outdoor activities and special events will delight everyone in the family. Kids will love taking a canoe trip on the Delaware River or a chance to try their hand at fishing. The Willowemoc and Beaverkill Rivers teem with trout, bass, shad, perch, and pickerel. The traditional opening of trout season is on April 1 at Junction Pool, Roscoe-Trout Town U.S.A. In July the city of Liberty stages a Civil War weekend where hundreds of reenactors transform Walnut Mountain Park into Union and Confederate battlefields. In August the Riverfest in Narrowsburg, a celebration of music and art, features crafts, live music, and a flotilla challenge. Kids will enjoy the excellent children's theater program on Saturday mornings at the Forestburgh Playhouse in Forestburgh. And any time of year, everyone in the family will enjoy a stop at the Bethel Woodstock Museum, home of the original 1969 music festival.

For further information, contact the **Sullivan County Visitors Association,** County Government Center, 100 North Street, Monticello 12701; (845) 794-3000, ext. 5010, (800) 882-CATS; www.scva.net.

What to See

MUSEUMS AND HISTORIC SITES

Bethel Woodstock Museum. The museum is located in the Bethel General Store, Route 55, Bethel 12720; (845) 583-4300. Open year-round, daily 10 A.M. to 5 P.M.; winter hours vary, so be sure to call before visiting. Free. This is the first and only museum of its kind at the home of the original 1969 music festival. Displays include photographs and articles from all over the world on events commemorating the concert over the past thirty-five-plus years. Woodstock aficionados of all ages will particularly enjoy making a stop here.

The actual Woodstock Festival Site is now part of Bethel Woods Center for the Arts, Hurd Road, Bethel 12720; (845) 295-2448 (not Woodstock, in Ulster County, which is over fifty miles away). This is where it happened; three days of peace, mud, and rock 'n' roll. A small monument marks the spot, and plenty of people stop and share stories. The area surrounding Bethel is beautiful, a nice place for a leisurely drive, a walk, or a picnic.

Catskill Fly-Fishing Center and Museum. P.O. Box 1295, Old Route 17, Livingston Manor 12758; (845) 439-4810. The museum and center are located on the Willowemoc Creek, between Roscoe (exit 94 from Route 17) and Livingston Manor (exit 96 from Route 17). The center is open every day year-round except Thanksgiving, Christmas, and New Year's Day. Call for hours, since they vary considerably by season. Demonstrations on weekends only in the summer. Admission. Special group tours by advance reservation.

This special site for fishermen of all ages is set in a beautiful spot on the world-famous Willowemoc Creek. This is the birthplace of fly-fishing in the United States, and it attracts sportspeople from all over the world to its pristine waters. The center was founded in 1978 as an educational resource, and today it carries on the tradition, offering classes in fly-typing and fly-fishing during July for eight- to sixteen-year-olds. Some of these workshops include overnight camping programs on the center's grounds, so Mom and Dad can fish while the kids learn about ecology and biology through hands-on experiments and classes. The museum contains continually changing exhibits about the lore and history of fly-fishing, and has entertained many famous anglers, including Jimmy and Rosalynn Carter. There are plenty of tackle shops in Roscoe and Livingston Manor, so you can outfit yourself and the kids for a day of fishing on the Willowemoc.

Facilities: *Restrooms. Strollers are easy to maneuver here, and the site is readily accessible to the disabled.*

Fort Delaware, Museum of Colonial History. Route 97, Narrowsburg 12764; (845) 252-6660. The museum is open weekends and holidays from Memorial Day weekend through June; the fort is open Wednesday through Sunday from the last week in June through Labor Day. Hours are 10 A.M. to 5:30 P.M. Closed Monday and Tuesday (except holidays). Admission. Group rates available.

Relive a part of New York's pioneer history at this re-creation of the first stockaded settlement in the upper Delaware Valley. Visitors to the fort will see life as it was during the mideighteenth century. This site reconstructs the everyday life of the average settler: no fancy houses, just log dwellings, an armory, blacksmith shop and animal pens, weaver's shed and fort. Costumed site interpreters around each area will explain the crafts and skills needed

to survive in the wilderness. Demonstrations are offered throughout the season, so children may see candle dipping, shingle making,
spinning, and musket and cannon firing. This site is particularly
appealing to young children, who have a chance to pretend they
are living in a wilderness fort in the days before Davy Crockett
and Daniel Boone. This rugged historic site is not the polished,
fancy restoration you see in places like Williamsburg, Virginia,
but this makes it even more appealing to the kids. Special events
held every weekend throughout the summer include Frontier
Living Days and a special military encampment, which is staffed
by members of the Fifth Connecticut Regiment of Continental
Life, a group that re-creates the daily life of soldiers and their
families.

Facilities: *Restrooms, picnic area outside fort, gift shop, snack bar.
Strollers can manage here, but you should call ahead if wheelchair
acessibility is a concern.*

Minisink Battleground Park. Located one mile northeast of State
Route 97 (recently designated as a Scenic Byway), at Minisink
Ford in the town of Highland on Route 168; (845) 794-3000, ext.
3066. Open mid-May through Columbus Day, 8 A.M. to dusk.
Free.

This fifty-seven-acre park is listed on the National Register and
is dedicated to the brave men who fought and died at the Battle of
Minisink, the upper Delaware's only major Revolutionary War
skirmish in 1779. The park features three self-guided trails of less
than two miles: the Battleground Trail, Woodland Trail, and the
Old Quarry Trail, which are mapped out in brochures available at
the information center.

This is an excellent place to combine history, nature study, and
hiking in a few hours of outdoor fun. Kids will be fascinated to

learn that this area was so wild and inaccessible that the bones of the dead were not collected for burial until nearly fifty years after the battle. The interpretive center contains displays that tell the story of the park and the trails, which wander through wetlands, fern gardens, berry patches, and rock shelters. The trails are great to walk with young children (over the age of five), since they are fairly flat and there are lots of interesting rocks and formations along the way.

Facilities: *Restrooms, picnic sites, picnic pavilion. Strollers and wheelchairs cannot maneuver through the trails.*

O & W Railway Museum. Routes 206 & Old Route 17, Roscoe 12776; (607) 498-4346/5500. Open Memorial Day weekend through Columbus Day from 11 A.M. to 3 P.M.; at other times, by advance reservation. Admission.

If you are stopping in Roscoe and your kids are train enthusiasts, this is a must. The O & W (Oswego & Weehauken) train line once ran from New Jersey northwest to Oswego on the shores of Lake Ontario. The museum complex contains a caboose at the site of the old Roscoe railroad station as well as a station building. The caboose contains changing displays of railroad memorabilia, and kids will have a chance to walk around a real red railroad ca-

---

Just across the street from the battleground entrance is the **Roebling's Suspension Bridge,** a National Historic Landmark built in 1848. This is the oldest suspension bridge in America. The wire cables were spun by hand on site, and the bridge was one of the few to ever carry a canal aqueduct above a river. The bridge has been restored and is open to visitors; the kids will enjoy being able to walk or drive into Pennsylvania.

boose. The station building has a self-operated model railroad kids can run on their own, as well as a theater that features an array of videos and slide shows describing the impact of the railroad on local history. On July fourth weekend there is always a parade and street fair in town as well as a colorful, fun-filled railroad festival.

Facilities: *Restrooms, gift shop.*

Sullivan County Museum. 265 Main Street, Hurleyville 12747; (845) 434-8044. Take Route 17 west to exit 100, then take Route 52 and follow signs to Hurleyville. Open year-round except January, Wednesday through Saturday from 10 A.M. to 4:30 P.M.; Sunday 1 to 4:30 P.M. Free. This small museum contains a great deal of local history and is very accessible to children who want to know what life was like in the nineteenth century. Dioramas with native animals, mining exhibits, railroads, and rafting all create a sense of living history in a not-too-formal museum setting. Old transportation vehicles in the form of trains and cars are on the site, as is a display of a general store. Children can also discover the story of Sullivan County's polar explorer, Frederick Albert Cook, who in addition to being a physician and anthropologist was the first American to travel to both the North and South Poles.

The town of Hurleyville itself is charming—a nice place to wander and enjoy art galleries, shops, and restaurants.

Facilities: *Restrooms.*

OTHER ATTRACTIONS

Apple Pond Farming and Renewable Energy Education Center. Box 371, 80 Hahn Road, Callicoon Center 12724; (945) 482-4764. Take the New York State Thruway to exit 16; pick up Route 17 west and go to exit 101, heading toward Ferndale. Make a right turn on Ferndale-Loomis Road; go another four miles and make a left onto Route 52 west. Continue for another six miles, and in Youngsville turn right onto Shandalee Road. Make a left turn on Stump Pond Road and then make another left onto Hahn Road. The farm is one mile up the road on the left. Watch for signs. Open daily year-round, 10 A.M. to 5 P.M. Admission. Groups can be accommodated by advance reservation.

This is a very special working farm and educational center. Much of the farm work is done by horsepower: all crops are grown organically, and most of the energy needs of the farm are provided by renewable energy including a wind turbine, solar thermal tubes, and photovoltaic panels. The tour begins with an explanation about how the farm works in harmony with the natural environment. The walking tour introduces children to the sheep, goats, and horses that are pastured next to the parking lot. The wind turbine, on a one-hundred-twenty-foot tower, is always within view, and as the tour progresses, the electric and solar thermal panels on the roof come into view. There is information on alternative energy sources available as the children visit the control area for renewable energy. Next comes a visit to the organic gardens where children can help make compost, learn to identify different kinds of foods and discover organic methods of growing crops. A visit the barn presents an opportunity for kids to milk one of the dairy goats and watch the horses being harnessed for the horse-drawn wagon ride. During the ride, children are treated to magnificent views. Sheep graze in the high meadows and some of the horse-drawn farming equipment is visible. The final part of the tour is a visit to the wool room where children try their hand at spinning wool and making bracelets to take home. Note that tours take a minimum of one hour and may be extended to two or more hours.

Facilities: *Restrooms, picnic area, gift shop with farm-made items such as wool hats and gloves. There is also a three-bedroom guest house on the premises that is available for rent.*

The Eagle Institute. P.O. Box 182, Barryville 12719; (845) 557-6162. Open weekends only, mid-December through March.

Sullivan County attracts more bald eagles than anywhere else on the East Coast, drawn by the open waters and virgin forests. Every winter more than one hundred eagles migrate here from

Covered Bridges. Sullivan County is well known for the surviving covered bridges that still span waterways throughout the county. Resembling small houses, the bridges are thought to have been covered with roofs for two reasons: to protect the timbers and to allow the horses and oxen that pulled the wagons to cross over the water without getting frightened. Some of the bridges are still in use, and children will enjoy seeing these remnants of old-time travel. At the Beaverkill State Campground, the **Beaverkill Bridge,** a lattice-type constructon, spans the river. Beaverkill State Campground is seven miles northwest of Livingston Manor on Johnston Hill Road. **Chestnut Creek Bridge** (from Route 55 north to Claryville Road) is a 128-foot long lattice bridge built in 1912 over the Neversink River. The **Livingston Manor Covered Bridge,** on County Road 179 north of Livingston Manor, is the county's only existing example of a Queen Truss bridge; it was built in 1860 and spans 103 feet over Willowemoc Creek. Also in the area is the **Willowemoc Bridge,** on Town Road 18, two miles west of Willowemoc, which hangs over the creek and was built by the same man who constructed the Livingston Manor Bridge. In 1913, this bridge, originally located at another site, was cut in half and moved to its present location.

Canada, and in the spring they return north. The county now has an information clearinghouse for eagle migratory and breeding data, and it is open to the public. On-site interpretive programs are offered on weekends during the winter months, when the eagles come south. The birds are sure to intrigue just about everyone, but children who have learned about eagles in school will particularly enjoy this stop. There are workshops, slide presentations, and guided eagle watches to habitat areas. Call ahead for schedule information. This is one of the few county attractions where winter is high season and it's a nice educational destination, as well.

Facilities: *Restrooms.*

Wurtsboro Airport. Route 209, Wurtsboro 12790; (845) 888-2791. Take Route 17 west to exit 113, then Route 209 north 3.5 miles to the airport. Open year-round, daily, 9 A.M. to 6 P.M. or dusk, whichever comes first, weather permitting. Free for observers; there is a charge for sailplane rides.

After visiting the airport, you may want to stop at the **Canal Towne Emporium,** Sullivan and Hudson Streets, in the town of Wurtsboro, a country store in a historic brick building that dates back to 1845. Open daily year-round, 10 A.M. to 5 P.M., the store was originally a dry-goods establishment near the Delaware & Hudson Canal. Now restored to its turn-of-the-century charm, the fixtures, furnishings, and equipment are all antiques, which include the first electric coffee mill ever used in the store, advertising prints, tins, and jars. Today the emporium sells furniture, handcrafted items, and decorative accessories, as well as books. The kids will enjoy the pickles and delicious penny candy!

Founded in 1927, this is the oldest place to go soaring in the United States. Visitors can take a ride in a sailplane, which is carried aloft by a Cessna tow plane, then released to soar quietly back to earth. For both adults and children who have flown before, the silence of sailplanes is relaxing and the closest you can get to flying like a bird. You can stay on the ground and watch the planes take off and land or sign up for a demonstration flight. The fifteen- to twenty-minute scenic rides over the Catskills are conducted by FAA-rated commercial pilots, who have lots of experience.

Facilities: *Restrooms (not wheelchair accessible). Snacks and drinks available in vending machines on the premises.*

What to Do

BICYCLING

Bicycle Club of Sullivan County. (845) 856-6899. Organized over thirty years ago, this club sponsors rides every weekend (usually on Saturday) from April through October. Many of the rides begin and end in Fallsburg, Liberty, and Neversink. Be aware that the county is rather hilly and that club excursions are advised only for older children who are enthusiastic bicyclists.

Lander's Mountain Biking Excursions. 5666 Route 97, Narrowsburg 12764; (800) 252-3925. If you are interested in taking a mountain biking trip along the Delaware River for a day, three days, or a week, this outfitter can make it happen and provide everything you will need from bicycles to tents. Such an outing is recommended for older children who have some biking experience.

CANOEING, KAYAKING, RAFTING
(RIVER TRIPS ON THE DELAWARE)

The Delaware River is the perfect place to canoe or kayak. It is wide and not too fast (it flows at about three miles an hour); the scenery is magnificent; and you can adjust the length of the trip as you like with many entry and exit points along the river. The Delaware is navigable from Hancock, New York, to Dingmans Ferry, Pennsylvania; it is now managed by the National Park Service—call (845) 252-3947 for information.

Sullivan County offers many places to rent canoes. As part of the standard retail package, you receive life jackets, a map, and pickup service along the river. The outfitters are accommodating, and there are many places where you can stop and rest or picnic. Anyone who takes a canoe trip must be able to swim. I recommend this kind of excursion for children over the age of ten, unless a younger child is very experienced on the water. Remember that the river has rapids and rocks and presents a more adventurous experience than a lake would. The best seasons are summer and early fall when the river is high enough without being flooded (the Delaware ranges in depth from two to five feet). Essentials for the river include a picnic lunch, liquids, and snacks, all packed in waterproof bags and containers. You should wear sneakers; in cooler weather, wear lightweight woolen clothes and always bring a change of clothing. Sun hats, sunscreen, and sunglasses will make you more comfortable. Don't let warnings scare you off: If you are new to river trips, tell the outfitter and he or she will suggest an appropriate journey, as well as show you how to maneuver. If you are experienced at paddling your own canoe or kayak, call the Upper Delaware River Conditions Information Line at (845) 252-7100 for the latest river report before you set out. The Delaware River can be dangerous during spring flood season.

Lander's Delaware River Trips (5666 Route 97, Narrowsburg 12764; (800) 252-3925), one of the largest outfitters on the river, offers rentals, overnight camping packages at four riverfront campgrounds, and shuttle service from twelve riverfront locations. They can arrange motel accommodations along the river for those who don't want to camp but who do want to paddle. Discounts are available for group outings. This company also offers rafting for adults and children over the age of five. With the rise in popularity of kayaking, they have also started offering tandem kayaks, a nice option for families to consider. **Kittatinny Canoes and Rafts** (102 Kittatinny Court, Dingmans Ferry, PA 18328; (800) FLOAT-KC) has sixty-four years of experience in providing quality service and equipment. Their seven bases are strategically located along the 135-mile river to ensure diverse trips and riverfront camping. There are day trips and calm-water trips for beginners, or overnights and whitewater trips for more advanced paddlers. Kittatinny has its own campgrounds along the river since much of the riverfront land is privately owned, it is sometimes difficult to find camping areas. They offer custom trips, groups discounts, and classes in canoeing and kayaking. **Cedar Rapids Kayak and Canoe Outfitters** (Cedar Rapids Inn, Barryville; (845) 557-6158) rents double and single kayaks, canoes, rafts, and tubes. There is also a nice riverside restaurant here, where you can enjoy refreshments and watch the fun from shore.

FISHING

Sullivan County is an angler's paradise and this part of the Catskills offers a broad selection of lakes, ponds, and streams to fish. The famed Willowemoc and Beaverkill streams produce prizewinning trout each year, augmenting the reputation of a county already known as the cradle of American fly-fishing.

All streams on state land are open to the public; other streams often have public fishing rights through state easements, which are clearly indicated by signs. New York State requires fishing licenses for anyone over the age of sixteen: these waters are patrolled quite well, and the fines for violations can be substantial. Licenses can be purchased at most tackle shops and town halls. You will receive a guide to fishing areas and a rule book when you purchase the license.

April 1 marks the opening day of fishing season, but in the Catskills, the weather can range from mild to snowy on that date, so dress accordingly. Sullivan County stocks three lakes: **Mongaup Falls Reservoir** (in Forestburgh, watch for signs), **Lake Huntington** (on Route 52 in Lake Huntington village), and **White Lake** (at the junction of Routes 17B and 55). If you want a real pioneer treat, try some shad fishing on the **Delaware River**— a good access point is Route 97, from Long Eddy to Barryville—in May and June: the run has been fished for over two hundred years.

Stream and river fishing present another challenge, and kids love casting from the sides of a willow-shaded bank; try the **Willowemoc** (Roscoe) and the **Basher Kill Marsh** (Routes 19 and 209 near Wurtsboro). If the kids have never fished before, you may want to spend the day in Roscoe, also known as Trout Town, which has everything you need, including tackle, licenses, information, and local fishing advice. One way to almost guarantee a catch is to try your cast at **Eldred Preserve** (Route 55, Eldred, (845) 557-8316), a private resort that opens its stocked ponds to the public for fishing. You pay both an admission fee and a per-pound price for the fish you catch, but because this is private property, a fishing license is not required. If you don't catch anything, schedule a stop at the **Catskill State Fish Hatchery**. Exit 96 off Route 17, Mongaup Road, DeBruce; (845) 439-4328. Open daily year-round from 8:30 A.M. to 4 P.M.; open until noon on weekends and holidays, July through September. More than 750,000 trout are raised here for stocking rivers and lakes throughout the state, and a series of hatching ponds holds the fish. Tours are available for groups with advance notice. Be aware that there are no public restrooms here.

PARKS

Lake Superior State Park. Dr. Duggan Road, Bethel 12720; (845) 794-3000, ext. 3066. The beach area is open from Memorial Day weekend through Labor Day from 11 A.M. to 7 P.M.; it is open weekends only through late June. The rest of the park is open from 8 A.M. to dusk. There is an admission fee at beach area only.

This beautiful 1,409-acre park is part of the Palisades Interstate Park System and provides families with a lovely stop in the summer. The sandy beach fronts the lake where there are boat rentals and abundant areas to picnic.

Facilities: *Restrooms, bathhouse, food concession, picnic areas, group picnic pavilion (fee charged), boat launch (electric trolling motors only).*

Mongaup Pond Public Campground and Day Use Area. 231 Mongaup/Fish Hatchery Road, Livingston Manor 12758; (845) 439-4233. Take exit 96 off Route 17 west; go seven miles northeast to DeBruce; then three miles north of DeBruce in the State Forest Preserve, and follow signs to the site. Open daily mid-May through Columbus Day, 9 A.M. to dusk. Admission. Groups accommodated; campsites available by reservation—call (800) 456-CAMP.

Located in the State Forest Preserve, this 275-acre facility is one of the nicest, most scenic recreation areas in the county for children. A small sandy beach lines Mongaup Pond, on a 120-acre site, where you can rent a rowboat, fish, swim, or build sand castles. Shady areas make this a comfortable beach, and when you are tired of water activities, you can hike and camp. The hiking trails are well marked and range in length from under a mile to several miles. This is a fine place to take young children for the day and keep them busy with outdoor activities. There are picnic areas with barbecue pits for day use and complete campsites with hookups for overnight use.

Facilities: *Restrooms, picnic area, overnight campsites (by reservation only). There are snowmobile trails for use in the winter months.*

Stone Arch Bridge Historical Park. Route 52, Kenoza Lake 12750. Open year-round from dawn until dusk. Free.

This three-arched stone bridge, spanning Callicoon Creek, is the only remaining one of its kind in America. Built in 1872 by two German stonemasons, the bridge was constructed from local stone and is supported without an outer structure. The bridge replaced an earlier wooden span that collapsed from the weight of continual use by heavy wagons. The Stone Arch Bridge became renowned for its unusual construction as well as for a murder that occurred near it in 1892. A local farmer, believing that his brother-in-law had put a curse on him, convinced his son to kill his brother-in-law. The young man committed the murder and dumped the body into the river near the bridge. Today, travelers fish from the banks of the creek, picnic on the grass, or stroll through the nine-acre landscaped park. Children will enjoy the small play area and nature trails.

Facilities: *Portable toilets, picnic area.*

SKIING

Holiday Mountain. 99 Holiday Mountain Road, Monticello 12701; (845) 796-3161. Exit 107 off Route 17 at Bridgeville. Open mid-December through mid-March, 9 A.M. to 9 P.M. on weekends; noon to 9 P.M. on weekdays.

There are fifteen slopes for all abilities at this family-oriented ski center. The vertical drop is four hundred feet, with 100 percent of the runs covered by snow-making capability, and the longest run is 3,500 feet. (There is also a cross-country skiing area.) Skiers and snowboarders of all abilities will enjoy the slopes here. The Winter Carnival in late February features snow softball, snow golf, a ski tug-of-war, hayrides, clowns, a pancake breakfast, and a chicken barbecue. Note that there is no nursery for the youngest children.

Facilities: *Restrooms, cafeteria, lounge, ski school, ski shop. Rentals available.*

Hanofee Park (off Route 52 east, Liberty 12754; (845) 292-7690) has one hundred ten acres of cross-country trails and offers rentals and lessons for all ages and abilities. The park is open daily 10 A.M. to 4 P.M., but the heated trail house is open on weekends only.

Town of Thompson Park (Old Liberty Road, Monticello 12701; (845) 796-3161, four miles past the Monticello post office) has trails throughout one hundred and sixty acres of parkland and is open from dawn to dusk. There are no facilities and you must bring all your own equipment if you want to ski here.

THEATER

Forestburgh Playhouse. 39 Forestburgh Road, Forestburgh 12777; (845) 794-1194. Open from late June through Labor Day. This summer-stock theater housed in a one-hundred-thirty-year-old barn offers drama, comedies, musicals, and children's theater. Call for the schedule in season.

Catskill Art Society. 263 Main Street, Hurleyville 12747; (845) 436-4227. Open year-round. This group sponsors theater, music, dance, and a variety of arts activities throughout the county. Some are specifically geared to young people. Call for locations and schedules of events.

Ulster County

The magnificent Catskill Mountains rise above the scenic Hudson River, making Ulster County a strikingly beautiful place to visit, a year-round family vacation destination alive with entertainment, outdoor activities, culture, and history. In the warm-weather months, take a boat ride on the majestic Hudson or plan a trip to go bicycling, hiking, or camping in the Shawangunks or Catskills. You can also visit the oldest street in America (New Paltz) or the first capital of New York State (Kingston).

The following attractions make for some of the best family outings in the county. A must-see is the **Hudson River Maritime Museum,** the only museum in New York State dedicated to preserving the maritime heritage of the Hudson River. For almost two hundred years the Hudson has been a major water highway between New York City and Albany, and kids will enjoy the ever-changing display of river vessels here, along with the weekend festivals held throughout the season. One of the most enjoyable ways for families to experience Ulster County is on the **Catskill Mountain Railroad,** a scenic six-mile rail ride along the Esopus Creek, which begins in Mt. Pleasant. It's a wonderfully relaxing way to take in the countryside, and kids love trains. The **Headless Horseman Hayride and Haunted House** in Esopus has become an autumn family tradition in the county. Named the best haunted hayride in the country, this thirty-five-minute experience is followed up with a four-acre scary corn maze and visit to a haunted house. The bears at **Widmark Honey Farms** in Gardiner have been raised somewhat like family pets, and they entertain visitors with their wrestling, climbing, and antics. This is a perfect spot to stop for anyone with small children. Don't miss **Forsyth Park Children's Zoo** in Kingston, one of the city's gems. There are llamas, deer, bulls, pygmy goats, and sheep along with an aviary. The adjoining playground makes this a wonderful outing.

Ulster is a region with a vast array of family-friendly events year-round. The Woodstock/New Paltz Art and Craft Fair is a tradition at the county fairgrounds on Memorial Day and Labor Day weekends. A Children's Festival at the Maritime Museum in Kingston is held in June with hands-on exhibits, demonstrations, boat rides, and more. The Artists' Soapbox Derby in August will delight everyone in the family with unique handmade vehicles that are as original as their creators who drive them down Broadway in Kingston. The annual county fair is held in early August in New Paltz, and one-price admission includes all entertainment, rides, and shows.

For further information, contact **Ulster County Tourism**, 10 Westbrook Lane, Kingston 12401; (845) 340-3566, (800) 342-5826; www.ulstertourism.info.

What to See

MUSEUMS AND HISTORIC SITES

Delaware & Hudson Canal Museum. Mohonk Road, High Falls 12440; (845) 687-9311. Take Route 213 to High Falls, and turn right onto Mohonk Road—the museum is located on the left side of the road. Open May through October, Thursday through Saturday and Monday, 11 A.M. to 5 P.M.; Sunday, 1 to 5 P.M. Admission.

This museum is dedicated to the history and lore of the great Delaware & Hudson Canal. Built in the early nineteenth century, the canal was used to ship coal from the mines in Pennsylvania to the factories of New York; later, cement was shipped south to be used for bridges and skyscrapers. The canal's designer was also responsible for the Erie Canal, and the locks, basins, and dams were engineering wonders of their era. In the museum, kids can discover a miniature setup of the canal and its operations. After leaving the museum, take the self-guided tour of the canal locks across the road, where you will see examples of stonework, locks, and loading slips.

Facilities: *Restrooms, gift shop.*

Hudson River Maritime Museum & Rondout Lighthouse. 50 Rondout Landing, at the foot of Broadway, Kingston 12401; (845) 338-0071. Open daily May through mid-October from 11 A.M. to 5 P.M. Admission.

This museum preserves the maritime heritage of the Hudson River. For almost two hundred years, the Hudson has been a major water highway linking Manhattan to Albany. One of the ports of call along the way was the Rondout Landing, once a bustling area of boatyards and rigging lofts that echoed with steam whistles and brass ships' bells. But when shipping on the Hudson fell into decline, so did the fortunes of the Rondout. In 1980, the museum was opened and has since restored several riverside buildings and historic vessels; kids will enjoy seeing a working part of the Hudson's legacy here. An exhibit hall features shows on maritime history. Outside there is a changing display of river vessels, including the 1899 steam tug *Mathilda* and the cruise boat *Indy 7*. Visitors to the landing have included the presidential yacht *Sequoia* and the sailing ships *Clearwater* and *Woody Guthrie*. Special weekend festivals are a great time to visit and they are held throughout the year. The season opens with a Shad Festival in May and there is a Harvest Festival in October, with lots of local color and fun activities for children.

   Facilities: *Restrooms, gift shop.*

Tours to the Rondout Lighthouse, a satellite museum, are offered from May through mid-October. During the months of May, June, September, and October tours are Saturday and Sunday at noon, 1 P.M., and 2 P.M. on the hour; in July and August, they are Thursday through Monday at noon, 1 P.M., and 2 P.M., and on Saturday and Sunday, there is an additional boat trip at 3 P.M. This tour gives visitors a glimpse into the former lives of Hudson River lighthouse keepers and their families.

Empire State Railway Museum. High Street, Phoenicia Station, Phoenicia 12464; (845) 688-7501. Open Memorial Day weekend through mid-September, daily, 11 A.M. to 4 P.M. Suggested donation.

   This museum brings to life the history of the Ulster & Delaware Railroad, their people, and the towns they served. Built in 1899, this historic structure is the center of restoration of these antique railway cars, and houses photos, films, and artifacts. Kids will enjoy seeing the old cars in the process of restoration. These same railway cars took city residents to boardinghouses in the mountains and returned to New York City with lumber, bluestone, and agricultural products.

Facilities: *Restrooms. Wheelchair and stroller accessible.*

Gomez Mill House. 11 Mill House Road, Marlboro 12542; (845) 236-3126. Open April through October, Wednesday through Sunday with tours at 10 A.M., 11:30 A.M., 1 P.M., and 2:30 P.M. You must take a tour to see the house. Admission.

Gomez Mill House is the oldest homestead in *Ulster County*, and is listed on the National Register of Historic Places. It is also the oldest surviving Jewish homestead in North America. This is truly an educational site, with a dam, wheel, bridge, and museum. A variety of programs are offered throughout the summer for young people that begin at 1 P.M. on Sunday. Call ahead for a schedule of events. School groups are welcome by advance reservation.

Facilities: *Portable toilets, picnic area.*

Kingston Heritage Area Visitors Center. 20 Broadway and 308 Clinton Ave., Kingston 12401; (845) 331-7517, (800) 331-1518. Open year-round Monday through Friday from 9 A.M. to 5 P.M.; from May through October, also open Saturday and Sunday 11 A.M. to 5 P.M. Free.

New York State has designated Urban Cultural Parks where there are urban settings of particular historic interest. Kingston is known for its importance in the history of transportation. The center is located in the Stockade area—once surrounded by walls of tree trunks thirteen feet high—and offers orientation displays that cover the city from its seventeenth-century Dutch settlement to the present. Directions for self-guided walking tours are available.

While in the uptown area you may want to stop by two nearby places of interest. (The Broadway location, on the Rondout, offers permanent exhibits on Kingston history and architecture, and is a clearinghouse for travelers filled with brochures, maps, and calendar of events.)

Senate House State Historic Site. 296 Fair Street, Kingston 12401; (845) 338-2786. Open mid-April through October, Wednesday through Saturday 10 A.M. to 5 P.M., Sunday 1 to 5 P.M. Group tours available by appointment year-round. Admission.

This site will appeal to older children with an interest in history. There are two buildings here: a modern museum and a seventeenth-century Dutch house where the first New York State Senate met. At the museum, a colorful display explains the American Revolution in New York State, and there are changing exhibits that tell the story of Kingston. At the Senate House, visitors will experience what a state senator would have seen during a stay in the eighteenth-century and see several rooms, including the kitchen with its huge fireplace. New York State's first constitution was adopted in Kingston, and the building, along with many others in the city, was burned by the British troops in October 1777. Outside, the Colonial gardens are delightful, especially in the month of June when the roses are in full bloom.

Facilities: *Restrooms, picnic area.*

John R. Kirk Planetarium. Coykendall Science Building, SUNY New Paltz Campus, New Paltz 12561; (845) 257-2121, ext. 3818. Located just off the ground-floor foyer. Take Route 32 south to Mohonk Avenue and watch for campus signs. Open year-round with weekend shows; call for schedule details. Admission. Group shows available.

This stop is recommended for the child who is fascinated by space, stars, and the universe. Some of the programs assume some knowledge of astronomy, while others introduce all ages and backgrounds to the joys of stargazing and skywatching. The planetarium boasts a powerful Spitz Space Systems projector, which allows a look at the universe past, present, and future. Shows have included exploration of an eclipse, a trip in a homemade rocket, the relationship of stars and Greek mythology, and the Christmas star in the Bible.

Facilities: *Restrooms. Strollers may be left in the lobby; if wheelchair accessibility is a concern, call ahead.*

Opus 40 and the Quarryman's Museum. 50 Fite Road, Saugerties 12477; (845) 246-3400. On Route 212 east of Woodstock or Route 9W north of Kingston; follow signs. Open Memorial Day weekend through Columbus Day, Fridays, most Saturdays, Sundays, and holidays, noon to 5 P.M. Some Saturdays are reserved for special events. Admission; children under the age of five free. Group tours available by advance reservation.

This environmental bluestone sculpture, rising out of an abandoned quarry, covers more than six acres and was built over a thirty-seven-year period by sculptor Harvey Fite. Visitors will be astonished by the amount of stone that was quarried, dressed, and moved into place to form the steps and monolith. Children will enjoy walking the pathways around the pools, fountains, and crannies. Stones curl around the trees, and wishing ponds abound, but it's best to wear rubber-soled shoes for walking. A stop at the Quarryman's Museum will introduce viewers to quarrying equipment and hand-forged "folk" tools; there's also a DVD show about the history of Fite and Opus 40 itself. The art gallery on the premises features the work of a different artist each month. Special events, including an occasional concert, are scheduled; call in advance for details since the events make for a fun-filled family outing and picnic.

Facilities: *Portable toilets, picnic areas (bring a blanket). Strollers can be used along the surrounding grounds, but are not permitted on the sculpture itself. Wheelchair access is extremely limited. No dogs allowed.*

Saugerties Lighthouse. Lighthouse Drive, Saugerties 12477; (845) 247-0656. From the center of town, follow Main Street to the end, heading north; make a right turn onto Mynderse Street, which becomes Lighthouse Drive, although there are no signs. Keep bearing to the left; the site is also accessible by boat from the Route 9W boat-launch area. Open Memorial Day weekend through Labor Day; tours given on weekends and holidays 2 to 5 P.M. Donation.

The kids will enjoy walking through the Ruth Glunt Nature Preserve and, at low tide, being able to walk out to the historic lighthouse (a short stroll), which has a museum with artifacts

If your children have any interest in art, make sure to make a brief stop at the **Samuel Dorsky Museum of Art** (SUNY New Paltz, 75 South Manheim Boulevard, New Paltz 12561; (845) 257-3844; open year-round Wednesday through Saturday, 10 A.M. to 5 P.M., Sunday, 1 to 5 P.M.; donation) before you leave the campus. There are changing exhibits of contemporary art in this rather new nine-thousand-square-foot addition to the campus, which opened in 2002. There is an emphasis on the cultural heritage of the Hudson Valley and Catskills as well as world cultures, so stop in if your children enjoy museums.

from the commerical heyday of the Saugerties waterfront. There is a live-in lighthouse keeper residing on the premises who will be glad to answer questions about days gone by.

Facilities: *Portable toilets; wheelchair and stroller access are difficult here.*

Trolley Museum. 89 East Strand, Kingston 12401; (845) 331-3399. Follow Broadway south to where it ends; turn left, and watch for signs. Open Memorial Day weekend through Columbus Day, weekends and holidays noon to 5 P.M. Admission.

Housed in an old trolley shed along the Rondout, this is a pleasant stop for anyone who remembers the ring of a trolley bell. The kids will love the ride along the Hudson River in a restored trolley car, from which you can see the Rondout Lighthouse. The museum offers displays that evoke lots of nostalgia.

Facilities: *Restrooms; the museum is stroller-accessible.*

OTHER ATTRACTIONS

Carousel at Beachview Center. 61 South Partition Street, Saugerties 12477; (845) 246-5388. Open many weekends and holidays from May through October, as well as Easter weekend and Thanksgiving weekend. Call for days and hours. Small fee.

The kids will love taking a ride on a historic wooden Allan Herschell Company carousel made circa 1946. This is a nice stop if you are in the Saugerties area, particularly for the youngest travelers. The Saugerties public beach here is a great stop for those traveling with small children.

Catskill Mountain Railroad. Route 28, Mt. Pleasant 12457; (845) 688-7400. Open Memorial Day weekend through the end of

October, 11 A.M. to 5 P.M.; trains leave every hour on the hour. Admission; children under the age of four ride free. Bus and group tours available by advance reservation.

Travel along the beautiful Esopus Creek by train. Take a six-mile round trip on the Esopus Creek Shuttle or a fourteen-mile round trip to Boiceville on the scenic train through the heart of the Catskill Mountains. Both trains operate on the tracks of the historic Ulster & Delaware Railroad. At Phoenicia, passengers can detrain and experience life in the Catskills both past and present by visiting the village merchants and the historic 1900 railroad station, home of the Empire State Railway Museum. Special events incude a September Teddy Bear Train Ride, and October brings a Haunted Halloween Ride. During the summer months, you can tube the Esopus and take the train back upriver (see tubing, p. 102) The train stops at the Empire State Railway Museum on High Street in Phoenicia (see p. 80), where riders can enjoy a guided tour. This is a wonderfully relaxing way to take in the countryside if you are traveling with children; just about everyone loves train rides!

Facilities: *Restrooms, snack bar, picnic tables, gift shop, parking area.*

Forsyth Park Children's Zoo. Lucas Avenue, on the right just beyond Millers Lane (which is on the left), Kingston 12401; (845) 339-3053. Open daily September through April, Monday through Friday 7 A.M. to 3 P.M., weekends and holidays 7 A.M. to 11 P.M.; May through August, Monday through Friday 7 A.M. to 7 P.M., weekends and holidays 9 A.M. to 5 P.M. Free.

There are nine species of mammals in this small zoo, including llamas, deer, bulls, pygmy goats, and sheep. An aviary on the premises is filled with a variety of birds. There is a large playground in the park, and the combination of activities and animals makes a terrific outing for those with young children.

Facilities: *Restrooms.*

Headless Horseman Hayride and Haunted House. 778 Broadway (Route 9W), Ulster Park 12487; (845) 339-2666. Open the last two weekends in September and all weekends in October, Friday through Sunday, dusk to 11 P.M.

One of the best haunted hayrides you will find anywhere, this thirty-five-minute traveling tale of terror will amuse and frighten the kids. There is also a four-acre Murder Corn Maze, which you can try to find your way through. There are three haunted houses on the premises as well. A special children's weekend, known as A Tiny Taste of Terror, is held on the third weekend in October, and makes a fun time to visit.

Facilities: *Gift shops, food concessions, live entertainment.*

HITS-on-the-Hudson Horse Shows. 454 Washington Avenue Extension, Saugerties 12477; (845) 246-8833. Open Memorial Day weekend through Labor Day, Wednesday through Sunday, 8 A.M. to 5 P.M. Admission on weekends only.

Located on nearly three hundred acres, horse-loving kids will enjoy seeing a horse show here (call for a schedule or check the Web site www.HitsShows.com). There are ten permanent all-weather hunter, jumper, and equitation rings, two amphitheaters and hundreds of stalls on the show grounds. A new addition to the horse show circuit (opened in 2004), HITS (Horse Shows in the Sun), is a fun place to visit for the entire family, especially during one of their special Saturday events like the Chili Cookoff in July or Kid's Day in August.

Facilities: *Restrooms, food concessions, retail shops.*

The Emporium at Emerson Place and Kaleidoworld. Route 28, Mt. Tremper 12457; (845) 688-5800. Open year-round daily 10 A.M. to 6 P.M., extended hours in summer. Closed Tuesday, January through June. Admission for Kaleidoworld.

The Emporium at Emerson Place is housed in a restored nineteenth-century building and has become synonymous in the county for fine dining, accommodations, shopping, and family entertainment. Kaleidoworld is where kids will enjoy seeing the world's largest kaleidoscope, at sixty feet in height. They will actually enter the scope, lean back on supports, and view the changing colors and patterns overhead while specially composed music plays in the background. The result is an indescribable sound and light show that kids will find impressive. After seeing the show, visit the variety of shops in the complex, one of them with an enormous collection of kaleidoscopes that range in price from a few dollars to $3,000. Adjacent to the shops is the Spotted Dog, an eatery designed to reflect old-time firehouses and to honor local volunteer firefighters. The restaurant is open for both lunch and dinner and the food is quite good.

   Facilities: *Restrooms, gift shops, restaurant; wheelchair and stroller accessible.*

Rondout Waterfront and Gazebo. At the end of Broadway, Kingston 12401. Open year-round.

At the on-site Hudson River Maritime Center (see p. 79), children interested in ships will enjoy the changing exhibits, which have featured tugboats, fishing, and sailing craft. Outside on the waterfront, both old and new ships tie up in port, and in the summer visitors have a chance to view some historically important vessels. At the gazebo on weekends there is often live music and the ambiance is festive and colorful. Strollers will have an easy time maneuvering through the streets and waterfront area. This is a great place to enjoy refreshments and ice cream on a hot weekend afternoon. This area was one of the leading maritime centers of Upstate New York during the nineteenth century, and today, restored buildings, the museum, and ships make this a bustling port once more.

Sports Connection. Washington Avenue, Saugerties 12477; (845) 246-4501. Open daily from April through September; call for hours. Admission.

This is an activity-filled fun place for kids who love go-carts; the track is a figure eight with some extra turns tossed in for good measure. Afer a ride, try the batting cages with adjustable speeds (softball and baseball), or play a round on the eighteen-hole miniature-golf course complete with waterfalls and fountains—a good way for the kids to expend extra summer energy!

Vintage Village. 128-138 Route 44/55, Highland, 12528; (845) 691-6000. Open year-round Saturday, 10 A.M. to 6 P.M.; Sunday, noon to 5 P.M.; Wednesday through Friday, 11 A.M. to 5 P.M.

Kids will enjoy seeing the past come to life with period displays covering three hundred years. A multibuilding complex combines historical exhibits wth an antique center, gift shop, formal gardens, and picnic area. This is nice relaxing place to stop.

Facilities: *Stroller and wheelchair accessible.*

Widmark Honey Farm. Route 44/55, Gardiner 12525; (845) 255-6400. Open daily year-round 10 A.M. to 6 P.M. for apiary tours. Admission (credited to any purchase in the shop). Group tours accommodated by advance reservation.

The bears that live at this farm are like family members (to the owners); this is not a zoo. The kids will delight in watching the black bears dance, wrestle, and climb. The baby bears are truly adorable. Be sure to closely examine the beekeeping exhibit and the apiary, where honey is produced and processed. The tours are informal. The retail shop has local farm goods, as well as many varieties of honey. Small children will love this stop.

Facilities: *Restrooms, picnic area, gift shop.*

What to Do

ARCHERY

Robin Hood Archery. 707 Fischer Lane, Accord 12404; (845) 626-0983. Open year-round; Wednesday through Friday, 4 to 9 P.M.; Saturday, 9 A.M. to 5 P.M. There are both indoor and outdoor ranges and shooting areas here. It's a great place to introduce children to the sport of archery, and an excellent activity for a rainy day.

BICYCLING

Hudson Valley Rail Trail. 12 Church Street, Highland 12528; (845) 483-0428 or 691-8666. Open year-round from dawn to dusk. This 4.2-mile nature trail extends from the Mid-Hudson Bridge through the town of Lloyd. There is a two-mile paved portion of the trail. A great spot for family bicycle outings, this trail is part of a network of over one thousand rail trails that cover ten thousand miles across America. Turnoffs along the way run to overlooks and down to the banks of the Hudson, and these are great places to get off your bicycle for a picnic.

Shawangunk Rail Trail. 14 Central Avenue, Wallkill 12589; (845) 895-2611. Open year-round, dawn to dusk. This three-mile section of unpaved rail trail with views of the Shawangunk Mountains provides easy access to the Wallkill River and village of Wallkill. It is also a nice ride for mountain bikers.

Wallkill Valley Rail Trail. P.O. Box 1048, New Paltz 12561. Open dawn to dusk year-round. This 12.2-mile trail is where a railroad line ran during the late nineteenth century. Once a busy link to New York City, used by both commuters to get to work and by farmers to ship their goods to market, it is now a popular recreational park. The rail trail, located between the New Paltz–Rosendale and Gardiner-Shawangunk town lines, officially opened to the public in 1993. Visitors of all ages are encouraged to walk, jog, or ride bicycles here. It provides an excellent place for children to learn to bike or roller-skate. The only motorized vehicles allowed are those used by the disabled. Write to the above address for a detailed brochure.

BOAT CRUISES

Hudson River Cruises. Rondout Landing, Kingston 12401. Open daily Tuesday through Sunday; in July and August there are cruises at 11 A.M. and 2 P.M. and Friday also at 8 P.M.; in May, June, September, and October, on weekends only at 11 A.M. and 2 P.M.

They offer two-hour cruises going south from Kingston for one hour toward the Hyde Park area, passing both the Kingston and Esopus Meadows lighthouses. Enjoy the roomy ship *Rip Van Winkle,* which features restrooms, plenty of seating, and a snack bar. Because the river tends to be less choppy than the ocean, the ride is smooth and pleasant. Some trips feature live music.

North River Cruises. Rondout Landing, Kingston 12401; (845) 339-1050 or 679-8205. The *Teal,* a medium-sized boat docked at Rondout Landing, is run by Captain John Cutten. The boat is fitted with rich wood and brass, and the atmosphere aboard takes you back to a time of genteel river travel; still, there are all the modern amenities, including restrooms and snack bar.

CANOEING AND KAYAKING

Atlantic Kayak Tours. 320 West Saugerties Road, Saugerties 12477; (845) 246-2187. Open April through mid-November for kayak trips on the Hudson River, Esopus and other local waterways, this outfitter will make an excursion fun; this is a particularly good way to go for first-timers.

PICK-YOUR-OWN FARMS AND MAPLE SYRUP

Arrowhead Farm. 5941 Route 209, Kerhonkson 12446; (845) 626-7293. The time for maple syrup tastings and tours is mid-February to mid-April. The owners of Arrowhead Farm will be glad to show you around and sell you their delicious syrup, maple cream, and honey. It's a good idea, however, to call before you go, since erratic weather can affect the sap season.

Jenkins-Leuken Orchards. Route 299 (four miles west of New Paltz), Gardiner 12525; (845) 255-0999. Open daily August through May from 9 A.M. to 6 P.M. You can pick your own apples and pumpkins here. They have a large variety of apples, including those marvelous Macouns. Pears, peaches, tomatoes, and vegetables are available in season. Honey and cider are produced on the farm as well.

Stone Ridge Orchard. 3120 Route 213, Stone Ridge 12487; (845) 687-0447. Open daily from mid-August through October, 9 A.M. to 5 P.M. for pick-your-own-apples, pumpkins, and raspberries.

They have over a dozen varieties of apples here, and the orchard is surrounded by hundreds of acres of forest and farmland. There are hayrides for the kids, picnic benches, and fresh cider. The shop on the premises offers maple syrup, home-baked pies, and other treats. This spot is easy to find, right off Route 209, and it's a beautiful place to spend a couple of hours on an autumn afternoon.

Wilklow Orchards. Pancake Hollow Road, Highland 12528; (845) 691-2339. From exit 18 off the NYS Thruway, turn right on Route 299 and go 2.3 miles; then turn right on New Paltz Road, go about one mile, and make a right on Pancake Hollow Road for another mile to the orchard.

One of the oldest family-run pick-your-own farms, Wilklow has been in business for more than one hundred years. They're open daily from Labor Day through October for picking apples (there are ten varieties offered) and pumpkins. The farmstand on the premises sells homegrown vegetables, fruits, and cider. Kids will enjoy seeing the farm animals.

FISHING

Ulster County is a good place to take young children going fishing for the first time since it's easy to get to many fishing areas that are well marked—and well stocked (so chances are good the kids will catch something and enjoy the outing!). The waters here offer a variety of fish—trout, bass, and pickerel, to name just a few. Remember that New York State licenses are required for anyone over the age of sixteen, and you must have a permit to fish in the **Ashokan Reservoir** (Route 28A, west of Kingston) and the **Kingston City Reservoir** (off Zena Road between Kingston and Woodstock). Call the **Department of Environmental Conservation Department of Fisheries** (845) 256-3161, in New Paltz, for information. There are few fishing guide services in the region due to the fact that the Esopus and other streams are so accessible.

Some of the better-known streams in the county include the following: The renowned **Esopus Creek** is easily accessed along Route 28 west of Kingston. The **Rondout Creek** has a number of access points along Route 209 south of Kingston. **Plattekill Creek** is easy to get to from Route 32 in Saugerties, and **Sawkill Creek** is close to Route 212 in Woodstock. Many of the access points are indicated by brown-and-yellow state signs, and some have parking areas.

HIKING

Black Creek Forest Preserve. Route 9W and Winding Brook Acres Road, Esopus 12429; (845) 473-4440.

This one-hundred-thirty-acre forest preserve lies along a major Hudson River tributary. Walkers will cross a suspension footbridge over Black Creek and pass through forest woodlands with vernal pools on the three hiking trails (a total of 2.5 miles) that have direct access to the Hudson River. This is a great place for a short hike with the kids; it always seems somewhat cooler here since much of the trail area is shaded.

Esopus Meadows Point Preserve. One mile from the intersection of Route 9W and River Road, Port Ewen 12466; (845) 454-7673. This one-hundred-acre site offers great views of the Esopus Meadows Lighthouse, three trails, and an environmental center. The trails are easy to walk, with gently sloping terrain, and they follow the Hudson River in many places.

Frost Valley YMCA. 200 Frost Valley Road, Claryville 12410; County Route 47 off Route 28, near Big Indian; (845) 985-2291. Open year-round, dawn to dusk.

This YMCA has over five thousand acres to explore and is a wonderful place for school groups and families to spend an overnight visit. Some of the activites in addition to hiking include ropes courses, astronomy, archery, and summer special events including workshops in the arts. There is an emphasis on projects that involve the entire family. In the winter this is a great place to go cross-country skiing. The lodge is built in the elegant style of the older Catskill camps, and the cafeteria even has an exhibit that focuses on nature writer John Burroughs.

Minnewaska State Park. Route 44/55, New Paltz 12561; (845) 255-0752. Open year-round for day use only. Admission. The Shawangunk trails here are beautiful with great views, although quite crowded on summer weekends.

Mohonk Mountain House and Skytop Observation Tower. Lake Mohonk, New Paltz 12561; (845) 255-1000. Open year-round. Admission. This Victorian-style resort surrounding a beautiful lake is world-famous and has been owned and operated by the same family for generations. The spirit of the resort revolves around preservation of the 22,000 acres located in the heart of the Shawangunk Mountains. You can visit Mohonk for a meal, a day, or overnight, although restrictions apply to day-use passes. It's a nice place to visit for a day hike; the trail around the lake is fairly flat and is easy for even the youngest children. Considering its old-fashioned ambience, Mohonk caters surprisingly well to families. Supervised children's programs are available on weekends year-round and daily in the summer season—for overnight guests only. Mohonk specializes in theme weekends and some are particularly suitable for children. If you need to get away with the kids during the winter, try a stay here during President's Day weekend, with snow tubing, cross-country skiing, ice-skating, snow sculpture contests, and more.

Overlook Mountain. Meads Mountain Road, Woodstock 12498. This trail is a moderate walk up a graded roadbed. From Tinker Street at the village green, take Rock City Road to Meads Mountain Road. The trailhead begins across from the Tibetan monastery on the right side of the road. The summit takes about an hour to reach, walking at a leisurely pace. You pass the ruins of the Overlook Mountain House on the way up; a lookout tower and picnic tables are at the top where the views are spectacular.

Wilson State Park. Wittenberg Road, Mt. Tremper 12457; (845) 256-3099. Take Route 28 west from Kingston thirteen miles to Route 212, and make a right. Wittenberg Road is the first right turn; follow to the park entrance on the right. Open daily, May through October from 9 A.M. to 5 P.M. Admission.

This is a small state park just outside of Woodstock, where you can enjoy a swim and activities on the sandy beach in the morning before visiting the colorful town in the afternoon. The park has a shallow lake with a nice beach that will keep the youngest toddlers digging for hours. Unfortunately, there is no shaded area nearby, so you may want to take a walk on the trails in the nearby woods. Wilson Park is an excellent place for a picnic and the mountain views are beautiful. Groups are welcome and there are campsites for overnight stays available by advance reservation.

HORSEBACK RIDING

Pine Grove Ranch. Cherrytown Road, Kerhonkson 12446; (800) 346-4626 or (845) 626-7345. Open year-round.

For more than thirty years, this family-owned-and-operated resort has provided an informal, inexpensive getaway for people of all ages. The six-hundred-acre property offers a host of activities. In addition to horseback riding, there is an indoor pool, an outdoor pool with a double-flume water slide, archery, handball, ping-pong, a rock wall, a fitness center, volleyball, paddleboating,

When you are finished at Wilson Park, head into **Woodstock**; follow Wittenberg Road east from the park, and make a left at the fork. Continue to the junction with Route 212; make a right and follow into the village of Woodstock. This is the town of the Aquarian Age, and there are often lots of unusual characters, musicians, and interesting shops to be seen along Tinker Street, the main thoroughfare. The kids will enjoy an ice cream, and on a summer day the village green is always packed with young people. At **Woodstock Wonderworks** (Route 375, in back of the elementary school; (845) 679-2316; open daily year-round dawn to dusk; free), kids will see a Robert Leathers– and children-designed playground. The multilevel wooden structure includes a castle maze, space tunnel, dragon slide, Viking ship, haunted house, and more—all designed to stimulate a child's imagination. This stop shouldn't be missed by those with active children. Facilities include picnic tables and wheelchair accessible areas, but no restrooms.

lake fishing, and a daily activity schedule offering guests a range of choices. Children from the ages of three to eleven can enjoy Li'l Maverick Day Camp, which runs from 9 A.M. until 5 P.M. while parents enjoy a game of shuffleboard, relax by the pool, or have a massage. There is a baby animal farm on the premises, as well. In-experienced riders will feel comfortable going on a leisurely be-ginner ride through the woods. More experienced riders may go on a cattle drive and enjoy the flavor of the Old West. With nightly entertainment, there is lots to amuse the entire family. A down-home atmosphere prevails, and all-inclusive rates incude three meals, snacks, and activites. All rooms have private baths, TV, and AC. A great getaway if the kids are horse lovers.

Rocking Horse Ranch. 600 Route 44/55, Highland 12528; (845) 691-2927 or (800) 64-RANCH. Open year-round.

For decades, this family-owned-and-operated ranch resort has offered a variety of vacation packages. The all-inclusive room rate incorporates sumptuous meals and horseback riding on acres of trails. During summer months, there is waterskiing and boating on the lake, tennis, miniature golf, and volleyball. The ranch also has heated indoor and outdoor pools, saunas, a gym, a petting zoo, and daily organized activities for the kids. There is entertainment in the lounge nightly. All rooms have private bath, TV, and AC.

ICE-SKATING

Kiwanis Ice Arena. Cantine Field, Saugerties 12477; (845) 246-2590. Open daily, October through March for both hockey and figure skating; weekdays, 8:30 A.M. to 6 P.M.; weekends, open after-noons only. Hours may vary, so call before you go. Sessions are one and a half hours long and there are rentals, restrooms, a snack bar, and bleachers at this enclosed rink.

SKIING

Belleayre Mountain. Route 28, Highmount 12441; (845) 254-5600 or (800) 942-6904. Open daily, November to April (weather permitting).

Belleayre is located in the heart of the Catskill Mountain Forest Preserve. Visitors can ride and ski on forty trails serviced by eight lifts, with close to 80 skiable acres and 97 percent snow-making capability. Came here to ski the highest skiable peak (3.429 feet) and the longest trail in the Catskills. The upper mountain lifts bring you to the summit, which is the start of twenty-six intermediate and expert trails. There is a half-pipe for snowboarding and a terrain park for the adventurous. The separate beginner/novice area boasts fourteen trails serviced by five lifts. Recognized as being one of the best places to learn to ski in the East, Belleayre has expanded its teaching facilities and increased its staff; they now offer free beginner lessons with the purchase of any lift ticket for those over the age of five. The ever-popular Kidscamp program for children from four to twelve has a new teaching device called the ski carousel, which greatly reduces the learning curve. There are nursery services on the premises for children from ages one to six.

Facilities: *Four lodges, two ski shops with rentals, two cafeterias, three snack bars, restrooms, and lockers.*

Sawkill Family Ski Center. 367 Hill Road, Kingston 12401; (845) 336-6977. Open from the day after Christmas through February, weather permitting. This is a privately-owned-and-run family ski center; in fact, its the smallest of its kind on the East Coast—the perfect place to go with the youngest skiers or snowboarders or those who have never tried these sports before. There are four trails serviced by one rope tow, as well as a terrain park. There are also three lanes of snow tubing with a separate lift.

Facilities: *Restrooms, snack bar, rentals, and a retail shop with both new and used clothing and equipment for sale.*

SWIMMING

Kingston Point Beach. Kingston Point Beach, Kingston 12401; (845) 331-1682. Take Broadway to the end, turn left, and follow East Strand (which becomes North Street), one mile to the park. The beach is open year-round, dawn to dusk. Free. Swimming is permitted from mid-June through Labor Day.

This small beach on the Hudson River is run by the city. There are no services, and it isn't advisable to swim in the Hudson River even now that it is much cleaner than it once was, but it is still a beautiful spot to sunbathe and enjoy the river views. Kids will love the sandy beach and small playground, as well as watching the boats pass by on the river.

Pine Hill Day Use Area. Route 28, Highmount 12441; (845) 254-5600 or (800) 254-5202. Open daily, mid-June through Labor Day. Admission.

This lovely lake offers swimming, boating, and fishing with a beach area, picnic pavilions, and snack bar. Bring your own canoe, or rent a kayak, paddle boat, or rowboat at reasonable prices. Run by the state, admission is charged by the car. The beach is roped off into different sections; there is a diving area and a special section for toddlers, which makes this area a good choice for those with very young children.

Ulster Landing Park. Ulster Landing Road (off Route 32), Kingston 12401; (845) 336-8484. Open daily, Memorial Day weekend through Labor Day from 10 A.M. to 8 P.M.

This county-owned-and-run park offers a small, quiet sandy beach area just north of the Rhinecliff Bridge with swimming in the Hudson River—although, as with Kingston Point Beach, swimming in the river is still not advisable. This spot is less popular, since it is a little off the beaten track. There are restrooms and a picnic pavilion.

THEATER

Backstage Studio Productions. 323 Wall Street, Kingston 12401; (845) 338-8700. Open year-round, daily, 10 A.M. to 6 P.M. This is the lab of an arts and entertainment complex with 75,000 square feet of space, a 2,000-seat concert hall, dance studio, and art gallery with changing exhibits. Call in advance for a schedule of children's events.

Unison Arts and Learning Center. 68 Mountain Rest Road, New Paltz 12561; (845) 255-1559. Open year-round, Monday through Saturday, 10 A.M. to 5 P.M. This multiarts center hosts performances of jazz, folk, dance, and children's theater, and has some excellent programs. Get on their mailing list for schedule updates. The center itself has a lovely outdoor sculpture garden.

UPAC. 601 Broadway, Kingston 12401; (845) 331-1613. Listed on the National Register of Historic Places, this renovated theater is the latest arts showcase in the county, offering a variety of theater and musical performances from March through December. Call for a schedule.

Woodstock Playhouse. Routes 212 and 375, Woodstock 12498; (845) 679-2764. This summer performing arts venue features a variety of events in music and theater. Children's performances are usually offered on Saturdays from Memorial Day weekend through Labor Day at 11 A.M.

TUBING

Town Tinker Tube Rental. Bridge Street, Phoenicia 12464; (845) 688-5553. Open daily, mid-June through Labor Day, 9 A.M. to 6 P.M.

If you want to try tubing, head to Phoenicia and spend the day floating the whitewater of the Esopus Creek. This makes an adventurous, fun outing for older children (at least twelve), who will enjoy bouncing along on a large inner tube. Although this is a popular activity, there are some caveats: the water is usually not more than 60 degrees, so pick a very warm day or rent a wetsuit to ensure that the trip is comfortable. Lifevests, helmets, and sneakers (for protection against the rocks) are required for those under the age of fourteen. Kids should never tube alone. July and August are the top months for this activity, and there are both novice and advanced river courses. On weekends, you can take the Catskill Mountain Railroad (see p. 85) back upriver to where you started your journey.

Facilities: *Portable toilets, picnic tables, free parking, changing rooms.*

Dutchess County

An area of eight hundred square miles with thirty miles of Hudson River shoreline, Dutchess County has something to please everyone in the family. Get back to simpler times on the farm; visit exotic animals at a zoo; or marvel at aerobatic demonstrations at a museum of antique airplanes. You can also experience nature's marvels at an environmental education center or attend a hot-air balloon festival. These are just some of the activities families will enjoy on a trip here.

County highlights include the **Hudson Valley Raptor Center** in Stanfordville, which is one of the largest centers in the nation dedicated solely to birds of prey. The **Trevor Zoo** in Millbrook has more than one hundred exotic and indigenous species in exhibits covering four acres on the grounds of the Millbrook School. The **Old Rhinebeck Aerodrome** showcases antique and replica planes in displays and theatrical airshows that include costumed performers and period cars. Families that yearn for the opportunity to feel connected to the natural world on vacation might visit pick-your-own farms, which allow visitors to enjoy fresh air, exercise, and plenty of delicious treats. Summer's bounty includes a variety of berries, while fall brings apples and pumpkins.

Nature and education centers are recommended for Dutchess-bound families seeking to combine fun and learning. The 756-acre **Stony Kill Environmental Center** in Wappingers Falls provides children's programs focusing on natural history, ecology, and farming. The **Mid-Hudson Children's Museum** in Pough-keepsie gives young people a chance to learn while they explore over fifty art and science exhibits including a computer center, interactive videos, and dinosaurs.

Whatever the season, Dutchess has a wealth of festivals and special events to celebrate the spirit of family fun. The Kids' Expo is held in March in Poughkeepsie, with more than one hundred hands-on projects and exhibitions at six different sites. The Mid-Hudson Balloon Festival takes place at a few sites in the county in May. And one of the biggest special annual events, the Dutchess County Fair, is held the third week in August in Rhinebeck—it's the second largest agricultural fair in New York State. If you visit in September, try to get to the Celtic Day in the Park (in Staatsburg), a cultural celebration featuring Scottish pipe bands, Irish dancing, caber tossing, and sheepdog herding.

Recent major cultural additions to the landscape include the **Fisher Center for the Performing Arts** at Bard College and **Dia: Beacon Arts Museum,** which both draw thousands of visitors to the county. The future looks bright for Dutchess, with the Hudson River Institute planned to open in Beacon toward the end of the decade.

For further information, contact the **Dutchess County Tourism Promotion Agency,** 3 Neptune Road, Poughkeepsie 12601; (845) 436-4000 or (800) 445-3131; www.dutchesstourism.com.

What to See

MUSEUMS AND HISTORIC SITES

Dia: Beacon. 3 Beekman Street, Beacon 12508; (845) 440-0100. Open mid-May through Columbus Day, Thursday through Monday, 11 A.M. to 6 P.M.; the rest of the year, Friday through Monday, 11 A.M. to 4 P.M. Located off Interstate 84 and Route 9D on Beekman Street; follow signs to the railroad station. Admission (children under the age of twelve enter free).

This 240,000-square-foot museum, which contains works from Dia's permanent collection, is housed in a renovated printing plant originally built in 1929 by Nabisco along the shores of the Hudson River. Kids will enjoy the exhibits of American art of the 1960s and 1970s (including works by Andy Warhol, Agnes Martin, and Richard Serra, to name just a few) since most of it is large scale. And if they are not engaged by the artwork, they will certainly appreciate the structure, which is fascinating in itself with its galleries illuminated almost entirely by natural light.

Facilities: *Restrooms, cafeteria, gift shop. Wheelchair and stroller accessible.*

Franklin Delano Roosevelt Home and Museum. 4097 Albany Post Road (Route 9), Hyde Park 12538; (845) 229-9115 or (800) FDR-VISIT. Open year-round, daily 9 A.M. to 5 P.M. Admission. The new Visitors Center, offers an orientation film and a wonderful gift shop as well as a café with refreshments of all kinds. Here you can purchase tickets for the tour.

The FDR house, which is in Victorian style embellished with Georgian touches, was the president's boyhood home and interests children studying American history. This is where Eleanor and Franklin raised their family, entertained heads of state, and shaped world history. Kids enjoy seeing how a child their own age lived a century ago. Toys, portraits, and even the stuffed birds that Franklin collected, help to make the president come alive for children. The site includes the house, the first presidential library, rose garden, and the site of the Roosevelts' graves. In the house once called the Summer White House by Roosevelt, family memorabilia are displayed, including photos, antiques, and the possessions of Franklin's iron-willed mother, Sara. Throughout the museum and house are photos, exhibits, and personal items that recall one of the most vibrant and troubled periods in American history. The museum contains model ships, books, manuscripts, and clothing, as well as a letter from Einstein to Roosevelt that led to the development of the atomic bomb. The gravesite is also where the rose garden is—a beautiful sight in June when the flowers are in full bloom. While it is sometimes difficult to introduce children to political history, this site is recommended as a good place to start. For those children who aren't tired of touring and may be interested in seeing more, a visit to Val-Kill and the Vanderbilt Mansion are suggested; tickets are sold at the FDR Visitors Center.

Facilities: *Restrooms, snack bar, gift shop. Wheelchair and stroller accessible.*

Locust Grove. 2683 South Road (Route 9), Poughkeepsie 12601; (845) 454-4500. Grounds open daily except Thanksgiving and Christmas Day. House open May through November, daily, from 10 A.M. to 3 P.M.; the museum and gift shop stay open until 5 P.M. Group tours by advance reservation. Admission. Children under the age of six are admitted free.

This charming house, a National Historic Landmark, was the

home of Samuel F. B. Morse, artist and inventor. The Italianate villa, designed by Morse and architect Alexander Jackson Davis, contains the extensive collection of furniture and decorative arts assembled by the Young family, who purchased the estate from the Morse heirs in 1901 and lived there until 1975. Children may know that Morse developed the telegraph and Morse code, but are surprised to learn that he was also a famous painter. In the museum galleries, several of Morse's paintings are on display along with antique telegraph equipment and interactive exhibits for young people to use. A tour of Locust Grove shows the life of a family in the early twentieth century, complete with fine examples of art-work, furniture, and even a billiards room. The house is fascinat-ing for children who enjoy history, but the tour is recommended for children over the age of five. The exquisite flower and kitchen gardens have been restored with flower-filled urns and lush plant-ings. The house is surrounded by one hundred and fifty acres of lawns and trees and miles of carriage roads and hiking trails accessible to children who like the outdoors and hiking through ravines and around ponds.

   Facilities: *Restrooms, gift shop, picnic area with tables, hiking paths with self-guided tour. Wheelchairs can be accommodated in the museum and on the grounds, but not in the house.*

Mid-Hudson Children's Museum. 75 North Water Street. Pough-keepsie 12601; (845) 471-0589. (At the waterfront, close to the train station.) Open Tuesday through Sunday 11 A.M. to 5 P.M.; special summer hours in July and August include Monday 11 A.M. to 2 P.M.

   This hands-on museum features permanent and changing ex-hibits that focus on the arts and sciences. Children ages two to twelve will enjoy these educational displays, examples of which include a horizontal rock-climbing wall, a huge play structure of the heart and lungs, and "science on wheels," which includes a bicycle gyroscope and giant bubble machine.

Facilities: *Restrooms.*

Hyde Park Railroad Station. 34 River Road, Hyde Park 12538; (845) 229-2338. Located at the foot of the hill that is formed by West Market Street and River Road, off Route 9. Open year-round on Monday from 7 to 9 P.M.; mid-June through mid-September, Saturday and Sunday, 11 A.M. to 5 P.M.; or by appointment. Free.

This railroad station was built in 1914, based on a design shown at the Pan American World Exposition of 1898. The building was nearly demolished in 1975, when the Hudson Valley Railroad Society acquired the station and set about restoring it. Almost thirty years later, the station is on the National Register of Historic Places and houses exhibits that tell the story of the area's railroads and their history. Model trains run throughout the building, and there are always people onboard to answer questions. This is a nice stop along historic Route 9, close to Mills Norrie State Park.

Facilities: *Restrooms.*

Warthin Geological Museum at Vassar College. 124 Raymond Avenue, Poughkeepsie 12603; (845) 437-7000. Open September through May, Monday through Friday, 8 A.M. to 4 P.M.; June, July, and August by appointment. Free.

The young rock hound will want to check out the scores of fossils, gems, and minerals that line this exhibit hall. Dioramas tell the story of the earth's formation and geologic history, and a demonstration geyser spouts every now and then. The Vassar campus is a nice place to walk, although it is busy during school semesters.

Facilities: *Restrooms. Call ahead to be certain the museum is open on the day you plan to visit.*

Culinary Institute of American Cooking Courses. Route 9, Hyde Park 12538; (800) 888-7850. Open for spring and fall sessions. Courses are held on Saturday morning. One-week, two-day, and one-day courses are offered.

The Culinary Institute of America is one of the nation's premier culinary colleges. Set above the Hudson River, the school site was formerly a seminary, and visitors are welcome to walk around the campus and dine in the five student-staffed restaurants (reservations are necessary, except at the Apple Pie Bakery and Café, open Monday through Friday 8 A.M. to 6:30 P.M.). In keeping with its educational goals, the school offers a wide variety of classes for the public, and among them are some fun workshops for kids. In Kids in the Kitchen or Kids Party Food children between the ages of nine and twelve spend time with professional cooks, who demonstrate and explain the art of making pizza, bread, salads, and other popular foods.

Facilities: *Restrooms, book and gift shop, restaurants. Wheelchair accessible.*

Fisher Center for the Performing Arts at Bard College. River Road, Annandale-on-Hudson 12504; (845) 758-7900. Cross the Kingston-Rhinecliff Bridge, and at the first traffic light make a left onto County Route 103 or River Road; drive north for 3.5 miles. Open year-round; call for a schedule of events.

Experience music and dance performances in the East Coast's only Frank Gehry–designed performing arts center, which opened in 2003. This unique and controversial venue, an architectural wonder that enchants kids, is worth a detour for all travelers, even if just to see the exterior. The building, with a performance space consisting of two theaters, is a work of art in itself.

Facilities: *Restrooms. Wheelchair accessible.*

Fun Central. Route 9, Wappingers Falls 12590; (845) 297-1010. Open late June through Labor Day, Sunday through Thursday, 10 A.M. to midnight; Friday and Saturday, until 1 A.M. The rest of the year, noon to 10 P.M.; Friday and Saturday, until midnight.

This multiactivity indoor and outdoor recreational facility with miniature golf, bumper boats, an arcade, a virtual-reality roller coaster, and laser tag, is a great place to stop if you are traveling with children, especially on a rainy day. At night, teenagers hang out here in large numbers; it's best to go early in the day with young children.

Facilities: *Restrooms, snack bar.*

Hudson Valley Raptor Center. 148 South Road, Stanfordville 12581; (845) 758-6957. From the Taconic Parkway, take the Route 199/Red Hook exit. Go east on Route 199 for quarter mile, and turn right onto County Route 53—South Road. The Raptor Center is one mile up the road on the right side. Open April through October, Saturday and Sunday, 1 to 4 P.M. July and August, also open on Fridays, 1 to 4 P.M. Call ahead, since hours may vary. Admission.

This unique and exciting center appeals to both children and adults who want to learn more about raptors, including bald eagles, red-tailed hawks, peregrine falcons, great horned owls, and more. Located on ninety-one scenic acres, the Raptor Center hosts over one hundred raptors of twenty species. It provides sanctuary and medical care for injured raptors, with the goal of rehabilitating injured birds and releasing them back into the wild when healthy. There are tours for visitors, and a birds-of-prey flight presentation is held on weekends from June through October. Additional programs are available by special arrangement for groups and organizations.

Facilities: *Restroom, picnic area, gift shop.*

Institute of Ecosystem Studies at the Mary Flagler Cary Arboretum. 181 Sharon Turnpike/Route 44A (off Route 44), Millbrook 12545; (845) 677-7600, ext. 317. Open April through September, Monday through Saturday 9 A.M. to 5 P.M.; Sunday 1 to 5 P.M. From October through March, closing time is 4 P.M. Free.

Founded in 1983, the IES is dedicated to research and education relating to ecological systems. The property, surrounding the Cannoo Hills in Millbrook, is open to the public through a free daily permit system. A visit should begin at the Gifford House visitor and education center where you receive a permit and maps of the grounds. First, enjoy lovely Gifford Garden, a model of natural gardening with labeled demonstration beds and a fish-filled water garden. Beyond the garden is the trailhead, from which you can explore the Wappinger Creek, Cary Pines, and Sedge Meadow Trails. Along the way, stop off at the Fern Glen, a lush native plant garden surrounding a pond; the Glen demonstrates the fascinating ecological relationships between plants and their environment, and is home to many turtles, frogs, salamanders, and other local creatures. The internal road system may be explored on foot, bicycle, or by car. Passing the Fern Glen along the way, you will wind through fields and lowland forests, which provide ample bird-watching opportunities. The roadway will lead you to the IES Greenhouse. At the Greenhouse, learn about its Integrated Pest Management program; follow the Economic Botany Trail; or just find a bench near a bubbling fountain, and bask in the tropical splendor. The IES-offers monthly ecology programs, continuing education classes, an ecology day camp in the summer months, and a variety of other ongoing programs. This is a wonderful excursion for school groups.

Facilities: *Restrooms, gift shop.*

Listening Rock Farm. 78 Sinpatch Road, Wassaic 12592; (845) 877-6335. Open June through October, Saturday and Sunday, 7:30 A.M. to 4 P.M. There is a charge for meals.

For those children who want to learn how cheese is made, as well as see farm life up close, this is an excellent excursion. Visitors may enjoy a simple farm kitchen breakfast; lunch is offered as well. There is a variety of envionmental and ecological programs on the schedule, so call before you go to see what's going on.

Facilities: *Restrooms, retail shop.*

Mills Norrie State Park and Staatsburgh State Historic Site. Route 9, Staatsburg 12580; (845) 889-4646. The park and mansion grounds are open year-round, free of charge, but hours vary with the season. Park is open from dawn to dusk daily. Mansion is open for tours April through October, Tuesday through Saturday, 10 A.M. to 5 P.M., Sunday 11 A.M. to 5 P.M. Open December for holiday tours, but hours vary; January through March, Sunday 11 A.M. to 5 P.M. Admission charged for mansion tour.

This unusual combination of state park and historic mansion is situated on over nine hundred acres along the Hudson River. Day-trippers will enjoy the outdoor activities of a park—there are hiking trails with lovely river views. If you want to picnic, the bluffs on the river are a great place to sit and watch the boats running up and down the Hudson. Fishing can be tried in any area of the park where there is access to the Hudson River. In the winter, cross-country ski trails snake around the park, and the mansion's hilly grounds are renowned for sledding, a sport that has been popular there for almost three hundred years. The park also contains a small environmental museum with displays of local plants and animals. Special educational programs are offered during the summer on birds, plants, and astronomy. Special events occur throughout the year. Everything from square dances to banjo bands, jazz ensembles, and bluegrass, take place as part of the county's summer Music in the Parks program. At holiday time, plan to visit and take in the elaborate arrangements of greens and flowers, including a huge Christmas tree. Any time of year, the mansion's furnishings and decorations exemplify the wealth of the Hudson River families at the turn of the century, and while adults and older children will enjoy the house tour, younger children may prefer to stay outside in the park.

Facilities: *Restrooms, picnic areas, boat-launch ramp, two golf courses, campsites, and cabins. The clubhouse at the golf course has a restaurant that is open to the public for lunch and dinner. There is some wheelchair accessibility within the park. Strollers can be used on the paved walkways, but they have to be carried upstairs in the mansion.*

Old Rhinebeck Aerodrome. Route 9, Rhinebeck 12572; (845) 758-8610. To find the aerodrome, take Route 9 north from Rhinebeck to Stone Church Road, and watch for signs. Museum open daily, mid-May through October, 10 A.M. to 5 P.M. Air shows are held only on Saturday and Sunday at 2 P.M. Admission; children under six admitted free; reduced admission for children from ages six to ten. Group rates available for fifteen or more.

I cannot recommend this site enough: it's colorful, corny, exciting, and full of activity, especially during the shows. Founded by the late Cole Palen, this is America's original living museum of old and restored airplanes, and it recaptures the thrill of flying that prevailed when the Red Baron and barnstorming were all the rage. The tour guides are enthusiastic experts on the finely restored planes housed in several hangars. A walking tour incorporates the Fokkers, Sopwith Snipes, and Curtiss airplanes, as well as old engines and many other vintage aircraft. Make sure you attend one of the weekend air shows, when the air hums and whines with planes, and the crowds cheer on the heroes and bad guys. Saturdays highlight the pioneer era of airplanes, with demonstration flights of old planes, and on Sundays, the battles of World War I are reenacted, complete with full costumes, a parade, and the best villains in the Hudson Valley. The planes are either original aircraft or powered with original engines of the period, and audiences are likely to feel that each show is especially for them. Announcers describe all the overhead antics. Brave souls can schedule barnstorming rides in a 1929 open-cockpit biplane before or after the shows for an extra charge. Spectators view the air shows from an outdoor stand, so sun hats in the summer and jackets in the fall are heartily recommended.

Facilities: *Restrooms, picnic tables, free parking. Snacks are available, and the area is navigable by strollers and wheelchairs.*

Splashdown Park/Adventure Island. 2200 Route 9, Fishkill 12524; (845) 896-6606. Open daily Memorial Day weekend through Labor Day, 10 A.M. to 7 P.M. Admission. Groups welcome by advance reservation.

Water parks are a wonderful break from sightseeing in the summer months, especially when younger children get hot and tired of traveling in the car. This park has three large water slides, an interactive shipwreck island pool, a large activity pool, a lazy river with a wave area, a pollywog pond kiddie activity area, two eighteen-hole miniature golf courses, a hoops miniature basketball court, a water balloon game, bumper cars, bumper boats, and an arcade area. Whew! There's something that will amuse just about every child in this place.

Facilities: *Restrooms, locker rooms, snack bars, picnic areas. Strollers are easily maneuvered here, and the park is wheelchair accessible.*

Stony Kill Environmental Center. Route 9D, Wappingers Falls 12590; (845) 831-8780. Grounds open daily from dawn to dusk. The Manor House interpretive center is open Monday through Friday, 8:30 A.M. to 4:30 P.M.; Saturday, 9:30 A.M. to 12:30 P.M.; Sunday 1 to 4 P.M. Free. Year-round weekend programs are offered to the public; call for a schedule.

Children who enjoy the outdoors or are studying the environment and nature should like this 756-acre facility, which offers a wide variety of habitats for local plants and animals. Rolling meadows, woodland, ponds, swamps, and vernal pools attract many species of wildlife. Five trails can be used for hiking, snowshoeing, or cross-country skiing. The working nineteenth-century replica farm includes a barn with livestock (cows, sheep, chickens, turkeys, and pigs), and the center has an Open Barn program for visitors from spring through fall. A community garden plot program is also offered to those interested in growing their own vegetables and food. Major annual festivals include the Fall Harvest Festival, the Holiday Open House (December), the Horse-Drawn Sleigh Rally (February), Backyard Maple Sugaring (March), an Earth Day Celebration (April), and a spring Butterfly Festival (June).

Facilities: *Picnic areas, perennial and herb gardens, fishing ponds, outdoor restrooms. Stroller and wheelchair accessible.*

Trevor Teaching Zoo. Millbrook School Road, Millbrook 12545; (845) 677-3704. Located on the grounds of the Millbrook School, six miles east of Millbrook on Route 44. Open year-round, daily, 8 A.M. to 5 P.M.; groups welcome by advance reservation. Free.

This small zoo, the only one in the region, is a part of the Millbrook School's curriculum, and visitors are welcome. On the four-acre site you will see seven endangered species, including red pandas and red wolves, as well as a collection of one hundred and twenty local and exotic species. The kids will also enjoy seeing hawks, snakes, deer, and badgers. The self-guided walk through the zoo is both stroller and wheelchair accessible.

Facilities: *Restrooms.*

Wing's Castle. 717 Bangall Road, Millbrook 12545; (845) 677-9085. Located five miles north of Millbrook on Bangall Road, a mile north of County Route 57. Open June through Labor Day, Wednesday through Sunday, noon to 4:30 P.M.; Labor Day until Christmas, Saturday and Sunday, noon to 4:30 P.M. Admission. Group tours by appointment.

This unique castle-in-progress has been under construction for the last thirty years. Visitors can see this fieldstone edifice on a tour conducted by owner and builder Peter Wing. He and his wife, Toni, have used salvaged materials from antique buildings to create this unique structure whose style they have dubbed Recycled Americana. An antique ship has been used as a balcony in the house, and children delight in the "cauldron" bathtub, complete with terra-cotta fountain. Youngsters will view the whole house as something out of a fairy tale, as they visit the many rooms and the grounds. You may even be lucky enough to meet the giant macaw, the castle's mascot. The house is crammed full of antiques, bric-a-brac, and collectibles, with carousel horses and suits of armor vying for space with stained-glass windows and military weapons. The details will keep everyone on the tour visually entertained, and Peter Wing is only too happy to answer any and all questions about his castle.

Facilities: *Strollers may be difficult to maneuver. Call ahead if wheelchair accessibility is a concern.*

What to Do

BALLOONING

Blue Sky Balloons. 99 Teller Avenue, Beacon 12508; (845) 999-2461. The best time of year for hot-air balloon trips is April through October, but flights are available year-round, weather permitting. This company organizes family-oriented outing. Flights are always within two hours after sunrise or two hours before sunset. FAA-certified pilots are in charge and the company has been in business for over thirty years.

BICYCLING

Harlem Valley Rail Trail. (845) 297-1224 or (518) 789-9591. Two paved sections of this twenty-mile rail trail are open, and the Dutchess County section, about eight miles, runs from Amenia to Millerton. There is access to the bike trail in both towns: in Millerton, at Railroad Plaza, across from the gazebo; in Amenia, at the Mechanic Street parking lot.

Mid Hudson Bicycle Club. (845) 635-1184. This club has a wealth of information about both road and mountain biking in the county; they also sponsor social events and an annual group ride. Call for a schedule or to receive their newsletter.

Wilbur Boulevard Trailway. (845) 451-4100. This trailway runs along Wilbur Boulevard in the city and town of Poughkeepsie. The paved length is 1.2 miles and it's a nice place to go with young children.

BOAT CRUISES

Hudson River Sloop *Clearwater*. 112 Little Market Street, Poughkeepsie 12601; (845) 454-7673. Call Monday through Friday,
9 A.M. to 5 P.M., from May through October, to find out dates, times,
and locations of departures, as well as the public sail schedule.

River Rose **Tours and Cruises.** Poughkeepsie and Newburgh
docks; (845) 565-4210. Operates May through October, call for
sailing schedule. The *River Rose* is a Mississippi-style paddle
wheeler that runs sightseeing cruises and charters. There is an
open upper deck and a fully enclosed, climate-controlled main
deck. This is a nice way to travel with the kids on a summer day.

Sloop *Woodie Guthrie*. Beacon Railroad Plaza, Beacon 12508;
(845) 297-7697. Open July through October, Monday through
Friday, 6:30 P.M. Free. This wooden boat is a replica of a Hudson
River ferry sloop; it goes out on weekday evenings only during the
summer and fall season. If you are in the area, head down to the
Beacon waterfront and take a ride.

CANOEING AND KAYAKING

Hudson River Kayak Tours—Rhinebeck Kayaks. Rhinebeck
12572; (845) 876-0246. Open May through October, 8 A.M. to
8 P.M. This outfitter/guide service provides kayaks and all other necessary equipment, as well as refreshments for up to six people per
group. They launch from Tivoli Bays, Rhinecliff, or Norrie Point.
For first-timers, this is a good way to go.

Hudson Valley Pack and Paddle Adventures. 361 Route 82,
Hopewell Junction 12533; (845) 896-7225. Open daily 10 A.M. to

5 P.M.; extended hours in season. This outfitter organizes kayaking tours on the Hudson River and its tributaries.

DRIVE-IN MOVIES

Only a few hundred drive-in movie theaters survive in America today, and two of them are in southern Dutchess County. Take the kids and lawn chairs for an evening of fun that the family will remember for years to come. Both drive-ins listed here have snack bars and radio sound.

Hyde Park Drive-in. 4114 Route 9, Hyde Park 12538; (845) 229-4738. Open April through September.

Overlook Drive-in. 126 DeGarmo Road, Poughkeepsie 12601; (845) 452-3445. Open April through September.

HIKING

Burger Hill Park. Route 9G, Rhinebeck 12572; (845) 473-4440. Park entrance is on the right, 2.5 miles south of the intersection of Routes 9 and 9G. Open daily year-round, 9 A.M. to dusk. Free.

There are seventy-six acres of open meadows and rural scenic beauty at this spot, a popular place for picnicking, hiking, and sledding during the winter months. Burger Hill is owned by Scenic Hudson. Rising to a 550-foot hilltop, it boasts panoramic vistas of the Hudson River, Shawangunk Ridge, and the Catskill, Berkshire, and Taconic Mountains.

Harlem Valley Rail Trail. (518)789-9591. There are twenty miles of scenic paved trail, linking villages and parks on the rail bed from Amenia and Millerton to Copake Falls in Columbia County. There is access to the trail at Railroad Plaza in Millerton, and in Amenia on Mechanic Street. Free. Open year-round.

Historic Hyde Park Trail. (845) 229-9115. There are 8.5 miles of hiking trails here connecting several parks and historic sites. Bikes are not permitted, and access is behind the FDR Presidential Library Visitors Center. Open year-round.

Poets' Walk Romantic Landscape Park. River Road (County Route 103), Red Hook 12571; (845) 473-4440. Crossing from west to east on Route 199, make a left at the first light and go approximately one mile; the park entrance is on the left. Open daily year-round, 9 A.M. to dusk. Free. Dedicated by Pulitzer Prize–winner John Ashbery in the summer of 1996, this park is located on one of the most beautiful roads in the Hudson Valley, only a few miles from the Kingston-Rhinecliff Bridge. This is a great place for organized nature walks and excursions for school groups. It is one of the few places that allows fairly easy access to the Hudson River. The walking paths consist of gently sloping terrain.

ICE-SKATING

McCann Ice Arena/Mid-Hudson Civic Center. 14 Civic Center Plaza, Poughkeepsie 12601; (845) 454-9800, ext. 212. Open year-round. Public sessions Monday and Friday 11 A.M. to 1 P.M.; weekends 2:30 to 4:30 P.M. Schedule varies with the season, so call ahead for times. Admission. Group rates. This indoor ice rink is part of the Mid-Hudson Civic Center, a recreation, entertainment and convention center that offers a variety of programs year-round. It is one of the best places to ice-skate indoors in the Hudson Valley. Kids will enjoy the large skating area, the skating music, and the bustling ambience. Inquire about figure skating lessons in the skating school office (ext. 205).

Facilities: *Restrooms, concession and snack bar, skate and locker rentals.*

PARKS

James Baird State Park. 14 Maintenance Lane, Pleasant Valley 12569; (845) 452-1489. Go one mile north of Route 55 on the Taconic State Parkway. Open year-round from dawn to dusk. Free.

This is a complete outdoor entertainment center with basketball courts, a playground, a volleyball court, a softball field, tennis courts, hiking trails, a golf course, and a full-service restaurant. The park is a great outdoor excursion destination for families, with picnic areas and hiking trails throughout the park. On weekends, the nature center is open with displays of live and preserved specimens of fish and wildlife native to the park. During the winter months, cross-country skiing is available, but bring your own equipment.

Facilities: *Restrooms, picnic areas, restaurant (open April through November). Wheelchair and stroller accessible.*

Riverfront Park. West Market Street, Hyde Park 12538; (845) 229-8086. Open year-round dawn to dusk. Free.

This small four-acre park along the Hudson River has a children's play area, educational programs, and nature trails; it's also easily accessed from Route 9. This is a nice place to take a break if you are sightseeing in the area.

Facilities: *Restrooms, picnic pavilion.*

Sylvan Lake Beach Park. 18 McDonnells Lane, off County Route 9, Hopewell Junction 12533; (845) 221-9889. Open Memorial Day weekend through Labor Day, daily 8 A.M. to 8 P.M. Parking fee.

This ninety-five-acre park boasts athletic fields, a sandy beach that's great for swimming, a children's play area, and fishing. It's a wonderful place to have a picnic, and kids who enjoy sports and the beach will love it here.

Facilities: *Restrooms, picnic tables, hot showers.*

Taconic State Park/Rudd Pond Area. 59 Rudd Drive, Millerton 12546; (518) 789-3059. Located east of the village of Millerton on County Route 62. Picnic area open year-round, daily dawn to dusk. Seasonal day-use admission charged per vehicle.

This is a wonderful place to take the kids swimming. Rudd Pond is a sixty-four-acre pond with a sandy beach, lifeguards, and rowboat rentals. Fishing is permitted as well, but you need a New York fishing license for anyone over the age of sixteen. There are over eight different types of fish in the pond. Camping season opens the first Friday in May and goes until Sunday night of Labor Day weekend; advance reservations are suggested. During winter families will enjoy cross-country skiing here, but you must bring your own equipment.

Facilities: *Restrooms, picnic areas, bathhouse, campsites.*

Taconic State Park/Copake Falls Area. Route 344, Copake Falls 12517; (518) 329-3993. Open year-round, daily, dawn to dusk.

In this area, there is an Ore Pit Pond for swimming, but no beach, as well as a wading pool for young children. Campsites can be rented, but reservations are suggested. There are ninety-six campsites, which can be reserved. For day visitors, there are hiking trails, a playground, fishing, access to the Harlem Valley Rail

Trail (bike path), and Bash Bish Falls. In the winter, the youngest cross-country skiers will enjoy the wild surroundings, but you must bring your own equipment.

Facilities: *Restrooms, picnic areas, bathhouse, campsites.*

Wilcox Park. Route 199, Stanfordville 12581; (845) 758-6100. Open Memorial Day weekend through Labor Day, daily 10 A.M. to 8 P.M.; closed the rest of the year, except by advance reservation for group outings. Admission.

This is one of the nicest parks to visit with young children during the summer. It has a small lake and sandy beach area. Paddleboats are a popular rental for older children, and when the water fun wears off, miniature golf and a special children's playground will keep the kids occupied. The hiking trails vary in length, so even the youngest in your party will enjoy taking a nature walk, on which you might come across deer and raccoons.

Facilities: *Restrooms, picnic tables, snack bar, bathhouse. Campsites (electric and water hookups available) by reservation.*

PERFORMING ARTS

Bardavon 1869 Opera House Children's Theater. 35 Market Street, Poughkeepsie 12601; (845) 473-5288. Open year-round; performance times and offerings vary. Admission by ticket; prices vary. Advance reservations for Daytime Performance Series are recommended.

This is one of the last (and best) of the old-time opera houses that once operated as cultural centers in small towns and cities all across in America. Built in 1869, Bardavon still operates as a lively theater and performing arts center, with a history of fine entertainment; past performers have included Mark Twain, Sarah

Bernhardt, Ethel Barrymore, and Milton Berle. The theater was re-furbished in the 1920s, and today it offers audiences a wide range of nationally known entertainers. It is a perfect place to introduce young people to musical performances and theater. In past years, life-sized puppet shows, incredible magic shows, musical revues, plays, ballets, and musicals have entertained youngsters. The selection of shows appeals to many different age groups, and Bardavon notes which performance is appropriate for what age.

Facilities: *Restrooms. The theater is wheelchair accessible, and there are special designated seats for the disabled, but you should call ahead about this service. Hearing-impaired children also can be accommodated with lightweight headphones for rent. Groups should inquire about special offerings, like the theater tours and question-and-answer sessions with the performers.*

Center for Performing Arts at Rhinebeck. Route 308, Rhinebeck 12572; (845) 876-3080. Open year-round. This multipurpose cultural and educational center features dramatic plays, musicals, dance, concerts, lectures, staged readings, and workshops. There are several children's shows as well.

Facilities: *Restrooms, wheelchair and stroller accessible.*

PICK-YOUR-OWN FARMS

Barton Orchards. County Route 7, Beekman Poughquag Road, Beekman 12570; (845) 227-2306. Open May through December for picking seasonal crops that include berries of all kinds, apples, pumpkins, Christmas trees, and vegetables. This is a great place to take kids since there are hayrides in the autumn and special events throughout the season.

Blueberry Park. 2747 County Route 21, Wingdale 12594; (845) 724-5776. Open July and August. They live up to their name, stocking only pick-your-own blueberries in the summer months. You can also get a farm tour with advance notice.

Greig Farm. Pitcher Lane, Red Hook 12571; (845) 758-1234. Located off Route 9G, three miles north of town; follow signs. There are acres of fields here available for self-harvesting, as well as a wonderful farm market. Berries, beans, apples, pumpkins, and peaches are only some of the seasonal treats to be gathered; you will also find a winery, greenhouse, and extensive herb and cut-your-own flower gardens on the site. This is one of the largest and most popular stops for pick-your-own in the county, and participating in all the farm has to offer could take a couple of hours if you spend time in the fields.

Keepsake Farm. East Hook Cross Road, Hopewell Junction 12533; (845) 897-2266. Open May through October. Call for hours. You can pick cherries, blueberries, raspberrries, strawberries, and peaches during the spring and summer, as well as apples and pumpkins in the fall. The market offers homemade baked goods plus freshly pressed cider and doughnuts in season. There's live entertainment and children's activities on weekends in autumn, as well as hayrides, a petting zoo, and hay bales for children to climb on. This is a terrific stop that the kids will love.

Secor Farms. 63 Robinson Lane, Wappingers Falls 12590; (845) 452-6883. Open June through August and the month of October, for picking strawberries, which they are famous for, as well as apples, berries, and pumpkins in autumn. The kids will enjoy going on a hayride here, as well.

Columbia County

Visit Columbia County and take a tour through American history. Rambling horse farms and stately center-hall Colonials with expansive lawns pepper the rolling countryside. Mansions of prominent early American families, the home of America's eighth president, the Moorish villa of a major Hudson River School painter, a Shaker settlement, and a museum of firefighting are just some of the places families can experience our unique American heritage. The county is also filled with pristine lakes, dense forests, mountain trails, and winding roads making it a giant outdoor playground. Whether your family loves swimming, boating, hiking, cycling, or skiing, this is the place to enjoy it.

Many of the Columbia's highlights combine education and recreation. **Clermont,** the ancestral home of the politically and socially prominent Livingston family, is one of the county's treasures. Situated along the Hudson River, children will be entranced by the special events offered on weekends, from Revolutionary War encampments to summer brass band concerts, Fourth of July celebrations, and autumn county fairs. At the **Old Chatham Sheepherding Company** youngsters can watch goats being milked and see the process of cheese making step by step at the largest sheep dairy farm in the country. Farm Day, the last Saturday in April, is a great time to visit with the kids. **Mud Creek Environmental Learning Center** in Ghent, open year-round, has a marvelous nature trail that wends its way through wetlands with two kid-friendly loops; children who are interested in nature will love this stop. **Lake Taghkanic State Park** is located on 1,569 wooded acres adjacent to the Taconic Parkway. The 156-acre lake offers families two beaches, boat rentals, and several picnic areas, and is great for swimming. The park also has playgrounds, a ballfield, volleyball courts, camping areas, and numerous hiking trails. Children of all ages will appreciate a visit to the **American Museum of Firefighting** in Hudson. It's packed with one of the nation's largest collections of colorful equipment and art relating to the fireman's trade.

Columbia County offers a number of wonderful family festivals throughout the year. Highlights include Summer Family Fun Weekends at **Olana,** June through August, featuring crafts, nature programs, games, and art projects at this beautiful state historic site just outside the city of Hudson. The **Shaker Museum** puts on a Strawberry Shortcake Festival in July. Last but not least, the Columbia County Fair in Chatham is a Labor Day tradition. The oldest continuously held fair in the country, the five-day celebration features prizewinning horses, sheep, cows, and other livestock, musical entertainment, midway games, and fabulous rides.

For further information, contact **Columbia County Tourism,** 401 State Street, Hudson 12534; (518) 828-3375 or (800) 724-1846; www.columbiacountyny.com.

What to See

MUSEUMS AND HISTORIC SITES

American Museum of Firefighting. 117 Harry Howard Avenue (next to the Firemen's Home), Hudson 12534; (518) 822-1875. Open daily 9 A.M. to 4:30 P.M.; closed on national holidays. Call in advance for group tours. Free, but donations welcomed.

Children of all ages will appreciate an hour in this museum, which is packed with one of the nation's largest collections of colorful equipment and art of the fireman's trade. As you step into the large display room called the Engine Hall, you will discover more than ninety pieces of antique fire engines, pumpers, and trucks, all in fine condition, and, of course, many of them painted bright red. The exhibit contains samples of equipment dating back to 1725, when fires were fought by bucket brigades. Elaborate engines include the Volunteer, which is like a Victorian fantasy. The walls of the museum are lined with old fire banners, lovely paintings that were used by the various companies in parades and at festivals. The image of the fireman (and -woman) is immortalized in paintings, advertisements, statues, helmets, and elaborate fire horns carried during processions. Each display is clearly marked, and there are often fire buffs around to answer your questions.

Facilities: *Restrooms, picnic area. The museum is wheelchair accessible.*

Clermont. 1 Clermont Avenue, Germantown 12526; (518) 537-4240. Off NY Route 9G, north of Tivoli; follow signs to Clermont State Historic Park. Open April through October, Tuesday through Sunday, 11 A.M. to 5 P.M.; November through March, weekends only, 11 A.M. to 4 P.M. Grounds open year-round, 8:30 A.M. to sunset. Admission. Group tours available by reservation.

This is the ancestral home of the American branch of the Livingston family, established circa 1730 and in use by the same family until 1964. Chancellor Robert Livingston, one of the five drafters of the Declaration of Independence, served as minister to France under Thomas Jefferson and was the partner of steamboat inventor Robert Fulton. Today, parents may wish to tour the elaborately restored house that overlooks the Hudson River and is filled with magnificent eighteenth- and nineteenth-century family heirlooms. Their children will enjoy the summer history day camp and special events offered many weekends throughout the year, including replica Revolutionary War encampments, music festivals, and Fourth of July festivities. The site offers a perfect place to picnic, with views up- and downriver, and children can run around and have a good time. School tours are welcomed all year, and at Christmastime there are special tours of the elaborately decorated house. Don't miss Clermont if you are traveling with children of any age.

Facilities: *Restrooms, picnic tables, barbecue pits. Pets are allowed in most areas if leashed. There are paths and miles of walking trails, but you may have trouble with a stroller or wheelchair on trails. While strollers and back carriers are not allowed in the mansion, the first floor is wheelchair accessible.*

Olana. Route 9G, one mile south of Rip Van Winkle Bridge, Hudson 12534; (518) 828-0135. Open April through October, Tuesday through Sunday, 10 A.M. to 5 P.M.; November until 4 P.M.; December through March, Saturday and Sunday, 10 A.M. to 4 P.M. or by apointment. Guided tours only, call to reserve tickets before you go. The grounds can be toured without a guide at no charge. Admission.

Frederic Edwin Church, a nineteenth-century American landscape painter, started construction on his Persian-style mansion overlooking the Hudson River in 1870. Children will be intrigued by the hand-painted roof tiles and colorful turrets. Inside they will have the opportunity to see Church's painting studio, set up just as it was in his day, as well as the interesting decor, which includes a pair of gilded crane lamps that look as if they stepped out of an Egyptian wall painting. Church and his wife, Isabel, traveled extensively throughout the Middle East and Europe and the treasures collected on their journeys may be seen throughout the thirty-seven rooms of the house. During holiday season Olana is decorated with elaborate greenery and Yuletide confections grace the tables. Older children will particularly enjoy the tour. There are special programs at Olana for young people year-round on weekends, so call in advance to see what is on the schedule before you visit.

Facilities: *Visitors center with restrooms, gift shop, and video on Church's life. Stroller and wheelchair accessible.*

Parker O'Malley Air Museum. 435 Old Route 20, Ghent 12075 (at the southwest side of Columbia County Airport); (518) 392-7200. Open on the first Saturday of every month, 10 A.M. to 4 P.M. Admission, but children under the age of twelve are admitted free.

The Parker O'Malley Air Museum has military and civilian aircraft from the 1920s, 1930s, and 1940s, as well as a varied collection of wartime memorabilia. Students of the Parker O'Malley band play music of the era. The foundation seeks to improve the academic, artistic, and social abilities of its young visitors through participation in a variety of activities and events. Call before you go to check the current schedule.

Facilities: *Restrooms.*

Shaker Museum. 88 Shaker Museum Road, Old Chatham 12136; (518) 794-9100. From Chatham, take 295 east to the East Chatham Post Office, and turn left; follow the road into Old Chatham Square, and bear left onto County Route 13; then, turn right onto Shaker Museum Road. Open mid-May through early November, Wednesday through Monday, 10 A.M. to 5 P.M. Admission. Group tours/rates available.

This Shaker museum is not as well known as its larger Massachusetts counterpart (see p. 264), but it offers children a unique look at the tools, farm equipment, and inventions of the Shakers, a sect that flourished in New York during the nineteenth century. The walk-through exhibits are well marked, and there are displays of Shaker baskets, clothing, and a large selection of woodworking tools. Children are given a guidebook that leads them through the museum on a detective search to find various artifacts; by following the clues, kids will learn about the life of Shakers. Outside they can visit the schoolhouse and walk through the herb garden. There are special events for children during summer and fall, and this museum is an enjoyable introduction to an often neglected part of America's social history.

Facilities: *Restrooms, picnic tables, gift shop, snack bar. Strollers are welcomed here and are easily maneuvered through the exhibits. Limited wheelchair accessibility.*

OTHER ATTRACTIONS

The Fields Sculpture Park. Letter S Road, Ghent 12075; (518) 392-7656. From Hudson, take Route 9H north; make a right onto County Route 22, then left onto Letter S Road. Continue to the second driveway on the left. Open daily, sunrise to sunset. Free.

Founded in 1988 as public grounds for viewing contemporary

sculpture, this spacious one-hundred-fifty-acre park contains over forty sculptures with works by renowned artists. Children will be able to explore freely at their own pace as they wander through the scenic rolling hills. The central path goes around a lovely pond and traverses a large expanse of fields. Some of the sculptures are located on farmlands so children will see crops growing amid the artwork, giving the Fields an interesting connection to the landscape. This is a wonderful place to expose children to the art of sculpture outside the confines of a museum setting. Throughout the year there are workshops and programs for children's groups.

Facilities: *Restrooms.*

Old Chatham Sheepherding Company. 99 Shaker Museum Road, Old Chatham 12136; (518) 794-7733 or (888) SHEEP-60. Open year-round, daily 9 A.M. to 5 P.M., but call before you go to find out what's happening at the farm. Free.

The kids will be enchanted by a visit to this working farm where they can watch goats being milked and see the cheese-making process from beginning to end. The farm produces several types of sheep's milk cheeses and yogurt—it is the largest sheep dairy farm in the country. In 1994, the operation started with one hundred and fifty sheep, and now there are more than twelve hundred East Friesian crossbred sheep grazing on six hundred beautiful acres of rolling pasture land. European methods are used to create new American cheeses, which have won culinary awards and have been praised in gourmet food publications. Farm Day, the last Saturday in April, is a great time to visit, as the place is bustling with activity.

Facilities: *Restrooms, retail shop where cheeses and yogurt can be purchased.*

Petting Zoo at Love Apple Farm. Route 9H, Ghent 12075; (518) 828-5048. Open July through November, daily 10 A.M. to 5 P.M.

This is a truly special place that kids will love. In addition to the petting zoo, there are dozens of varieties of apples to pick in season, along with pears, prunes, cherries, and peaches. The doughnuts and home-baked fruit pies are first-rate and are for sale on the premises.

Facilities: *Restroom, farm market.*

Taconic Sculpture Park. Stever Hill Road, Spencertown 12165; (518) 392-5757. Open year-round, daily, 10 A.M. to 5 P.M. Free.

Roy Kanwit, a working sculptor, has forty of his pieces exhibited on the grounds. His home/studio is a stone castlelike structure. The park attracts a few thousand visitors every year. Children will thoroughly enjoy this stop where they can go inside many of the enormous sculptures.

Facilities: *None.*

What to Do

BICYCLING

Harlem Valley Rail Trail. Undermountain Road, off Route 22, Ancram 12501; Valley View Road, Copake 12516; Taconic State Park entrance near Depot-Deli, Copake Falls 12517.

When completed, this paved bicycle/pedestrian path will stretch from Wassaic in Dutchess County to Chatham in Columbia County, and run some forty-six miles. It was built on the old railroad bed that connected New York City, the Harlem Valley, and Chatham. New York State purchased twenty-two miles of land to build this linear park, about half of which lies in southern Columbia County. The area is ideal for hiking and bicycling. Kids will enjoy seeing many species of birds on the trail, as well as deer, coyotes, foxes, hawks, turtles, and beavers (or at least their dams). The trail passes through the hamlets of Amenia and Millerton in Dutchess County, as well as Copake Falls in Columbia County.

CANOEING AND KAYAKING

Keep in mind that Columbia County doesn't have an array of outfitters where visitors can rent canoes or kayaks. The state parks are the best places to canoe or row on a lake. However, if you have your own equipment, the following two spots are excellent places to explore with the kids.

Rogers Island (under the Rip Van Winkle Bridge). Row or paddle out to this paradise for bird-watching. There are eagles, water fowl, and an amazing array of birds that inhabit this intriguing island in the Hudson River between Greene and Columbia Counties.

Stockport Flats. Station Road, Greenport. If you are traveling north on Route 9, look for Station Road, which is on the left, just after crossing the Columbiaville Bridge. This state land offers the perfect place to explore by canoe. There are 250 acres here. The waters of these flats are easy to navigate and a good place for beginners and young canoe enthusiasts to practice paddling.

FISHING

The county is filled with deep lakes, clear streams, and stocked creeks, making it a fine destination for a fishing outing with the kids. Remember that a New York State fishing license is required for anyone over the age of sixteen. The following creeks are stocked by the Department of Environmental Conservation and are fairly easy to find. To get to the **Claverack Creek** turn onto Roxburgh Road, off Route 217, and look for the bridge that crosses the creek; this is a good spot to fish. There is also access on Route 23 at Red Mills, off the south side of the bridge only, and on County Route 29 halfway between Webb and Hiscox Roads. A nice spot to try your luck is **Kinderhook Creek.** From Route 66 in the town of Chatham there is easy access at Bachus Road; you can also get to the creek at the bridge in Malden Bridge. **Roeliff Jansen Creek** is accessed from County Route 2 between Elizaville and the Taconic State Parkway; another place to fish this creek is off Route 22, two miles south of Hillsdale on Black Grocery Road.

HIKING

When walking through wooded and grassy areas be aware that Lyme disease is transmitted by deer ticks and is extremely prevalent in this county. Wear appropriate clothing and check yourself and the kids if you wander off marked trails for any reason. The following are some nice places with relatively short trails to comfortably hike with kids.

Borden's Pond Preserve. Off Route 203, just outside the village of Chatham. Open year-round from dawn to dusk, this fifty-two-acre preserve provides a nice change of pace after shopping in town and is within walking distance of the main village streets. This is a relatively new area, with an old woodland mill pond surrounded by forest land and a series of gently sloping trails.

Greenport Conservation Area. (518) 392-5252. Open year-round dawn to dusk. Heading south on Route 9 to Greenport, go right onto Joslen Boulevard, across from a condominium complex; then make a right onto Daisy Hill Road. There is a parking area and information kiosk with interpretive brochures detailing the 3.5 miles of trails marked in red, blue, and green. This is a wonderful place to take kids who want to go on a short hike; the trails wend their way through meadows, woodlands, and wetlands along the Hudson River. A hand-hewn cedar gazebo overlooking the river is a great spot to rest and enjoy the view.

Mud Creek Environmental Learning Center. Route 66, Ghent 12075; (518) 828-4386. Building open year-round, weekdays, 8 A.M. to 4:30 P.M., and on one Saturday each month when a public walk is scheduled; other times, by appointment. Groups by advance reservation. Trails are open dawn to dusk daily. There are two short trails that lead through forests, fields, and wetlands, which are detailed in a self-guiding pamphlet. The environmental center building has a Hudson River estuary exhibit, other educational displays, and restrooms.

Pachaquack Preserve. Elm Street, off Route 203, Valatie 12184; (518) 758-9806. Open year-round, dawn to dusk. This forty-three-acre preserve is operated by the town of Valatie, and it's a beautiful spot for a walk any time of year. There are two miles of walking trails, picnic tables, and a gazebo. The walking is extremely easy, so even the youngest travelers will feel comfortable here; three trails follow the Kinderhook Creek, where there is excellent fishing.

Wilson M. Powell Wildlife Sanctuary. Hunt Club Road, off County Route 13, Old Chatham 12136. Open year-round, dawn to dusk.

This 130-acre sanctuary offers a variety of walks with lovely views of the mountains; some trails meander around a pond. One marked trail leads you on a half-mile walk to the observation area called Dorson Rock. Kids enjoy watching the ducks and birds at the pond.

PARKS

Lake Taghkanic State Park. 1528 State Route 82, eleven miles south of Hudson, at the Taconic Parkway, Ancram 12502; (518) 851-3631. Open year-round for day use. Vehicle use fee from Memorial Day weekend through Columbus Day.

The park is a delightful getaway with its 1,568 acres of lush rolling hills and 156-acre lake. There are many recreational opportunities for the entire family to enjoy year-round. During the summer months, visitors can enjoy boating, kayaking, swimming, picnicing, fishing, and guided hikes. The nature center operates during the peak season and offers children educational programs to explore plant and wildlife. During the winter, families can enjoy cross-country skiing, ice-skating, and snowshoeing. There are also cabins and campsites in the park for those who wish to camp overnight.

Facilities: *Restrooms, bath houses, picnic tables, rowboat and paddleboat rentals, snack bar, tent sites, cabins and cottages (available May to October). Pets must be kept on a leash and are restricted to special areas.*

Taconic State Park. Route 344 (off Route 22), Copake Falls 12517; (518) 329-3993. Open year-round, dawn to dusk.

A twenty-five-mile network of hiking trails ranges from very easy to difficult in this five-thousand-acre park, one of the largest in the Hudson Valley. The park spans two counties (Dutchess and Columbia) and borders Massachusetts and Connecticut, running for sixteen miles along Taconic Ridge with spectacular views in many places. This is a good stop for families; there's a small nature center with displays, and camping areas are open from May through November; cabins may be rented year-round. Older children may be interested in the historical section of the park, which includes the Copake Iron Works, a relic from 1845, when iron-making was the main industry in town. For over sixty years, iron ore, limestone, and hardwood were extracted locally with water power from Bash Bish Creek; 2,500 tons of blast iron, much of which was used for making car wheels, was taken out of the "park." In the 1920s the owner of the foundry sold the site to the state. The cabins that once housed laborers are now rented out as overnight lodging to travelers.

Facilities: *Restrooms, limited swimming, campsites, cabins, hiking trails.*

PICK-YOUR-OWN FARMS

The Berry Farm. Route 203, Chatham 12037; (518) 392-4609. Call for hours. The Berry Farm is a haven for berry lovers, offering everything from gooseberries and currants to boysenberries, strawberries, and even kiwi fruit. Call the farm to find out when the crops are ripe for the picking.

Golden Harvest Farms. Route 9, Valatie 12184 (one mile north of the junction of Routes 9 and 9H); (518) 758-7683. Call for hours. This farm provides pick-your-own or already-picked apples, as well as a large roadside stand.

Love Apple Farm (see Other Attractions, p. 133).

SKIING

Catamount. Route 23, Hillsdale 12539; (518) 325-3200. Open weekends and holidays, 8:30 A.M. to 4 P.M.; night skiing on Wednesday and Thursday, 5 to 9 P.M.; Friday and Saturday, 5 to 10 P.M. Charge for lift ticket, but age six and under ski free when accompanied by ticketed adult. Group rates.

When you ski at Catamount you can see three states (New York, Massachusetts, and Connecticut) from the top of the runs. There are twenty-nine trails, along with seven lifts and snowmaking on 100 percent of the mountain. This is a full-service ski area with all the amenities. The varied terrain suits all ages and skill levels, and a full children's ski program is offered. The Mountain Cats program is for skiers from age four to twelve, and for snowboarders from age seven to twelve. The nursery will care for children ages two to six, 8:30 A.M. to 4 P.M., while parents enjoy the slopes.

Facilities: *Restrooms, picnic tables, ski shop, retail shop, restaurant, snack bar, full equipment rentals, nursery.*

SWIMMING

Knickerbocker Lake. Route 9, just outside the village of Valatie. Open late June to mid-August. This large lake, managed by the town of Kinderhook, has a nice beach, making it a popular place to swim among residents, especially those with young children. It is also open to the public for a fee of $10 per car.

THEATER

MacHaydn Theatre. Route 203, Chatham 12037; (518) 392-9292. This theater specializes in summer-stock musical productions. This intimate setting is the perfect venue for all-time crowd pleasers like *Oliver, Oklahoma, Fiddler on the Roof*, and other performances that the kids will enjoy.

Spencertown Academy. Route 203, Spencertown 12165; (518) 392-3693. Built in 1847 as a private school, Spencertown is now a cultural arts center where visitors can enjoy films, dance, theater, and a variety of other cultural events. The academy has a reputation as a leading venue for great folk music and jazz. Groups of local, regional, and national renown play this intimate setting at all times of the year. There are also workshops, performances, and a variety of classes geared to children. Two galleries on the premises feature changing arts and crafts exhibits. Call for a schedule of events here if you will be in the area.

Greene County

Greene County offers the perfect family outdoor experience at any time of year. During the winter, families can visit the slopes at Hunter or Windham Mountain, which provide some of the best downhill skiing in the East. Spring brings an annual tour of homes, farms, and estates run by the county historical society. Summer celebrates its warmth with the pleasures of icy brooks for feet tired from hiking, as well as a flood of cultural festivals. Come autumn visitors wonder at the colors that transform the hills and villages into paint pots full of orange and red. The magic that enchanted Rip Van Winkle in Catskill still impresses visitors today.

Watch your children's eyes light up as they pet and feed a baby deer or llama at the **Catskill Game Farm,** home to thousands of domestic and exotic animals from alligators and lions to lambs and peacocks. When it's 90 degrees in the shade, splash down in the **Zoom Flume Water Park** in East Durham. The Raging River ride and Zoom Flume let the kids slosh and slide their way down beautiful Shady Glen Canyon. **Armstrong's Elk Farm** is a fascinating educational detour where you can learn how the elk's velvet antlers are harvested and used for a variety of drugs and natural remedies. The owner loves to show visitors around the farm and explain about the business of raising these gentle animals. **Bear Creek Landing Family Sports Complex** in Hunter is a licensed fishing preserve, which also has a challenging sport-putting course and driving range. In winter there is an outdoor skating rink and snowmobiling at this lovely recreational area surrounded by mountains. **North and South Lakes** provide breathtaking scenery and a multitude of activities. Kids can swim in a mountain lake with a clean sandy beach. Boat rentals and fishing are also available. A short hike away from North Lake is Kaaterskill Falls, one of the highest waterfalls on the East Coast and a popular subject for Hudson River School artists.

The following are just a few of the wonderful celebrations held annually in the county that may fit into your travel plans. On Memorial Day weekend, the Annual Irish Festival in East Durham is a great stop if you love music and dance. In July, the Mountain Culture Festival sponsored by the Catskill Mountain Foundation celebrates regional arts and crafts; there's plenty to amuse the kids including performers of all kinds, demonstrations, bike races, food vendors, and craftspeople selling their wares. The county fair in Catskill, also in July, is a festive event—amusement rides, lawn mower races, and live entertainment are all part of the fun.

For further information, contact **Greene County Promotion Department,** (518) 943-3223 or (800) 355-CATS.

What to See

MUSEUMS AND HISTORIC SITES

Zadock Pratt Museum (Homestead) and Pratt's Rocks. Route 23, Prattsville 12468; (518) 299-3395. Open Memorial Day weekend through Columbus Day, Thursday through Monday, 1 to 4 P.M. School and group tours may be arranged year-round by appointment.

The museum/home of Zadock Pratt, a ninetieth-century community leader who owned a thriving leather-tanning business, may be of interest to older children. However, just about all kids will enjoy visiting Pratt's Rocks, just outside town on Route 23, a memorial carved by a stonemason into the wall of rock. The park-like setting is free and open year-round, and the huge stone reliefs show Pratt's son, his favorite horse, and Zadock Pratt himself. There is a short hiking path, great views from the summit, and a nice picnic area overlooking the Schoharie Creek.

Facilities: *Restrooms (in the museum only), picnic tables (at Pratt's Rocks).*

OTHER ATTRACTIONS

Armstrong's Elk Farm. 936 Hervey Sunside Road, Cornwallville 12418; (518) 622-8452. Take the NYS Thruway to exit 21; pick up Route 23 west for twelve miles; and make a right onto Hervey Street. Open year-round by appointment. Free.

This is a captivating educational detour for just about anyone. There are over forty Rocky Mountain elk in their own habitat at this farm, and spring is when the baby elk are born. Learn how the velvet antlers are harvested and used for a variety of drugs and natural remedies that prevent bone deterioration. The farm is an excellent place for bird-watchers—the kids will enjoying identifying orioles, finches, bluebirds, and many more species. Owner Les Armstrong loves to tell visitors about the farm and the business of raising elk. He is a fascinating character and makes this a special stop for families.

Facilities: *Restrooms.*

Bear Creek Landing Family Sports Complex. Located at the junction of Routes 214 and 23A, Hunter 12442; (518) 263-3839. Open year-round, Monday through Thursday 10 A.M. to 10 P.M.; Friday and Saturday, until 11 P.M.; Sunday, 9 A.M. to 10 P.M. Call for winter hours, which vary. Admission fee for activites.

This licensed fishing preserve, with rainbow, brown, and golden trout also has a challenging putting course featuring eighteen holes of dramatic rock waterfalls, sand traps, and terrific views of the Catskills. There is a four-hundred-yard golf driving range, and lessons are available in season. In the winter months a small outdoor ice skating rink delights children of all ages (with rentals available); there is also snowmobiling here. The restaurant and pub on the premises is a delightful place to relax and enjoy a drink or lunch.

Facilities: *Restrooms, restaurant, skate rentals.*

Catskill Game Farm. Game Farm Road, Route 32, Catskill 12414; (518) 678-9595. Take Route 32 and watch for signs. Open May through October daily, 9 A.M. to 5 P.M. Admission; children three and under free. Additional charge for train ride and amusement rides. Group tours and rates can be arranged.

One of the oldest game farms in the country, with more than two thousand animals and birds, this is a great place to spend an entire day. Lions and giraffes roam the grounds, and the not-to-be-missed special shows include elephants. The petting zoo is inhabited by friendly deer and llamas that can be fed by hand if you purchase the farm's crackers. Very young or small children may feel overwhelmed by the loose animals which crowd in if you have food in hand. The petting zoo also has lots of small baby animals like pigs and lambs, which can be bottle fed. Visitors can take a train from the petting zoo to the birdhouse, a trip that delights small children. Although the admission charge is on the high side, the grounds are expansive, and a family easily can find a day's worth of activities. After the children tire of the animals and the show, there is an amusement park with rides and a playground, in addition to a huge sandbox area and a splashpad water spray area with lounging deck.

Facilities: *Restrooms, picnic areas, gift shop, snack bars. The paved pathways and stroller areas make this an excellent place for moving about with infants. Wheelchair accessible.*

Catskill Mountain Wolf Center. Route 32 (three miles north of the Catskill Game Farm and two miles south of Cairo), Cairo 12413; (518) 622-8013. Open Memorial Day weekend through Labor Day weekend, Thursday through Tuesday, 10:30 A.M. to 4:30 P.M. Admission.

This nonprofit organization is dedicated to the preservation of the wolf population through education. It offers a chance to see the gray wolf in a forest setting and to learn about wolves in the wild. A twenty-minute video will be of interest to older children; all the kids will enjoy the room with computer stations that feature wolf games.

Facilities: *Restrooms.*

Hull-O Farms. 3739 County Route 20, Durham 12422; (518) 239-6950. A stay at this farm is an authentic experience that will be long remembered by your children. You can live the country life on this three-hundred-acre working dairy farm that has been in the same family for seven generations. Milk a cow; collect chicken eggs; feed pigs and baby calves; go fishing; or take a nature walk. The hands-on experience is fun for everyone. There are pumpkins to be picked and hayrides in the autumn, as well as barbecue dinners during the warm weather months. There are three cozy guesthouses on the premises and home-cooked meals are served in the homestead. Nightly rates include a full breakfast and dinner. Children under the age of two stay free; those two to twelve are less than half price. There is a two-night minimum stay.

Junior Speedway. 7399 Route 32, Cairo 12413; (518) 622-4050. Open July through Labor Day, daily, 10 A.M. to 10 P.M.; May, June, and Labor Day through Columbus Day, weekends only, noon to dusk.

This mini-amusement park has go-carts, a miniature golf course, baseball batting cages, and a game room to entertain kids. Those four to nine years of age will enjoy the battery-operated Jeeps and roller facers (boards with roller-skate wheels that can be steered).

Facilities: *Restrooms, snack bar, gift shop, picnic area.*

Mountaintop Arboretum. Route 23C, Tannersville 12485; (518) 589-3903. Open year-round, but call about guided tours, which may be arranged in advance.

This nonprofit organization features a collection of exotic and native trees and shrubs on a lovely ten-acre site. Each season brings new sights, from the flowering height of spring to the brighly colored autumn foliage. Many of the plants have identification markers, and there are educational workshops throughout the year, some of which appeal to children. Those kids who always want to know "What is that tree?" will enjoy this stop. The arboretum serves as a botanical research facility and a place for programs on a variety of horticultural topics.

Winter Clove Inn. Winter Clove Road, Round Top 12473; (518) 622-3267. Open year-round. Group rates.

This is a great family vacation resort that has been run by the same family for four generations. Located in Winter Clove, a deep valley that holds the winter snows until early spring, guests are housed in an old-fashioned (but comfortable) lodge, which has been updated and restored to provide all the modern amenities. Escape to the charm of the country, a place where time moves at a more leisurely pace. Indoor and outdoor pools, tennis courts, volleyball, golf, bowling alleys, and a game room are all on the premises, so that there is always something fun going on for every age group. Kids will love the country picnics, hayrides, movies, and bonfires that are offered in the warm weather months. During summer evenings, guests can also visit with friends and enjoy the inn's large front porch, complete with rocking chairs. Visitors are welcome to enjoy the many beautiful pools and waterfalls that surround Winter Clove. The chef prepares three meals daily, and the choices on the menu include children's entrees. During the winter, access to cross-country ski trails and equipment are included in the room rate. The Catskills offer many exciting recreational activities nearby. There are also farmers markets, country fairs, and covered bridges to explore.

Facilities: *Complete facilities, including a bowling alley, indoor and outdoor pools, tennis courts, nine-hole executive golf course, and hiking trails.*

Zoom Flume Aquamusement Park. Shady Glen Road (just off Route 145), two miles north of East Durham 12423; (518) 239-4559. Open mid-June through Labor Day, Monday through Friday, 10 A.M. to 6 P.M.; Saturday and Sunday, until 7 P.M. Admission.

This lovely "aquamusement" park is set in Shady Glen Canyon, a natural formation of steep walls and running water, so the site itself is beautiful and worth a stop, even if you are going to observe rather than participate in the array of water activities. The Raging River Ride and Zoom Flume let you slosh and slide your way down the canyon; there's also an enormous activity pool with several slides of all sizes, a game area, and a toddler section for one- and two-year-olds. The Black Vortex Speed Slide takes three at a time through an exciting water adventure that older kids will appreciate. There are nature trails, scenic overlooks, and waterfalls, as well as a restaurant with an observation deck and a sizable outdoor food court and picnic area.

Facilities: *Restrooms, picnic tables, changing rooms, snack bar/restaurant, lockers.*

What to Do

CANOEING AND KAYAKING

CD Lane Park. 281 County Route 56, Maplecrest 12454; (518) 734-4170. Open Memorial Day weekend through Labor Day. Free.

This small lake has a sandy beach area and the park itself offers soccer and baseball fields, a picnic pavilion, and a beautiful environment the kids will love. You should bring your own canoe or kayak to the lake; there are no rentals available.

North and South Lake State Park. County Route 18, Haines Falls 12436; (518) 589-5058. Open May through October, 9 A.M. to dusk. Admission. There are canoe and rowboat rentals here; the lakes both have beach areas with lifeguards on duty during the summer swimming season.

FISHING

There are approximately sixty streams with wild trout in the county, as well as lakes, ponds, and, of course, the Hudson River. Route 23A passes Rip Van Winkle Lake in Tannersville, Schoharie Creek, and the Schoharie Reservoir, all easily accessible and great places to fish with young children. Route 145 leads to Lower Catskill Creek, Upper Catskill Creek, and Ten Mile Creek, while Route 296 offers easy access to the Batavia Kill boat launch and the East Kill Trout Preserve. Public fishing places in the county are marked by yellow signs and most have designated parking areas. Permits and licenses can be obtained at most bait and tackle shops or town clerks' offices. For more detailed information, contact the **Department of Environmental Conservation** at (845) 256-3000.

Fins and Grins. 5571 Cauterskill Road, Catskill 12414; (518) 943-3407. They offer fishing charters as well as scenic rides on the Hudson River. Captain Bob Lewis supplies all the equipment you need for the excursion.

HIKING

Cohatate Preserve. Route 385, Athens 12015; (518) 622-3620. This nature preserve with a self-guided tour on trails that run along the Hudson River is a perfect gentle hiking spot, even with young children. You can see the sign for the preserve on the right side of the highway if you are heading from Catskill toward Athens.

4 Miles Point Preserve. Route 385, Coxsackie 12051. This preserve is about eight miles north of the Rip Van Winkle Bridge, a

7.6-acre riverfront area that offers picturesque shoreline vistas and a tranquil inland pond. There are nature trails, and this is a wonderful place to observe several types of birds. Kids will be comfortable on the gently sloping terrain.

RamsHorn-Livingston Sanctuary. Route 9W, Catskill 12414. Go 2.5 miles south of the Rip Van Winkle Bridge on Route 9W; then make a left onto Grandview Avenue; and go one-half mile to the parking area. Here there are 480 acres of the Hudson's largest tidal swamp forest, which is a breeding ground for shad and bass. There are about three miles of trails that can be easily hiked by even the youngest children.

HORSEBACK RIDING

Bailiwick Ranch/Catskill Equestrian Center. Castle Road, next to Catskill Game Farm, Catskill 12414; (518) 678-5665. Open year-round. In business for over forty years, there is riding here for all ages and abilities. Scenic mountain trail rides are offered for either one or two hours. For those who would like something more intensive, there are all-day mountain trips and overnight camping excursions. The youngest kids will have fun on the pony rides and playing in the petting zoo. There are both English and Western riding lessons offered in the indoor and outdoor riding arenas.

K&K Equestrian Center. Route 67, East Durham 12423; (518) 966-4829. Open May through October. A family-owned-and-operated business for over three decades, they offer guided scenic trail rides, pony rides, lessons, and overnight trips. There is an informal atmosphere here, so everyone feels comfortable and welcomed.

Rough Riders Ranch. Route 23C, East Jewett 12424; (518) 589-9159. Open year-round. Ride with a cavalry sergeant, and experience the spirit of the Old West on one of the theme rides here. There are trail rides, pony rides, a petting zoo, and overnight adventures. Lessons in both Western and English are offered, as well.

PERFORMING ARTS

Catskill Mountain Foundation. Route 23A, Hunter 12442; (518) 263-4908, ext. 202, or (518) 263-5157.

This nonprofit organization has revitalized the town of Hunter. Stop in at the performing arts center, bookstore, and gallery on Main Street, and pick up a current schedule of events that include classical, folk, and jazz concerts, dance performances, art exhibits, film series, festivals, and more. There is a green market open year-round, daily, 10 A.M. to 6 P.M., featuring local organic produce, pasta, grains, eggs, cheeses, and other gourmet specialty foods; it's held in a restored country barn at the foot of Hunter Mountain. This is the place to find out what is happening culturally in the mountaintop region. It's a good idea to check their Web site (www.catskillmtn.org) if you are planning a visit and want to include some cultural events. They sponsor the **Sugar Maples Center for Arts and Education** in Windham, which includes state-of-the-art facilities for ceramics, fiber arts, and painting, as well as hotel accommodations.

Dutchman's Landing. Catskill Point, Main Street, Catskill 12414; (518) 943-3223.

This area once served as a boat landing for the Hudson River craft, and today visitors can enjoy spectacular views of the river and eastern shore. There is often musical entertainment here during the warm weather; a farmer's market and crafts market operate on weekends summer through fall; there are also displays of the cultural history of the Catskills, travel information, a picnic and dining area, and riverfront festivals. This is a wonderful place to hang out with the kids with easy access to the Hudson River.

Greene Room Players. P.O. Box 535, Hunter 12442; (518) 263-4233 or (518) 589-6297. This theater group has been presenting professional musicals, revues, children's shows, comedies, and drama for over a decade. The performances are given year-round and take place at the Dancing Bear Theater in the center of the village of Hunter.

Impulse Theater and Dance. Woodstock Avenue, Palenville 12463; (518) 797-3684 or (518) 678-3205. Performances take place from May through August in Palenville. This quality summer theater puts on contemporary musicals, comedies, and dramas. Call to see if any family shows are on the schedule during your stay in the area.

SKIING

Cortina Mountain Resort. Route 23A, Haines Falls 12436; (518) 589-6378 or (866) 9-CORTINA. Open Friday through Sunday in season, 10 A.M. to 10 P.M. Admission. This ski area sits on 280 acres with a base elevation of 1,925 feet and a summit of 2,650 feet. There are eleven trails and four lifts, many of them conducive to young children and novice skiers. There is a challenging terrain park that will appeal to both beginners and more advanced snowboarders. A refurbished twenty-room inn and snow-tubing park opened in 2002.

    Facilities: *Restrooms, snack bar/cafeteria, rental shop, paintball, outdoor horseback riding year-round.*

Hunter Mountain. Route 23A, Hunter 12442; (518) 263-4223. From exit 21 on the NYS Thruway, the trip is approximately twenty-four miles; take Route 23 east to Route 9W south, then 23A west; or it's eighteen miles from exit 20 by taking 32 north to 32A north to 23A west. Open Thanksgiving through April, depending on the weather, 8:30 A.M. to 4 P.M.; Hunter West open 9:30 A.M. to 3:30 P.M.

Hunter Mountain's reputation as the snowmaking capital of the East is well deserved. There are three mountains—Hunter One, Hunter West, and Hunter Mountain—and all offer skiers of all skill levels a chance to test themselves on over fifty trails. Runs at Hunter can extend more than two miles, with a 3,200 foot summit elevation and vertical drops of 1,600 feet; there are some very difficult areas, even for expert skiers. Double, triple, and quadruple chairlifts (there are now eleven lifts) cut some of the lines down to size, but this is such a popular area that there are always crowds on holidays and weekends. Check out the special discounts during weekdays when there are usually no lift lines. Hunter offers ski and snowboard lessons for all levels of ability. There is a Terrain Park for snowboarders with a one-thousand-watt stereo system that blasts music, and a hot dog stand at the base of the halfpipe brings new meaning to the term *fast food*. There are also snowshoeing and snow tubing areas.

Facilities: *Restrooms, food court, café, deli, full-service restaurant, slope-side barbecue, ski shop, rentals, lockers, ski school, baby-sitting.*

Windham Mountain. Route 23, Windham 12496; (518) 734-4300. Open late November through early April, Saturday, Sunday, and holidays, 8 A.M. to 4 P.M.; Monday through Friday, 9 A.M. to 4 P.M. Night skiing Thursday through Saturday, 4 P.M. to 10 P.M. Children under six ski for just $10.

With its forty-one trails ranging from beginner to expert serviced by seven chairlifts including a high-speed quad lift, Windham Mountain has all the ingredients for great family fun. Children between the ages of one and seven who do not wish to ski can spend the day in the learning center with activities such as arts and crafts and games; lunch is included. Younger skiers (ages four to seven) can join the Mini Mogul program for lessons, and children from the ages of eight to twelve can take a half day or full day of lessons with the Mountain Master program. Windham Mountain is a great place to take the family and enjoy real togetherness. Night skiing is offered on weekends and holidays, and there is a fully equipped tubing park.

Facilities: *Restrooms, cafeteria, lodge, ski shop with rentals, children's learning center.*

Mountain Trails Cross-Country Ski Center. Route 23A, Tannersville 12485; (518) 589-5361. Located one-half mile west of the traffic light on Route 23A in the village of Tannersville. Open December through March, 9 A.M. to 4:30 P.M. Always call before going, since weather conditions are always changing.

Cross-country ski enthusiasts will want to visit Mountain Trails. There are thirty-five kilometers of state-of-the-art Snowcat-groomed and track-set woodland trails (beginner to expert) in the beautiful Catskill Mountains. There is also snowshoeing and pull-sled rentals. Lessons are available with certified instructors. The trails are patrolled on weekends and during holiday weeks by the ski patrol.

Facilities: *Restrooms, lodge with fireplace, ski shop with rentals, snack bar.*

SWIMMING

North & South Lakes. County Route 18 (off Route 23A), Haines Falls 12436; (518) 589-5058 or (518) 943-4030. Open late May through early December daily, 9 A.M. to dusk. Admission (with extra charge for campsites).

This recreational area has breathtaking scenery and a multitude of activities. The highlight of a visit here is swimming in these mountain lakes with their clean, sandy beaches. Boat rentals and fishing are also available, making this a wonderful spot for a family outing. A short hike from North Lake is Kaaterskill Falls, one of the highest waterfalls on the East Coast and a popular subject for Hudson River School artists. The area also has a campground with hookups for recreational vehicles. On summer weekends the place gets very busy, so if you plan to stay overnight, make reservations early.

Facilities: *Restrooms, picnic area, changing room at the beach, showers, boat rentals, campsites, two beaches with lifeguards.*

Delaware County

Delaware County, with more than 64,000 acres that are state owned and proclaimed "forever wild," is an ideal place to go for families that enjoy outdoor recreation. The region is filled with places to fish, canoe, kayak, hike, and bike. And at the end of an activity-packed day, visit one of the county's charming villages, which seem as if they were plucked from a nineteenth-century picture book. This is a county that cherishes its past and a visit here brings back a sense of community celebration that is rare to find in twenty-first-century life.

Any itinerary to Delaware County should include some special places children will particularly appreciate. There is no better way to sample the fun of old-time travel than to hop aboard any of the vintage trains on the **Delaware and Ulster Railride,** which begins in Arkville. Kids will love the whistles, the bells, and the clickety-clack of the train as it weaves along the tracks, through meadows and up mountains. **Hanford Mills** in East Meredith is a restored sawmill and woodworking shop where kids will be able to watch as water power is harnessed to produce wood products and animal feed. A huge ten-foot waterwheel is still used to make the machinery run and visitors are guided through the rambling mill to watch the antique machines. The beautiful, huge red barn at **Healing Waters Farm** in Walton holds a collection of antique carriages, but the big attraction for kids is the petting zoo that includes a baby camel, buffalo, zebra, emus, llamas, sheep goats and a variety of exotic pets. **Plattekill Mountain Resort** in Roxbury is known for its big mountain skiing (and biking) terrain and small mountain charm. Family owned and operated, the resort caters to what they know best, families.

Since Delaware County is still a rural area, the special events here tend to take place during the "better weather" months, from late spring through summer. June brings the Meredith Dairy Fest, complete with exhibits, games, tractor pulls, music, crafts, hayrides, butter making, ice cream, and all things dairy. Firemen's Field Days, a July tradition in Margaretville, features carnival rides and entertainment, along with games of skill and chance. The second week of August is the Delaware County Fair in Walton, where the emphasis is on agriculture. On Labor Day Sunday, "Turn of the Century Day" brings vintage baseball to Kirkside Park in Roxbury. The clock is turned back to 1898 and all the pursuits of Victorian times are offered, including period dress, croquet, sack races, horseshoes, a barbershop quartet, and a chicken barbecue. This day-long event commemorates the renowned Roxbury Nine's last baseball game of the season.

For further information, contact the **Delaware County Chamber of Commerce**, 114 Main Street, Delhi 13753; (607) 746-2281 or (800) 642-4443; www.delawarecounty.org.

What to See

MUSEUMS AND HISTORIC SITES

Delaware County Historical Association. Route 10, Delhi 13753; (607) 746-3849. House open late May to mid-October, Tuesday through Sunday, 11 A.M. to 4 P.M. Library and exhibits are open year-round. Admission. Group tours are available by advance reservation.

Kids who love the past will enjoy becoming a part of it when they visit this historic site. The Frisbee House, which is on the grounds, was the birthplace of Delaware County's government, but the site itself is much more than dry history. In the house, kids will get a chance to see a children's room from the mid-nineteenth century as well as a selection of old toys, clothing, furniture, and a tavern from the 1800s. Out in the barn, a permanent exhibit introduces viewers to the rhythm and patterns of nineteenth-century farm life. A dog churn might interest children, along with the enormous collection of wagons and large farming tools, like rakes, flails, and apple presses. Also on the grounds are the blacksmith shop, a gun shop, a one-room schoolhouse, a toll-house, and a small family cemetery. Young nature lovers will enjoy walking the short trail that begins at an old farm path and winds down to Elk Creek. The plants and flowers are marked, and lucky observers may even spot a raccoon or two. Even the youngest visitors will be able to complete this trail, so don't hesitate to take the walk, especially in the summer. Special events at the site are well suited to children's interests. Teachers may want to inquire about the program called "Produce, Preserve, and Play," which offers school groups a chance to spend a day here.

Facilities: *Restrooms, picnic tables, gift shop (stocks many old-*

fashioned toys). Pets are not allowed. Most of the buildings are wheel-chair accessible.

Hanford Mills Museum. P.O. Box 99, East Meredith 13757; (607) 278-5744. The museum is located at the intersection of Delaware County Routes 10 and 12, ten miles east of Oneonta. Open May through October daily, 10 A.M. to 5 P.M. Admission. Group tours at special rates available by advance reservation.

Once a busy, noisy sawmill, gristmill, and woodworking shop, this pastoral site has been restored to its original use, and visitors will be able to watch as water power is once again harnessed to produce wood products and animal feed. Situated alongside a serene millpond, the buildings reflect the pace and industries of a century ago. A huge ten-foot waterwheel is still used to make the machinery run, as Kortright Creek provides the power. Visitors are guided through the mill building to watch the waterwheel and the antique woodworking machines. The staff is friendly and will answer questions about procedures; the tour will interest adults and children, who never seem to tire of watching the waterwheel grumble and roar its way around in circles. Outside, fifteen other notable structures include barns, lumber sheds, and an icehouse. Hanford Mills is well known for its special children's events. On July Fourth, an old-fashioned Independence Day celebration features traditional music, homemade ice cream, games, and rides; President Teddy Roosevelt himself often pays a visit. There are fly-fishing clinics at the millpond. The museum is also open the first Saturday in February for its annual ice harvest, when visitors of all ages can try their hands at sawing and harvesting ice for the July Fourth ice cream social.

Facilities: *Restrooms, picnic tables (the pond is a lovely place to have lunch, but bring your own; there are no nearby restaurants), gift* *shop (children's games and books are available, as well as many local food products). Pets are not allowed. There are gravel paths, but it would be difficult to maneuver a stroller inside the buildings. The mill, some exhibits, and bathrooms are wheelchair accessible.*

Healing Waters Farm, Carriage Museum and Petting Zoo. Route 206, Walton 13856 (one mile west of town); (607) 865-4420. Open April through December, Thursday and Friday, 11 A.M. to 5 P.M.; Saturday, 10 A.M. to 4 P.M., and Sunday, 11 A.M. to 4 P.M. Admission. Hayrides and special-themed group and educational tours available by advance reservation.

The beautiful, huge restored red barn here holds a collection of antique carriages from New York State and Pennsylvania, while the petting zoo includes a baby camel, buffalo, zebra, emus, llamas, sheep, goats, pheasants, and a variety of exotic pets. This is a working farm; in addition to raising horses, owner Ken Schrider, has egg-laying chickens, sheep for shearing, honeybees, and free-range turkeys. The antique carriages seem as though they have just been unhitched from a team of horses. An Amish man in Pennsylvania, who still drives and builds horse-drawn buggies today, restores and repairs these carriages, which include double-benched covered carriages, winter sleighs, speed wagons, a doctor's buggy, and a rare hearse. All were in use during the nineteenth and early twentieth century.

Facilities: *Restroom, picnic area. There are four shops on the premises: one for antiques, another for herbs (formerly the chicken coop), a toy shop, and a tack shop.*

OTHER ATTRACTIONS

Delaware & Ulster Railride. Route 28, Arkville 12406; (845) 586-DURR. Open late May through October; schedules vary, so call ahead. Entrance to the site and depot is free, but admission is charged for the ride. Group rates are available by advance reservation.

All aboard for a ride on the old *Doodlebug*, a self-propelled mail and freight car that was used more than seventy years ago on the Catskill rail lines. Painted bright red, the car is one of several pieces of old railroad stock that have been restored to provide fun rides for all ages. Even the youngest children will be delighted with the whistles, the bells, and the clickety-clack of the train as it weaves along the tracks through meadows and up mountains. Along the way, the friendly train crew points out interesting sites and tells stories of what travel was like before automobiles. The Catskill Mountains were once a daily stop for tourist and milk trains from New York City, but when the service stopped in the 1960s, many believed the echo of the train whistle was gone forever from the region. But the Railride has resurrected some of the favorite trains that once rattled along the tracks. Try to visit the DURR on a special-events weekend that caters to kids. Sometimes costumed train robbers stop the train to hold up the crew and passengers. Other days fiddlers and storytellers entertain everyone with songs and tales. There are Halloween ghost trains and foliage runs during the autumn months.

Facilities: *Restroom, snack caboose, gift shop. Wheelchair and stroller accessible.*

Pakatakan Farmers Market. Kelly Round Barn, Route 30, Halcottsville 12438. Open May through October Saturdays, 9 A.M. to 3 P.M. Free.

Kids will enjoy a stop at this farmers market, which is likely to yield a shopping bag full of local vegetables, fruits, and crafts. The market is housed in a historic round barn that was designed to make maintaining the stock less work. Indoor and outdoor vendors provide the best in produce, complete with free samples at many booths and a chance to chat with a farmer about his or her life and work. Special events, which take place just about every week through the summer, have included musical performances, dances, visits from farm animals and raptors, and the famous cow-pie derby. This is a nice way to spend a country morning, and a great way to experience rural life that continues to survive in Delaware County.

Facilities: *Restrooms, picnic tables. Pets are allowed if leashed. Strollers can manage on the grounds, but wheelchair accessibility may be a problem, especially in inclement weather.*

What to Do

BICYCLING

Catskill Scenic Trail (CST). (607) 652-2281. This nineteen-mile trail is great for off-road trips and can be accessed at various points where there are designated parking areas. One place to get on the trail is the historic Stamford Depot at the intersection of Railroad Avenue and South Street in the village of Stamford. There is also a parking lot north of Route 10, just east of the village of Bloomville. The CST is marked with octagonal signs that show the distance to the trailhead in the direction you are facing. There is only a four-hundred-foot change in elevation over the entire nineteen miles, which makes it a pleasant, relatively easy ride for all. Stamford is the peak, and it is downhill in both directions from that point, so I suggest you begin the tour there.

Bike Plattekill Mountain Resort. Plattekill Mountain Road, Roxbury 12474; (607) 326-3500. Open April through November,

10 A.M. to 5 P.M. This mountain biking center offers rentals, instruction, and trails in the surrounding valleys and mountains. There are also hiking and chairlift rides. If you are a first-timer, this is a great place to go to try out the sport. However, there is a variety of terrain to suit all levels of ability.

CANOEING AND KAYAKING

Al's Sport Store. At the junction of Routes 30 and 206, Downsville 13755; (607) 363-7740. Al's is a clearinghouse for canoe, kayak, and fishing information; they rent equipment and have tours in season.

Catskill Outfitters. Delaware and North Streets, Walton 13856; (800) 631-0105. This shop is able to supply everything you need to rent for a canoe or kayak outing.

Smith's Canoe and Drift Boat Rental. Route 97, Hancock 13783; (607) 637-2989. Smith's rents both canoes and kayaks for day trips.

HIKING

Americorps Outdoor Education Center. Route 28, Delhi 13753; (607) 746-4051. This facility offers woods walks and educational excursions in a nature preserve with marked trails, making it an excellent place to introduce children to hiking.

Catskill Forest Preserve. 65561 State Highway 10, Stamford 12167; (607) 652-7366. The regional office of the preserve is a good place to get information regarding the more than three hundred miles of trails that vary in length from a half mile to almost one hundred miles. Even novice hikers will find comfortable trails, whether for a day trip or an overnight. Trail brochures are available upon request.

Catskill Scenic Trail. Railroad Avenue, Stamford 12167; (607) 652-2821. This trail has a marked nineteen-mile stretch with a hard-packed surface and gentle grade perfect for hiking, biking, and cross-country skiing. This is an excellent choice for those with young children.

Kirkside Park. Main Street, Roxbury 12474; (607) 326-3722. This historic eleven-acre treasure was formerly the estate of Helen Gould-Shepard, daughter of railroad magnate and Roxbury native son Jay Gould. Rich in natural beauty and history, and recently restored to its glorious splendor, Kirkside has rustic Adirondack-style bridges, graceful paths along the east branch of the Delaware River, and lush plantings to admire in the warm-weather months.

Oquaga Creek State Park. Route 20, Masonville 13733; (607) 467-4160. There are 6.5 miles of marked hiking trails here that will delight those of all abilities. The park itself is actually in three counties: Delaware, Broome, and Chenango.

PERFORMING ARTS

Delaware Heritage. P.O. Box 442, Downsville 13755; (607) 363-7360. This organization focuses on programs dealing with the history and cultural heritage of the county. There are several concerts, plays, and a wonderful youth theater with presentations throughout the summer months. Call for a schedule of events.

Facilities: *Restrooms. Wheelchair and stroller accessible.*

Roxbury Arts Group. Vega Mountain Road, Roxbury 12474; (607) 326-7908. This arts organization offers year-round children's programs that include concerts, puppet shows, crafts workshops, and a week-long summer day camp that incorporates nature and arts activities. Call in advance for a schedule.

Facilities: *Restrooms. Wheelchair and stroller accessible.*

Stamford Performing Arts Center. 76 Main Street, Stamford 12167; (607) 652-3121. There is the full range of performance art here—plays, concerts, mime, children's theater. Call for a schedule of events.

Facilities: *Restrooms. Wheelchair and stroller accessible.*

West Kortright Center. Turnpike Road, West Kortright 13757; (607) 278-5454. During May through October, enjoy everything from Bach to bluegrass and zydeco, at this cultural center, which sponsors performance workshops, concerts, art exhibits, and community gatherings in a historic country church. Concerts are held both outdoors, in the green fields, and indoors, where guests sit in unique rounded pews. The intimate setting makes all events delightful. There is an annual young people's showcase performance in both theater and dance; call for a schedule of events.

Facilities: *Restrooms. Wheelchair and stroller accessible.*

SKIING

Bobcat Ski Center. Gladstone Hollow Road, Andes 13731; (607) 676-3143. Located 2.5 miles off Route 28 on Gladstone Hollow Road; follow signs. Open December through March, Friday through Sunday and holidays, 9 A.M. to 4 P.M.

This ski center has a vertical drop of 1,050 feet and a top elevation of 3,345 feet, making for a great mix of expert and novice terrain; there are nineteen trails and slopes in all. The center attracts a smaller crowd than many mega-ski mountains, and is a good place to enjoy a weekend ski with the kids. Because their snowmaking capability is limited, it is a good idea to check conditions before planning a trip.

Facilities: *Restrooms, cafeteria, rentals (snowboards and skis), lockers, ski school.*

Ski Plattekill Mountain Resort. Plattekill Mountain Road (two miles off Route 30), Roxbury 12474; (607) 326-3500. Open December through March, 8:45 A.M. to 4:15 P.M.

Plattekill Mountain has been called the Catskills best kept secret, and is known for its big-mountain terrain and small-mountain charm. This family-owned-and-operated resort caters to families. There are thirty-five trails and three lifts serving 1,100 feet of vertical drop. The mountain has something for everyone, from two-mile-long beginner cruising runs to some of the steepest double-black-diamond slopes in the region. The resort also offers a full-service ski school with lessons in skiing and snowboarding, and a special children's program called Snowkidding for those under the age of eight. This program is geared for youngsters to learn the fundamentals of skiing in a relaxing, fun atmosphere. A racing program and freestyle mogul camp are also available for more advanced skiers. Plattekill is a fine place to escape overcrowded slopes and enjoy a laid-back, family-friendly atmosphere.

Facilities: *Restrooms, cafeteria, ski school, retail shop, nursery (hourly and day rates available).*

Otsego County

Otsego County is a timeless place where heritage and natural beauty merge in the rolling foothills of the northern Catskills, the land of James Fenimore Cooper's Leatherstocking Tales. If you love baseball, you will love Cooperstown, the heart of the county and the birthplace of the sport. Folklore has it that Abner Doubleday, on an afternoon in 1839, was inspired to invent a game that soon became our national pastime. The county is well known for its maple syrup production, and during the season at many farms throughout the area visitors are invited to watch the sap being boiled into syrup, before going indoors to enjoy a hearty pancake breakfast.

Otsego is a place where past meets present, from hands-on history museums and Native American art to baseball games and soccer tournaments. The **National Baseball Hall of Fame** is a must-see for baseball lovers of all ages. Three floors are filled with thousands of pieces of baseball history—memorabilia, clothing, photos, cards, and equipment. Everyone in the family will appreciate the **Farmers' Museum,** a "village" assembled during the last fifty years by importing buildings from across central New York State. A highlight is the Cardiff Giant, known as America's greatest hoax. "Feet-on" action-oriented games, video monitors, and interactive exhibits are an exciting part of the **National Soccer Hall of Fame and Museum**. The thirty-thousand-square-foot building contains the sport's historic treasures, from the world's oldest soccer ball to the 1999 Women's World Cup trophy. The **Science Discovery Center** at the State University of New York at Oneonta has more than eighty hands-on exhibits for kids, who marvel at the array of gadgets and gizmos. **Glimmerglass State Park** is a great place to spend time swimming, fishing, or camping overnight. James Fenimore Cooper called Otsego Lake Glimmerglass because of its serene beauty; it's the perfect place to end a busy day of sightseeing.

Try to coordinate your visit to Otsego with one of the many special events in the region. In mid-July, the Hall of Fame induction ceremonies are held at the National Baseball Hall of Fame. Cooperstown is bustling, and it's an exciting time to visit. The county celebrates its traditions every August at the annual county fair in Morris. And in September, the **Fly Creek Cider Mill** hosts its annual Antique Tractor Festival.

For further information, contact **Otsego County Tourism**, 242 Main Street, Oneonta, NY 13820; (800) 843-3394; www.otsegocounty.net.

What to See

MUSEUMS AND HISTORIC SITES

American Baseball Experience. 99 Main Street, Cooperstown 13326; (607) 547-1273. Open Friday through Monday, 10 A.M. to 5 P.M. Here you will find the only wax museum featuring baseball greats and a virtual-reality exhibit featuring Roger Clemens's fastball. The place is filled with autographed items and features Tom Catal's Tribute to Mickey Mantle.

Facilities: *Restrooms, café.*

Farmer's Museum. P.O. Box 30, Cooperstown 13326; (607) 547-1450 or (888) 547-1450. The museum is located on Lake Road, Route 80, one mile north of the village of Cooperstown. Open daily from mid-May through Columbus Day, 10 A.M. to 5 P.M.; April through mid-May and the last two weeks in October, Tuesday through Friday for guided tours and Family Fun Saturdays, 10 A.M. to 4 P.M.; Saturday and Sunday of Thanksgiving weekend, 10 A.M. to 4 P.M. for Family Fun after Thanksgiving. Admission; children under the age of seven are admitted free. Group rates and tours available by advance reservation.

Although this "village" looks as if it has been in Cooperstown forever, it was really assembled during the last fifty years by importing buildings from across central New York State. Split rails and stone fences guard the landscape; heritage breeds of animals grace the farmyard; and children have a wonderful time in this nineteenth-century historic village and farm. You enter the site through the huge stone barn that houses several exhibit galleries worth the price of admission by themselves. Four exhibit areas highlight aspects of life in rural Upstate New York, including hops production, traditional handcrafts, and architectural styles. The family activity center provides parents and children with exciting learning opportunities.

Housed in his brightly striped tent is the Cardiff Giant, known as America's greatest hoax. A huge stone carving that was buried by night, and then dug up by an enterprising con artist/farmer who publicized it as a petrified giant of biblical times. P. T. Barnum eventually bought the giant.

Outside, the village itself has much to explore and see; the buildings house enough to keep all ages interested. There is a printer's shop, where much of the village's printing is still done; a doctor's office; a pharmacy; a blacksmith shop with working smith; a tavern; church; eight heritage gardens including a children's garden; and more. Heritage breeds of farm animals include Devon cattle, chickens, ducks, sheep, pigs, turkeys, and a patient pair of oxen. Special weekend events highlight the season including Sugaring Off Sundays in March, Spring Festival in May, Independence Day in July, Harvest Festival in September, and Candlelight Evening in December. Kids should not miss a stop at the village green, where they can walk on stilts or roll a hoop along the grounds.

Facilities: *Restrooms, restaurant, gift shop, picnic tables. Strollers can manage here, and the paths can be negotiated by a wheelchair, but call ahead if access is a concern.*

Fenimore Art Museum. Route 80 (Lake Road), Cooperstown 13326; (607) 547-1400. Open mid-May through Columbus Day daily, 10 A.M. to 5 P.M.; April through mid-May and the day after Columbus Day through December, Tuesday through Sunday, 10 A.M. to 4 P.M. Admission; children under the age of seven are admitted free.

This museum houses one of the most outstanding collections of folk art in America. Children and their families will enjoy learning about art and history with a truly hands-on approach here. The galleries reflect and complement permanent and temporary exhibits in the museum and encourage learning through visual, tactile, and auditory activities. Children are encouraged to relax, sit back, and interact in gallery spaces constructed especially for them. The labels for many paintings have corresponding text for kids—and at their eye level. There is even a corner where children can stop and create artwork of their own, which is posted on one of the gallery walls.

The museum also houses the Thaw Collection of North American Indian Art, one of the finest private collections in the country, now accessible to all. Children will be intrigued by the colorful, powerful art created by Native American tribes, including huge paintings on hides, carved kachina dolls, and striking beaded clothing.

Facilities: *Restrooms, gift shop (with a wonderful selection of books and activity kits for children), restaurant. Stroller and wheelchair accessible.*

National Baseball Hall of Fame. Main Street, Cooperstown 13326; (607) 547-7200 or (888) HALL-OF-FAME. Open daily, year-round, except Thanksgiving, Christmas, and New Year's; from Memorial Day weekend through Labor Day, 9 A.M. to 9 P.M.; rest of the year, 9 A.M. to 5 P.M. Admission; children under the age of seven are admitted free. Group rates are available by advance reservation.

This is it: the promised land for baseball lovers of any age. Three floors are filled with thousands of pieces of baseball history—memorabilia, clothing, photos, cards, and equipment. From the time you enter, where the hand-carved lifelike wooden statues of Babe Ruth, Ted Williams, and other greats greet you, until you leave, everything you see is related to great and not-so-great moments in America's favorite pastime. Pictures of current players and the uniforms from all the modern major leagues in the Today's Highlights room will gain the attention of young fans, as will the large baseball, gum, and tobacco card collection on display. The Hall of Fame gallery holds the plaques of inductees; there is a section devoted to the early African-American leagues;

and the new wing's state-of-the-art theater offers a short film all about the excitement and tradition of baseball. Kids who love statistics will enjoy the Records room, filled with memorabilia and displays concerning the records set by the greatest players, and a chronological history of baseball displays with many bats, balls, and gloves that were involved in the greatest plays. The museum's interactive exhibits let kids call up information on the Hall of Fame members, and additional displays focus on women in baseball, umpires, and the World Series. Throughout the summer, a series of baseball films is screened in the Library Building, which faces Cooper Park. The National Baseball Hall of Fame is a comfortable museum, especially on a hot summer's afternoon, but be aware that it is always crowded on the Fourth of July, and when the annual Hall of Fame induction is held, also in July.

Facilities: *Restrooms, gift shop with lots of baseball memorabilia. Strollers can manage here and the museum is wheelchair accessible.*

National Soccer Hall of Fame. 18 Stadium Circle, Oneonta 13820; (607) 432-3351. Take I-88 to exit 13; take State Route 205 north, and turn left at third traffic light. Open daily 10 A.M. to 5 P.M.; during July and August open until 7 P.M. Call for winter hours, which vary. Admission. Group rates are available by advance reservation.

The history of soccer in America goes back to the 1860s and is filled with memorable moments and interesting personalities. This museum preserves the story of the sport in displays of photos, trophies, uniforms, and other soccer memorabilia. There are also "feet-on" action-oriented games, video monitors, and interactive exhibits in this thirty-thousand-square-foot-space. The Hall of Fame features the sport's treasures from the world's oldest soccer ball to the 1999 FIFA Women's World Cup trophy, and will delight soccer aficionados of all ages. Every October the induction ceremony is held and honors players with games and special events. Throughout the summer there are tournaments on site, and during the winter there are indoor activities for children. If you have a soccer lover in the family, you may want to inquire about the soccer camps sponsored by the museum during the summer months.

Facilities: *Restrooms, gift shop, café. Strollers and wheelchairs can maneuver fairly easily here.*

OTHER ATTRACTIONS

Clark Sports Center. Susquehanna Avenue, Cooperstown 13326; (607) 547-2800. Open May through September, Monday through Saturday 6:30 A.M. to 9 P.M.; October through April, Monday through Friday 6:30 A.M. to 10 P.M.; Saturday to 9 P.M.; Sunday 9 A.M. to 6 P.M. Admission for daily pass; additional charge for use of Nautilus equipment.

An outstanding stop for families, this sports center is state-of-the-art and open to the public. There are indoor and outdoor swimming pools, a bowling alley, indoor running tracks, an indoor horizontal climbing wall, and the area's only Outward Bound–designed adventure ropes course and climbing wall. For a rainy day, this action-filled stop will keep the kids busy. Not all the facilities are available for use all the time, so if the kids have a special interest, call ahead for the schedules. Classes and workouts are available as well.

Facilities: *Restrooms, lockers, towels.*

Cooperstown & Charlotte Valley Railroad. P.O. Box 681, Oneonta 13820; (607) 432-2429. Open daily Memorial Day weekend through Labor Day. Call for schedule. Admission.

Take a ride along the scenic Susquehanna River with the

Leatherstocking Railway Historical Society's rail journey back in time. The two-hour sixteen-mile round-trip train ride also features special events that will delight the kids.

Facilities: *Restrooms.*

Cooperstown Family Campground. 230 Petkewec Road, Cooperstown 13326; (607) 293-7766 or (800) 959-2267. Take Route 28 2.5 miles south from Cooperstown; turn right onto County Road 11, and go four miles. Watch for signs. Open May through October, but call ahead for exact dates and times which are subject to change. Admission.

This is a large (hundred-unit) campground that offers a great deal to families. The campsite is only minutes away from the village of Cooperstown, so visitors can enjoy the outdoors and still be near all the museums and attractions. On summer evenings children will love the free pony rides and hayrides. The small working farm on the premises allows kids to help milk the cows in the morning, feed the chickens, and get up close to the animals, which include camels, peacocks, deer, cougar, and many miniature mammals. There are on-site fishing ponds and a pool for swimming. The youngest hikers will enjoy the short, marked nature trail, and afterward can play miniature golf, ride in a paddleboat, or play games in a recreation hall in the event of rain. This is a busy place, but it's one of the few campgrounds that offers such a variety of activities. It is necessary to make reservations in advance on summer weekends.

Facilities: *Restrooms, snack bar.*

Cooperstown Bat Company. Pioneer Alley, Cooperstown 13326; (607) 547-2415. Open May through October, Monday through Saturday, 10 A.M. to 5 P.M.; July and August, Monday through Saturday, also 7 to 9 P.M. and Sunday noon to 4 P.M. Free.

This company specializes in making custom and fine bats and bat accessories, such as display racks. They issue commemorative bats, personalized bats, and even autographed bats. Each bat is handmade, and you can often watch the staff working on a custom order if you visit during the summer months.

Facilities: *Restrooms.*

Doubleday Batting Range. Main Street (next to Doubleday Field), Cooperstown 13326; (607) 547-5168. Open Memorial Day weekend through Labor Day, daily, 10 A.M. to 5:30 P.M.; Labor Day through Columbus Day weekends only 10 A.M. to 5:30 P.M. No admission, but there is a charge for the pitching machines.

The batting range is not connected with the Hall of Fame, but it is an interesting, fun commercial stop for baseball-hungry kids. Here you can use the same pitching machines used by the pros and check your throwing speed with a radar gear. It's the only place in the village where kids can actually throw a baseball!

Facilities: *Restrooms, snack bar.*

Fly Creek Cider Mill and Orchard. 288 Goose Street, Fly Creek 13337; (607) 547-9692. Fly Creek is located on Goose Street, three miles from Cooperstown; follow the signs from Routes 28/80. Open May through Christmas daily, 9 A.M. to 6 P.M. Free.

This site offers visitors a chance to see apple cider produced as it was a century ago, with one of the oldest water-powered mills in the state. Built in 1856, the mill is still run with a 1924 engine for the grinder and an 1889 hydraulic apple press. Mill-made fudge, cheese, and cider samples are offered to visitors, and the last weekend in September is the big Applefest, with baked goods, kids activities, and, of course, apples, apple wine, and cider for sale. The mountain views are lovely in autumn, and you may want to combine a stop at the mill with a day in nearby Cooperstown.

Facilities: *Restrooms, gift shop, snack bar featuring gourmet specialty foods. The ground floor of the mill is accessible to strollers and wheelchairs.*

Royal Llamas. 515 Old Stone Robbie Road, Oneonta 13820; (607) 432-5827. Open year-round, but call in advance to check on hours. Group tours by advance reservation.

This farm has a large herd of llamas with a variety of species and children will enjoy the chance to take a llama ride. There is almost always someone on hand to give a barn tour.

Facilities: *Portable toilets.*

Science Discovery Center of Oneonta. Physical Science Building, State University, Oneonta 13820; (607) 436-2011. Open Thursday through Saturday, noon to 4 P.M.; closed Thanksgiving, Christmas, and New Year's Day. Free. Group tours by appointment.

This unique center places the emphasis on practical science; kids will have a chance to test and explore more than eighty touchable exhibits. They can explore sound, electricity, magnetism, and chemistry; make noise; or just watch as the gadgets and gizmos prove that science is for everyone.

Facilities: *Restrooms. Wheelchair accessible.*

What to Do

BOAT CRUISES

Classic Boat Tours. P.O. Box 664, Cooperstown 13326; (607) 547-5294. Tours run from Memorial Day weekend through October and leave daily several times a day on the hour. Do call for current schedule before you go. There is an admission fee.

Cooperstown lies at the foot of Otsego Lake, and there is no better way to see the lake and surrounding landscape than from the water. Lake tours take you past scenes from James Fenimore Cooper's novels, Kingfisher Tower (a small water tower from the nineteenth-century built in the shape of a castle), well-manicured lakeside estates, Sunken Island (which disappears when the water is high), and James Fenimore Cooper's home. Older children will love the stories of pioneers and Native Americans told by the boat guides, and the lake is beautiful on a summer afternoon. I recommend you bring along sun hats and sweaters, especially if it is a breezy day. Boat tours leave from the bottom of Fair Street in Cooperstown, near the Baseball Hall of Fame. They have one-hour tours aboard two classic boats, 1902 and 1912 launches. These are beautiful boats, and older children may even feel they have been whisked back in time, when sport boating was only for the rich.

Sam Smith's Boatyard. Route 80 (2.5 miles north of Cooperstown); (607) 547-2543. Open daily in the summer months. Here you can rent a boat or canoe for an outing on the lake to get far away from the bustle of Main Street. The nautical gift shop is fun, and fisher-kids can select their own tackle.

MAPLE FARM TOURS

Otsego County is well known for its maple syrup production, and at many farms throughout the county visitors are invited to watch the sap being boiled down into syrup. The saphouses are usually small affairs that are steamy, hot, and sweet, and there is nothing like the taste of warm maple syrup to usher in spring for you and the kids. Tours consist of a stop in the sugarbush (the maple trees), a visit to the saphouse, and sometimes, the candy-making area. The tours are usually informal, and I suggest you put on boots and a hat before you venture out into the woods and the mud of an Otsego County March. Make sure to call before you go since the season is highly weather dependent. The following farms offers tours in maple season, which usually runs from March to mid-April. **Brodies Sugarbush**, Westford 13488; (607) 264-3225. Take Route 165 to route 34 and go one mile up the road; watch for signs. **Captain's Grove Maple Products**, 654 U.S. Highway 20, West Winfield 13491; (315) 822-5835. **Dale Gates**, Unadilla Forks Road, West Winfield 13491; (315) 855-4129. South of Route 20 between West Winfield and Bridgewater.

PARKS

Gilbert Lake State Park. Oneonta 13820; (607) 432-2114. The park is located between Routes 205 and 51, twelve miles northwest of Oneonta. Open Memorial Day weekend to Labor Day, daily, 8 A.M. to 10 P.M.; from dawn to dusk the rest of the year. Fee for camping. Groups and camping by reservation only.

This large (sixteen-hundred-acre) state park is located in one of the loveliest areas of central New York State. Lush forests and open meadows surround Gilbert Lake, with its sandy beach, where kids will enjoy swimming and boating. There are children's play areas in the park, and several marked nature trails and hiking trails will tempt the adventurous. A special recreation program is held in the park through the summer, and there are often storytellers, puppet shows, and other entertainers to amuse the youngsters. Camping is available on-site, in either campgrounds or cabins, but note that the cabins must be reserved nine months in advance. The action doesn't stop at Labor Day, however—cross-country ski trails, snowshoeing, and snowmobiling are all popular sports at this park during the winter.

Facilities: *Restrooms, snack stand in summer, picnic areas. Strollers*

are not recommended here. The beach is wheelchair accessible, with a
ramp down to the lake, and several of the bathrooms have access as well.

Glimmerglass State Park. 1527 County Highway 31, Cooperstown 13326; (607) 547-8662. The park is located seven miles
north of Cooperstown on the east side of Otsego Lake. Open
year-round, 9 A.M. to 5 P.M. for day use. Small use charge. Groups
are welcome by reservation; camping by advance reservation only.

James Fenimore Cooper called Otsego Lake "Glimmerglass" because of its serene beauty, and you can see why at this lovely park
where you can spend the day or camp overnight. You can swim
and fish from lakeside spots; watch sailboats go by; or enjoy some
time with the kids in the children's playground areas. There are
hiking trails throughout the six-hundred-acre park, as well as a
short nature trail for younger naturalists. A picnic area is complete
with fireplaces and covered pavilions for bad weather, but be fore-
warned: Because of the small number of campsites (only forty)
and the popularity of the lake, this campground fills up quickly
in the summer. Even day-trippers should bring along their own
portable chairs and tables. If you are in Cooperstown on a weekend during the winter months, there is a lot to do in the park, including snow tubing (the tubes are free), cross-country skiing,
ice-skating on the lake (bring your own skates), and snowshoeing.
Five kilometers of trails snake through the park and the skiing is
free, but you must bring your own equipment.

Hyde Hall Mansion, a covered bridge and several outbuildings
are contained within a fifteen-acre historic site within the park.
The fifty-room mansion, a restoration in progress, is considered
one of the finest surviving examples of classical revival architecture in the country. There are occasionally concerts on the grounds,
so inquire about any special events when you enter the park.

Facilities: *Restrooms, picnic areas, fireplaces, campsites, playground, snack stand. On winter weekends, the restrooms are open, and there are hot drinks and snacks for sale. The park has limited access areas for strollers and wheelchairs, although six of the campsites are accessible to the disabled.*

PICK-YOUR-OWN FARMS

Ingall's Berry and Vegetable Farm. State Highway 28, Cooperstown 13326; (607) 547-5481. There are seasonal harvest delights here, ranging from asparagus in May to apples in autumn. You can pick berries, tomatoes, and a variety of other crops. Call in advance to see what is ripe for picking. Children will love the corn mazes and hayrides.

Willy's Farm and Cider Mill. 329 Badeau Hill Road, Schenevus 12155; (607) 638-9449. This family-owned-and-operated cider mill and pumpkin farm is located on one hundred scenic acres, with lots of room for the kids to run around. There are pumpkins to pick in season, hayrides, a corn maze, and home-baked pies and other tempting treats for sale on the premises.

Schoharie County

Schoharie County history has been entwined with the history of emerging America from the beginning. The Schoharie Valley was so important to the revolutionary cause that the U.S. Army's first cavalry charge took place here. General George Washington stationed several regiments of Continental soldiers—troops he could ill afford to spare—to protect the valley's harvest, which supplied his army.

What is now known as the **Old Stone Fort Museum** withstood a fierce attack by the British during the Revolutionary War. Located in the village of Schoharie, it first opened its doors to visitors in 1889. Today, children enjoy touring the eighteenth-century Dutch barn and nineteenth-century one-room schoolhouse. At the **Iroquois Indian Museum** a self-guided tour takes visitors through a series of interactive displays that include an archaeological dig and tell the story of the earliest people who lived along the Cobleskill Creek some nine thousand years ago. Kids will also learn about the Mohawks who had a village in the Schoharie Valley in the 1700s. No visit to the area would be complete without a trip through the fantastic subterranean worlds of the county. Two popular and spectacular caves—**Howe Caverns** and **Secret**

Caverns—offer visitors a unique underground adventure filled with winding passageways and massive geologic formations. There's plenty of fun aboveground at the New York Power Authority's **Blenheim-Gilboa Power Project Visitors Center.** Housed in a nineteenth-century dairy barn, the state-of-the-art exhibits and interactive displays show kids how hydropower is created and used.

With rolling hills, waterways, and wide open spaces, Schoharie County offers visitors a vast outdoor recreational area. With two state parks, three state forests, and miles of nature trails, it is paradise for families who love to hike, bike, and camp. The five-hundred-acre **Mine Kill State Park** offers a relaxing site for picnicking, softball, volleyball, basketball, and water sports. Winter activites include tobagganing, sledding, snowshoeing, and cross-county skiing. For something a little different, visit the **Landis Arboretum** in Esperance to see one of the Northeast's most magnificent collections of trees and shrubs. The two-hundred-acre public garden is the perfect place for kids who are curious about plants, animals, and natural history. The grounds contain ponds, a wetland, open fields, trails, and phenomenal views.

A number of kid-friendly special events take place year-round and reflect the way of life in the county. The fourth weekend in April is the annual Maple Festival in the village of Schoharie. The Strawberry Festival takes place at the Old Stone Fort on the last Wednesday in June. For six days beginning on the first Tuesday in August, enjoy the Cobleskill Sunshine Fair, which is filled with activities for children of all ages. Labor Day weekend brings the annual Iroquois Festival at the museum, and Haunted Howe Caverns is scheduled just before Halloween.

For further information, contact **Schoharie County Tourism, 315 Main Street, Suite 1, Schoharie 12157; (800) 41-VISIT; www. schohariechamber.com.**

What to See

MUSEUMS AND HISTORIC SITES

Iroquois Indian Museum. P.O. Box 7, Caverns Road, Howe's Cave 12092; (518) 296-8949. Take exit 22 off Interstate 88, and follow state signs on Route 7 for one mile. Go left at the Howe Caverns arrow on Caverns Road; then continue one mile to museum entrance. Open April through December, daily, 10 A.M. to 5 P.M.; closed January through March and national holidays. Admission. Group rates and tours available by advance reservation.

This colorful museum has won awards for its design, which evokes the longhouses of the Iroquois nation, and it contains a marvelous collection of ancient and modern Iroquois art and artifacts. The Iroquois were the most powerful tribe of native peoples in the region and included the Six Nations: Mohawk, Oneida, Onondaga, Cayuga, Seneca, and Tuscarora. The self-guided museum tour takes visitors through a series of displays that include an archaeological dig, Iroquois creation myths, crafts, and artwork. There are shelves and displays filled with beadwork, basketry, paintings, soapstone carvings, cornhusk weavings, and costumes. Silverwork glints in another section, and there are ceremonial objects like pipes and clothing. Changing exhibits highlight living Iroquois artists and their works, and a visit here on a summer weekend will often include the delights of a traditional storyteller or doll maker, or the chance to join in a community dance. In the lower section of the museum, the children's section offers visitors a chance to participate in hands-on crafts demonstrations or try on Native American clothing. The gift shop deserves special mention, since it stocks only Iroquois arts, crafts, and publications, and there are lovely gifts for all ages and budgets. Outside, there are nature trails and an Iroquois log cabin and garden to explore. Special festivals are held every Memorial Day and Labor Day weekend and include entertainment, educational displays, craftspeople, and traditional foods. School groups may request special programs about the modern Iroquois, but any young visitor will come away from this museum knowing more about the Native American heritage.

Facilities: *Restrooms, gift shop, picnic area, snack stand. Wheelchair and stroller accessible.*

Old Stone Fort. 145 Fort Road (from Route 30), Schoharie 12157; (518) 295-7192. Open May through October, Tuesday through Saturday, 10 A.M. to 5 P.M.; Sunday, noon to 5 P.M.; open on Mondays, 10 A.M. to 5 P.M. during July, August, and holidays. Admission. Children under the age of five are admitted free. Group tours available by advance reservation.

The Old Stone Fort is a marvelous museum complex that gives young visitors a glimpse into Schoharie County's past. First of all, there is the fort itself, which withstood an attack by the British during the American Revolution in an unsuccessful attempt to rout two hundred settlers. The exhibits are done up in the old-curiosity style—rows of glass cases alternate with open displays of some odd and quirky items. An old hand-pump fire wagon from the eighteenth century is shown (it was built before George Washington was born), as are foot warmers, farming tools, bear traps, musical instruments, specimens from a nearby fossil forest, and tools from prehistoric cultures. Also in the complex is a re-created blacksmith shop, farming equipment, a law office, a barn, and an eighteenth-century house. There is a complete one-room schoolhouse where kids can sit at the desks and try out the slates and other sample lessons, as well as the century-old car owned by the first female mayor in New York State, Eleanor Taylor. Kids can even try on period clothing here. The Scribner Exhibit of Twentieth-Century Communications features radios, cameras, projectors, recording devices, and a 1947 television set. Children appreciate the unstructured feeling of this museum and the jumble of collections here. Their annual visitor-interactive Columbus Day weekend event features music, old-fashioned food, and costumed militiamen. It is a true living history event that will please children of all ages.

Facilities: *Restrooms, gift shop, picnic area.*

OTHER ATTRACTIONS

Caverns Creek Grist Mill. Caverns Road (one mile off Route 7), Howe's Cave 12092; (518) 296-8448. Open mid-May through Labor Day daily, 10:30 A.M. to 6:30 P.M.; September through mid-October, weekends only (same hours). Admission for the mill tour. Group tours available by reservation.

A restored 1816 gristmill, this charming, bright red working "museum" still grinds corn with a water-powered millstone. There are three floors of exhibits here, all related to the history and art of milling, including stone dressing, grinding, and waterwheels. The miller on duty can answer questions about the operation of the mill, and there is a short tour of the site. Children will enjoy watching the wheels go round and listening to the rush of water as it pours into the mill through the elaborate series of gutters and races. Outside, there is a lovely picnic area along the millpond, and a series of short hiking paths leads along the millrace. The overshot waterwheel is located at the side of the mill and is just as fascinating to younger visitors as the mill itself.

Facilities: *Restrooms, picnic tables, gift shop stocked with locally ground flours. Overall, not suitable for strollers or wheelchairs, although the grounds have some accessible paths.*

Cobleskill College Agricultural Tour. Route 7, Cobleskill 12043; (518) 234-5323. Open year-round daily, for self-guided tours. Free. Group tours available by advance reservation.

This college is part of the State University of New York (SUNY) system. It contains more than fifty buildings over a 550-acre campus, which contains a 300-acre working farm. Cobleskill has a national reputation as a fine agricultural college, and a tour of the campus can introduce children to the workings of a modern farm. Tour stops include visits to the cattle barn, a greenhouse (with crops and flowers), the plant science building, the horse barn, and the dairy barn. Kids love the farm machinery that's on view, especially the tractors, and although this is a walking tour, children as young as four should be able to manage it easily. There is a small fisheries and wildlife museum on campus, with displays and exhibits of local plants and animals; the museum is open only when school is in session. Because many of the tour stops are actual work areas, you may have a chance to see milking or harvesting in progress, but what you see depends upon the season and the time of day. The campus is lovely, and this is a nice stop for kids interested in farm life.

Facilities: *Restrooms, gift shop in the student center, picnic areas. Strollers and wheelchairs can manage on campus.*

Cooper's Ark Farm. 145 Ark Lane, Schoharie 12157; (518) 295-7662. Open daily 7 A.M. to 7 P.M., but call ahead to arrange a visit and get directions. Free. This beautiful working farm is home to over four hundred laying hens, four llamas, an alpaca, a donkey, and forty goats. Children can get involved in farm tasks as well as learn to use a pitchfork.

Facilities: *Restrooms, farm shop.*

Easter Egg Exhibit. Intersection of Routes 30 and 433, Schoharie 12157; (518) 295-8696. Open Palm Sunday through Easter Sunday, daily, 10 A.M. to 5 P.M.; the rest of the year, weekends only, 1 to 5 P.M. Small donation.

Everyone will be delighted by this amazing collection of five thousand colorful, hand-painted Easter eggs exhibited in groups, on trees, and in historic and storybook settings. There are several egg doll characters displayed in scenes from favorite children's stories like Cinderella, the Wizard of Oz, and Alice in Wonderland. Marvel at the First Thanksgiving, a replica of Disney World characters, and several popular nursery rhyme scenes. This is certainly a novel and intriguing place to stop.

Facilities: *Restrooms, gift shop.*

George Landis Arboretum. 174 Lape Road, Esperance 12066; (518) 875-6935. From the center of town, follow signs to the arboretum. Open daily, dawn to dusk. Free. Group tours by advance reservation.

This 163-acre public garden is home to hundreds of rare shrubs and trees from around the world. It is on the site of a nineteenth-century farm, the home of Fred Lape, the arboretum's founder, an amateur botanist, poet, English professor, and writer, who established the arboretum in 1951 as a memorial to George Landis, a faculty colleague at RPI and fellow amateur botanist. There are plantings, gardens, and pathways lined with trees from Russia, Japan, China, and other exotic lands, as well as common trees native to the area. There are several hiking trails and a short walking path that is perfect for a family stroll. The plants are all well marked, so you may enjoy spending some time identifying plants and trees with the kids. It's really peaceful and lovely here on a summer afternoon, and the kids will enjoy running around and letting off some steam. The arboretum offers special children's workshops in botany and nature studies during the summer months, but call ahead for a schedule.

Facilities: *Restrooms, picnic area, barn, greenhouse, and meetinghouse. This site is not recommended for wheelchairs or strollers, although the restrooms and parking area are accessible.*

Howe Caverns. 255 Discovery Drive, Howe's Cave 12092; (518) 296-8900. Take exit 22 from I-88 and follow signs. Open daily, 9 A.M. to 6 P.M., except Thanksgiving and Christmas Day; hours are extended during July and August, 8 A.M. to 8 P.M. Admission. Group rates, private tours, and "lantern tours" available by advance reservation.

One of the oldest "tourist" caves in the Northeast, Howe Caverns has been introducing people to the underground since the nineteenth century; a local farmer, Lester Howe, discovered the site in 1842. Today you can still see what millions of years have created underneath your feet. The tour begins with an elevator ride from the visitor center, which descends 156 feet to the subterranean walkway that takes you through the lighted caves. The year-round temperature is a constant 52 degrees Fahrenheit, and the array of formations are fascinating to see. Children will enjoy the Bridal Altar, with its heart-shaped stone (more than five hundred weddings have taken place here), and the unique wall formations, including the Old Witch and the Chinese Pagoda in Titan's Temple. But the best part of the tour is the boat ride on the underground Lake of Venus, where tour guides turn off the lights and let you experience total darkness. The cave is brightly and safely lit. Bring a sweater or a light jacket, because the cave is damp and the tours last about eighty minutes. In general, kids enjoy the rock formations, tunnels, and, in particular, the Winding Way's narrow passages. The rock hounds in the family can purchase bags of mining rough and wash away the soil to reveal semiprecious gems, which are theirs to keep; they can also watch as the geode they select is cut in half to reveal its prized contents!

Facilities: *Restrooms, picnic tables, retail shops, homemade fudge and snack bar, motel, restaurant. The caves are not stroller friendly or wheelchair accessible. Note that backpacks and other large bags are not allowed in the cave.*

Mine Kill Falls Overlook and Environs. Route 30 between Mine Kill and Blenheim. Open daily weather-permitting, 10 A.M. until dusk. Free.

You can park and walk along a path to the overlook, where the falls drop dramatically to the stream. This is not a good walk for very young sightseers, since it is a quarter-mile trek that climbs uphill on the return trip. If you want to picnic at an unusual site, try to find the longest single-span covered bridge in the world, which is located just north of the Power Authority entrance in Blenheim (the bridge is on your right). Also, the remains of a **petrified forest** with the oldest known fossils in the world are found on County Route 342 off Route 30 in Gilboa; watch for county road markers. The "forest" is really only a pocket-sized park, but there is a bronze marker at the site, and it is an unusual stop for kids who are interested in what life was like in the times of the dinosaurs.

New York Power Authority Visitors Center. 1378 State Route 30, North Blenheim 12131; (800) 724-0309 or (607) 588-6061. Watch for signs on Route 30. Open daily 10 A.M. to 5 P.M., except national holidays; Lansing Manor is open daily May through October, except Tuesdays, 10 A.M. to 5 P.M. Free. Group tours available by advance reservation.

Housed in a nineteenth-century dairy barn, the Blenheim-

Gilboa Power Project visitors center has recently undergone a complete renovation. State-of-the-art exhibits and interactive displays demonstrate how power is made and used. Video and computer technology help explain the science of energy and electricity to both children and adults. The hands-on computerized displays make kids part of the action. They can hop on a bicycle generator and turn pedal power into electricity, or test their energy smarts with a touch-screen video quiz. The Power Authority provides some of the lowest-cost electricity in the state; it operates seventeen generating facilities and maintains more than fourteen hundred miles of transmission lines. The project supplies more than 1 million kilowatts of energy at times of peak demand by recycling water between two reservoirs. Each of the reservoirs—one atop Brown Mountain, the other at its foot—holds 5 billion gallons of water. When generating power, the water cascades down a vertical shaft five times taller than Niagara Falls. When storing water— usually at night or on weekends—the process is reversed and water is pumped back up the shaft for storage.

Next to the visitors center is Lansing Manor, an early American country estate built in 1819 by John Lansing, a New York State delegate to the 1787 Constitutional Convention. The manor house was restored by the Power Authority in 1977 and fully refurbished in 2002. It is filled with authentic furnishings from the first half of the nineteenth century, and showcases the simple yet gracious lives of the families that first lived there. After a tour, take a stroll along the 2.5-mile Bluebird Trail, so named because of efforts to restore populations of New York's state bird. The trail traverses a rolling hillside between the visitors center and nearby Mine Kill State Park. There is also a two-acre wetlands area that serves as an outdoor classroom to explain the function and benefits of wetlands to air and water quality.

Facilities: *Restrooms, picnic tables, wheelchair accessible.*

Schoharie Pharmacy and Ice Cream Fountain. Main Street, Schoharie 12157; (518) 295-7300. Open daily 9 A.M. to 6 P.M., except holidays. Free.

This old-fashioned ice cream parlor, soda fountain, and drugstore is at the site of the historic Throop Pharmacy from days long past. It makes a wonderful stop on a hot summer day. The building housing the pharmacy is the oldest store in the county and offers kids a look at apothecary items of the past. Those with a sweet tooth can try one of the ice cream treats; their Black Forest sundae is a favorite choice among local residents. There are also several bakery items and soups available.

Facilities: *Restroom.*

Secret Caverns. Cavern Road, Cobleskill 12043; (518) 296-8558. The caverns are five miles east of Cobleskill, between Routes 7 and 20 on Cavern Road. Open daily, May, June, and September, 9 A.M. to 6 P.M.; July and August, 9 A.M. to 8 P.M.; April and October, 10 A.M. to 5 P.M. Admission. Group rates and tours available by advance reservation.

These causes are a totally different underground experience from Howe Caverns. The two cave companies have been competing for years, and Howe wins hands-down as the more sophisticated tourist attraction. However, if you and the older kids are looking for somewhat more adventure and Tom Sawyer–like experiences, then by all means, visit Secret Caverns; don't bring younger kids unless they like to walk. The tour begins not with an elevator ride but instead with a walk down more than one hundred thirty steps to the cave floor. Then you trek alongside the underground river to see wonders such as Alligator, the Cavern's Monster, City of the Future, and Wonderland. The rock formations are all lighted, and a misty one-hundred-foot waterfall is impressive. Kids will love the stalagmites and stalactites—the latter "stick tight" to the ceiling—and the colorful wall deposits called flowstone. The caverns are a constant 50 degrees Fahrenheit, so bring along a sweater for the forty-five-minute tour.

Facilities: *Restrooms, picnic area, restaurant, motel. This site is not stroller or wheelchair accessible.*

What to Do

MAPLE SYRUP FARMS

Many of the maple syrup producers and sap houses in Schoharie County are run on an intermittent basis; however, there are a few places that have been in business for many years and welcome visitors.

Buck Hill Farm. Fuller Road, Jefferson 12093; (607) 652-7980. Take Route 10 to Jefferson and watch for signs to the farm. Open daily. Free.

This farm has a complete maple production setup, including a candy-making area. There are tours of the sugarbush, sap house, and shop during maple season, and the staff will even mail maple gifts to your friends. There are pancake breakfasts from 8 A.M. to 2 P.M. on Sundays, October through April. The sap season runs from March to mid-April but is weather dependent, so call ahead.

Maple Hill Farms. Grovernors Corners Road, Cobleskill 12043; (518) 234-4858. Located three miles northeast of town at the junction of Cromie Road and Grovernors. This farm is only open for tours during the maple season, but they sell maple products year-round in a shop on the premises. Call for opening hours.

Stone House Farm. 305 Lynk Road, Sharon Springs 13459; (518) 284-2476. From Sharon Springs take Route 20 west 1.5 miles; make a right on Lynk Road. The farm is on the left about one mile up the road. This small family farm has forty Jersey cows and a one-thousand-tap maple operation. You will find pure maple syrup, cream, candy, and sugar on sale year-round. There are pancake breakfasts in the saphouse from 8 A.M. to 1 P.M. on weekends during February, March, and April.

PARKS

Max V. Shaul State Park. Route 30 (watch the signs), Fultonham 12071; (518) 827-4711. Open year-round, daily, 8 A.M. until dusk. Small use fee. Group rates and camping available by advance reservation.

This small, wild state park is only fifty-seven acres, but it packs a lot into its space. The park straddles Schoharie Creek, which is renowned for its fishing, and this is the perfect recreational stop for a summer's day when you are traveling with the kids. Campsites are available for overnight use, and there are barbecue pits for day-trippers as well. Short nature trails let you take the kids on a walk through the woods on quiet paths filled with plants and birds. There are playgrounds on the site, and movies are offered on Friday evenings in the summer. Cross-country skiing trails are opened in winter, but you must bring your own equipment. I recommend this park as a nice place for a picnic, or to get away from the summer tourist bustle in some of the larger towns in the region. If you don't want to stop here for a picnic, just travel north a mile or so above the park on Route 30; there is a charming picnic and rest stop on the left, which is set along the creek and has covered table sites.

Facilities: *Restrooms, campsite, picnic areas. The restrooms are wheelchair accessible.*

Mine Kill State Park. Route 30, North Blenheim 12131; (518) 827-6111. Open daily, year-round. Hours of operation vary with the season. Summer pool hours are July and August, daily, 10 A.M. to 6 P.M. There is a small day-use fee from Memorial Day through Labor Day.

This is an excellent day-use park (no overnight camping allowed) that is often quiet, even on holiday weekends. Located on Schoharie Creek, which is part of a reservoir system, the park overlooks the water and provides many hiking trails, picnic areas, and other seasonal delights. The summer offers pool swimming, complete with locker rooms, a snack bar, and sunbathing areas. A boat-launching ramp for the reservoir is open from May through Labor Day, and the park has cross-country and snowmobile trails in the winter. Kids will enjoy walking the trails, which wind down through the forest to the water's edge.

Facilities: *Restrooms, picnic tables, athletic fields, playgrounds, snack bar, locker room. Wheelchair accessible.*

Vroman's Nose Nature Preserve. Mill Valley Road, Middleburgh 12122; (518) 827-5747. Open year-round, dawn to dusk.

This preserve has a 1.5 mile walking trail through woodlands that brings you out to a cliff facing the lovely Schoharie Valley, a view you will always remember. This is a nice place to stop while driving through the county. Look for signs on Route 30.

Facilities: *Restrooms, picnic area.*

PICK-YOUR-OWN FARMS

Barber's Farm. 3722 State Route 30, Middleburgh 12122; (518) 827-5452. Located 3.5 miles south of Middleburgh on Route 30. Open May through October, daily, 10 A.M. to 6 P.M.

You can pick your own tomatoes, peppers, and eggplants here, and the kids will enjoy visiting the cows in the dairy barn. During the autumn there is a corn maze, and a retail market on the premises sells an array of plants starting in spring. This farm has been family owned and operated since 1857 and is a wonderful place to show children farm life.

Facilities: *Restroom, picnic area.*

Pick a Pumpkin Pumpkin Patch. Creek Road, Central Bridge 12035; (518) 868-4893. Open during October only, Monday to Saturday, 10 A.M. to 5 P.M.

The kids will love the free hayrides out to the fields to pick pumpkins and gourds. There is a hay tunnel and a Storybookland, as well as specialty foods and crafts.

Facilities: *Restroom, picnic area.*

Sharon Orchards. 573 Chestnut Street, Sharon Springs 13459; (518) 284-2510. From Route 20 west in Sharon Springs, turn left onto Chestnut Street; the orchard is on the right two miles ahead. Open May through October daily, 10 A.M. to 5 P.M.

The orchards here produce apples, cherries, peaches, pears, and plums, and visitors can pick their own or buy from the farm stand. This particular orchard is unusual for the variety of fruit offered.

Facilities: *Restroom, picnic area.*

Terrace Mountain Orchard. Terrace Mountain Road, Schoharie 12157; (518) 295-8212. Open September through November, daily, 9 A.M. to 5 P.M. Take Route 30 to Schoharie, and make a left on Bridge Street; the next right is Terrace Mountain Road, and the orchard is two miles ahead on the right.

There are sixteen apple varieties on offer here, as well as excellent cider, doughnuts, pies, and specialty foods available in the shop on the premises.

Facilities: *Restroom, picnic area.*

Wellington's Herbs and Spices. 649 Rickard Hill Road, Schoharie 12157; (518) 295-7366. Open April through November, Wednesday through Saturday, 10 A.M. to 4 P.M.; Sunday, 11 A.M. to 4 P.M. Monday and Tuesday, by appointment only. Call for directions.

While you cannot pick your own crops here, this family-friendly place is a nice oasis. There are spectacular hillside views, a 2,500-square-foot country store, lovely herb and flower gardens, a children's petting zoo, ponds, and a tea room.

Facilities: *Restroom, picnic area.*

Albany, Schenectady, and Rensselaer Counties: The Capital Region

The city of Albany is the oldest chartered city in the United States, and long before the city received its charter in 1686, the settlement was an important river stop and trading center. Henry Hudson discovered the area in 1609 while seeking a route to the Far East. Gradually, the Dutch settled there, attracted by the area's fertile farmland and abundant game. Trade and industry burgeoned, since the city was located where the navigable Hudson River ended and the Erie Canal began. Today the capital region is a dynamic place where you can revisit the past with a trip to a children's museum; stop at a planetarium; enjoy an outing at a state park; or watch lawmakers at work in the state capitol building. The region is firmly rooted in history, which provides a strong foundation for its continuing growth in the twenty-first century.

A tour of Albany is best begun at the city's **Heritage Area Visitors Center,** which offers a spectacular orientation show, suggested walking and driving tours, and a planetarium. During the summer this is the starting place for city trolley tours of the capital's attractions. One of the best places to take kids in Albany is the **New York State Museum.** The changes in the state over the centuries are displayed in a series of realistic, lifelike dioramas. Mastodons, wild birds, bear, and deer are shown in their natural habitat, while street scenes of old New York show subways, fire engines, and shops of the past. Don't miss a tour of the **New York State Capitol,** one of the most beautiful government buildings in the world. Some of the art most appealing to kids can be found on the famous staircases here. Older kids will enjoy watching the lawmaking process from the Senate galleries if you happen to visit when a legislative session is taking place.

For a break from sightseeing in the city, head out to **Grafton Lakes State Park** for year-round sports and outdoor activities. Over two thousand acres provide a full range of playgrounds, ball fields, and picnic areas, and four lakes may be enjoyed in the park, with swimming at Long Pond, which has a lovely sandy beach. Another recreational gem, the **Hudson-Mohawk Bikeway,** is one of the capital region's most popular features, a forty-one-mile path traveling along the Hudson and Mohawk rivers and connecting Albany, Schenectady, and Troy.

Heading over to Troy, the **Junior Museum** is a must-see with its fantastic Exploring Hudson River Life exhibit. Kids can follow all 315 miles of the Hudson River in this 75-foot interactive display. Recently renovated, the **Schenectady Museum and Planetarium** hands-on oriented museum features interactive exhibits that tell the story of the city's role in world-changing innovations such as refrigeration, radio, and television.

To enliven your stay, check out a few of the special events that coincide with your visit. Seasonal celebrations abound and there are many that are perfect for families. Every May in Albany's Washington Park, the annual Tulip Festival features arts and crafts, children's games, and live entertainment. Also in May,

Schenectady's Festival of Nations celebrates the cultural richness of the city and features international food, music, dance, and storytelling. August brings the Riverfest to the banks of the Hudson in Albany, an all-day event offering continuous water activities, children's games, and fantastic fireworks at dusk.

For further information, contact the **Albany County Convention and Visitors Bureau,** 25 Quackenbush Square, Albany 12207; (518) 434-1217; www.albany.org.

What to See

MUSEUMS AND HISTORIC SITES

Albany Heritage Area Visitors Center and Henry Hudson Planetarium. 25 Quackenbush Square, Albany 12207; (518) 434-1217 or (800) 258-3582, (518) 434-0405 for the planetarium. Open daily 10 A.M. to 4 P.M. Free.

This site offers visitors a series of changing exhibits, as well as interactive displays that highlight history and culture in the capital city and provide an overview of the region. The planetarium features star shows on Saturday mornings at 11:30 A.M. for children and at 12:30 P.M. for adults; there are special programs during the summer months and at other school vacation periods throughout the year.

Facilities: *Restrooms, gift shop.*

Albany Institute of History and Art. 125 Washington Avenue, Albany 12210; (518) 463-4478. Open year-round, Wednesday through Saturday, 10 A.M. to 5 P.M.; Sunday, noon to 5 P.M.; Tuesday is for preregistered groups only. Admission; children age five and under admitted free. Group tours by advance reservation.

This museum was founded in 1791 as a repository for science and history materials. Today the Albany Institute of History and Art (AIHA) celebrates five centuries of the history, art, and culture of the upper Hudson Valley. It is housed in a complex of three historic buildings connected by a glass atrium. The Museum Explorers Gallery, a special hands-on museum experience for families, offers a great introduction to the Albany Institute. Activities include Crack the Code (how to read and understand museum labels), the Mini-Museum (design and install your own exhibition in a scale-model of a museum gallery), Guess the Mystery Object (discover the stories original objects can tell), and Try on History (dress up in eighteenth-century clothing). Kids will also enjoy exercising their imagination in the art-making corner or at the computer station.

The first floor of gallery space is dedicated to temporary exhibitions, with the exception of three galleries that highlight AIHA's permanent collections: the Entry Point Gallery, the Open Storage Viewing Room, and the Sculpture Gallery. On the second floor, visitors experience the best of AIHA's permanent collections, including "The Landscape That Defined America: The Hudson River School," which features some of AIHA's finest landscape paintings from the first American school of painting. Other permanent exhibits focus on trading culture and eighteenth- to nineteenth-century painting and sculpture. Kids will especially enjoy the Ancient Egypt gallery, which is like entering an ancient tomb. Albany's own beloved mummies have the place of honor among objects that explore the themes of the Nile, daily life, and the afterlife.

Special programs and workshops for children and families are an important part of the museum's activities. Kids can make their own valentines or try their hand at creating Egyptian art. Teachers should note that special lectures can be arranged for classes if reservations are made in advance.

Facilities: *Restrooms, café, gift shop. Wheelchair and stroller accessible.*

Crailo State Historic Site. 9½ Riverside Avenue, Rensselaer 12144; (518) 463-8738. From I-787, take Route 20 east to Rensselaer; at the first traffic light, turn right and go one block further to the site. Open April through October, Wednesday through Sunday, 10 A.M. to 5 P.M. Admission. Groups welcome by advance reservation only.

Crailo was a Dutch-fortified farmhouse built circa 1704 by the Van Rensselaer family. It soon became the center of a vast patroonship, or estate, which contained more than 700,000 acres. Although the building has undergone many changes over the past three hundred years, serving at various times as a home, a boarding school, a church rectory, and even a cinder-block factory, today the restored building contains exhibits about the history of Dutch culture in the upper Hudson Valley. Young visitors will see how the Dutch lived, slept, worked, and ate (school groups can arrange for a cooking demonstration), and they also can see the two gun ports that were cut into the walls in the 1700s. There are displays of art and furniture, and while the museum is lively enough, very young children will not be entertained unless they have a strong interest in history or everyday life of long ago. Archaeological artifacts from the Fort Orange area are on display and are used in conjunction with the tours to explain the historical significance of the Dutch influence in present-day New York State. If the weather is warm, make sure to wander around outside. It is here, legend says, that in 1758 a British surgeon composed a funny song about American soldiers and then set the words to an old drinking tune. The result is the still-popular song known as "Yankee Doodle"!

Facilities: *Restrooms, park area for picnics. Strollers are difficult to maneuver in the house, but the museum is accessible to wheelchairs.*

Empire State Aerosciences Museum. 250 Rudy Chase Drive, Glenville 12032; (518) 377-2191. Open year-round, Wednesday and Sunday, noon to 4 P.M.; Thursday through Saturday, 10 A.M. to 4 P.M. During school vacation hours of operation are extended, so call ahead. Admission.

The mission of this facility is to educate but also to entertain and excite young people with experiences of air and space. The museum consists of nine buildings on twenty-seven acres located at the western perimeter of the Schenectady County Airport (where Charles Lindbergh landed in 1927). Visitors will learn about the history of flight, as well as New York State's importance in the development of aviation. There is an impressive collection of aircraft on display outdoors that includes a F-14A Tomcat, a A-6E Intruder, a A-4F Skyhawk II, and a Huey helicopter. The main galleries contain some of the more fragile aircraft, detailed models, dioramas, historical artifacts, memorabilia, and photographic displays. The Amelia Earhart exhibit should not be missed. There are a few hands-on exhibits, including a mock-up of a 1910 Von Pomer airplane and a simulated-reality vehicle (SRV), which treats kids to a video and "ride" that makes them feel as if they were part of the action. Aviation Adventure programs are held during school vacation weeks, as well as throughout the summer. Call for a schedule.

Facilities: *Restrooms, gift shop, cafeteria. Wheelchair and stroller accessible.*

Empire State Plaza. Albany 12242; (518) 474-2121. Located off exit 23 of the NYS Thruway (go through the tollbooth to I-787 and take Empire State Plaza exit) and bounded by Swan, Madison, State, and Eagle Streets. Open daily 6 A.M. to 6 P.M. Free.

Popularly called the Plaza, this is really a government complex that includes office buildings, a convention center, a performing arts center known as the Egg, a concourse, and the state museum. Built at a cost of more than $2 billion and finished in 1978, the Plaza fulfilled Governor Nelson Rockefeller's dream of a government center that would draw people in, an urban park for all seasons. It has achieved world renown as an outdoor arts center. There is enough open space that kids can enjoy the outdoors, and all family members will find something to amuse them. Scattered across the plaza (or the esplanade) are a series of reflecting pools, where kids can ice-skate in the winter; in warmer weather they can roller-skate on the walkways. Along the mall are plantings and modern sculpture, fountains, waterfalls, and an excellent play area known as the Children's Place, which has outdoor activity areas, a sandbox, and a separate toddler area. Next to the play area is the environmental sculpture called the Labyrinth, where you can sit on benches and take a break from walking. The New York State Vietnam Memorial, at the courtyard in the Justice Building, is a quiet park with memorial panels for the people from New York State who served in the war. Inside the concourse you will find fine examples of modern art on permanent display, which can introduce older kids to colorful canvases by great masters. For a bird's-eye view of it all, head to the observation deck on the forty-second floor of the Corning Tower. From the deck, which is free and open from 9 A.M. to 4 P.M., you can see the Catskills, the Adirondacks, and the Berkshire Mountains in the distance on a clear day. At the end of the mall, near the huge stairway that leads up to the New York State Museum, concerts and special events are held throughout the summer, including an Independence Day celebration, the Tulip Festival, and the Northeastern Wildlife Expo.

Facilities: *Restrooms, three cafeterias, restaurant, food concessions, gift shops, skate rentals. There are many shops inside the concourse. Stroller friendly and wheelchair accessible.*

The Junior Museum. 105 8th Street, Troy 12182; (518) 235-2120. Open year-round, Thursday, 10 A.M. to 2 P.M.; Friday through Sunday, 10 A.M. to 5 P.M. Admission. Groups by advance reservation.

Where can you see the 315 miles of the Hudson River in an impressive 75-foot exhibit, complete with waterfall and live animals? At the Junior Museum's fantastic "Exploring Hudson River Life" exhibit. Kids will enjoy following the waterway from an Adirondack tributary to estuary and salt-marsh tanks, then to a tidal pool. They will feel as if they were right at the river's edge watching live trout, bass, catfish, puffer fish, and a snapping turtle. At the seawater filled Tide Pool, a museum educator shares fascinating facts about the starfish, horseshoe crabs, and sea urchins that live there. The museum also has a wonderful bee exhibit. The hands-on learning experience, "Turtles, Geckos and Snakes!" gives young visitors the opportunity to touch live reptiles and giant insects. The resident barred owl may hoot at overnight groups sleeping in the Mohican wigwam near the dugout canoe. The museum's Digistar II Planetarium offers multimedia shows on space exploration, constellations, and molecules. The Learning Loft has a variety of interactive displays from computers and Legos to fun-house mirrors and art supplies. Exciting exhibits and shows fill all four floors of this award-winning museum. Workshops, group tours, overnights, and school-break camps are available by advance arrangement.

Facilities: *Restrooms. Wheelchair and stroller accessible.*

New York State Capitol. State Street, Albany 12224. Located at the State Street end of the Empire State Plaza; (518) 474-2418. From I-787, take the Empire Plaza exit; the plaza is bounded by Swan, Madison, State, and Eagle Streets, and the capitol is on State Street, at the northern end of the plaza. Open Monday through Friday for tours at 10 A.M., noon, 2 P.M., and 3 P.M.; Saturday and Sunday at 11 A.M., 1 P.M., and 3 P.M. Tours leave from the Empire State Plaza visitors center courtyard. Free. Group tours available by advance reservation.

The New York State Capitol Building is considered one of the loveliest government buildings in the world, and rightfully so. Built between 1867 and 1899, the intricate carvings and decorative motifs are still as fresh and fascinating as they were almost a century ago. The tour is designed to introduce children to the workings of the state legislature, and, along the way, they have a chance to see architecture, art, and even some live lawmakers at work! Surprisingly enough, some of the art most appealing to children can be found on the famous staircases. The Senate Staircase is also called the Evolutionary Staircase because of the wonderful carvings of animals that decorate its sides, a variety of wildlife from single-cell creatures to lions. The Great Western Staircase is the most elaborately carved and is also known as the Million-Dollar Staircase for both the cost of its construction and its wealth of carvings. In fact, many of the carvings are of famous people including Abraham Lincoln, Ulysses S. Grant, and Harriet Beecher Stower, and the stone-carvers included their own portraits as well. The East Lobby holds a fine collection of flags that date back to the Civil War, as well as changing exhibits. Older kids will enjoy watching the lawmaking process at work from the Senate galleries (call before you go to see when sessions are taking place). There is enough to see for all ages, and the capitol is always buzzing with activity, so this is not a boring tour. Outside, parks at either end of the building offer magnificent flower gardens and great spots for picnic lunches and rest stops.

Facilities: *Restrooms, cafeteria, wheelchair access. Strollers are welcome, but the building has many staircases.*

New York State Museum. Madison Avenue, Empire State Plaza, Albany 12230; (518) 474-5877. To reach the plaza, take exit 23 off the NYS Thruway; pick up I-787 and get off at the Empire State Plaza exit. Open year-round, except national holidays, 10 A.M. to 5 P.M. Free. Group tours available by advance reservation.

This is by far one of the best places to take kids in the Albany region. The changing life and history of New York State over the centuries is shown in a series of realistic, lifelike dioramas. Mastodons, wild birds, bear, deer, and other wildlife are shown in their natural habitat, while street scenes of old New York show pushcarts, subways, fire engines, and shops of the past. A popular stop for younger kids is the original *Sesame Street* set, with a video featuring Oscar the Grouch, Kermit, Count Von Count, and Big Bird. A Native American section has displays of everyday life as experienced by a variety of New York tribes. The Discovery Place offers kids hands-on learning with a science theme. Rotating exhibits like Prehistoric Mammals provide a unique and fun approach to education. The famous Cohoes mastodon is a special attraction, and a moving September 11 exhibit was installed in 2002. There are a number of shows given in the museum's theater. Special events are scheduled throughout the year; you may get to enjoy a Victorian holiday, a children's sleep-over in the museum, or a visit with an American artist.

Facilities: *Restrooms, cafeteria, gift shop. Wheelchair accessible and stroller friendly.*

Scotia Glenville Children's Museum. 303 Mohawk Avenue, Scotia 12302; (518) 346-1764.

This is a truly unusual children's museum—you don't go to it; it comes to you, in the form of a museum teacher and tote bags filled with objects, artifacts, and project materials. The museum travels to twelve counties within a fifty-mile radius of Scotia, and if you are a teacher or a leader of a children's group, you can make arrangements to have your own museum visit for a day. There are also birthday party visits, with special programs for such celebrations. Founded by three women who believed that museums should offer hands-on participatory exhibits, the museum has traveling programs for schools, fairs, festivals, summer recreation sites, and after-school programs. The exhibits are more than just displays; children are encouraged to become involved as geologists, explorers, musicians, and artists.

Schenectady Museum and Planetarium. 15 Nott Terrace Heights, Schenectady 12308; (518) 382-7890. Located off Route 5 in the downtown area. Open Tuesday through Friday, 10 A.M. to 4:30 P.M.; Saturday and Sunday, noon to 5 P.M. Planetarium shows on weekend afternoons; call ahead for schedule. Admission. Group tours by advance reservation.

This Schenectady treasure celebrates the region's creativity in both technology and culture. The museum is notable for the strength of its collections, including artifacts and photographs from the history of General Electric and the Marjorie Bradt Foote Costume Collection, with approximately six thousand costumes. The collection of 1.5 million photos covering GE's history ranks among the top ten private collections in the nation. Permanent exhibits invite visitors to celebrate the birthplace of radio and television by testing the technology of a variety of items from a lightbulb to a refrigerator. There are also changing exhibits of art, history, and technology.

MVP Kid's Place is a permanent exhibit that focuses on community life and is geared to kids between the ages of four and nine. Children can step into the role of a General Electric scientist (Schenectady is the home of GE), try on clothes at Barney's Department Store, and put on their own puppet shows in the WRGB puppet theater. They will also encounter a child-sized kitchen, a soap-box derby car from the 1950s, and a full-size model of a Mars Rover developed at RPI. The exhibits combine hands-on activities and objects from the museum's collection to help young children discover their own communities and to give new meaning to the diverse people, places, and things around them.

The Suits-Bueche Planetarium, newly renovated and reopened in 2003, has been automated with state-of-the-art computer technology, including dozens of brand-new projectors, two video projectors, and an amazing sound system. In addition, the Spitz A3P Star Projector, the workhorse of the planetarium, continues to display some of the most spectacular views of the stars. The planetarium has a new lighting system that shows off magnificent sunrises and sunsets, a wraparound silhouette of the capital-district skyline, and plush new carpeting. Two forty-two-inch plasma screen video monitors showing astronomical images—from the latest Hubble pictures to NASA TV footage—flank a fiber-optic star curtain and futuristic display welcoming visitors to an unforgettable show.

Facilities: *Restrooms, gift shop.*

OTHER ATTRACTIONS

Albany Trolley. Visitors Center, 25 Quackenbush Square, Albany 12207; (518) 434-0405. Open daily, July and August only; call for schedule. Admission. Free parking.

This is a great way to see the historic sites of the city during the summer months and to get oriented upon arrival. A narrated tour tells the story of the city and the legends behind several stately landmarks and important attractions. All tours begin with a video, *Albany: A Cultural Crossroads.*

Facilities: *Restrooms, gift shop.*

Amtrak Train Station. Herrick Street, Rensselaer 12144; (518) 462-5763. Located just over the Dunn Memorial Bridge. Free, but there is a charge for a train ride. Open daily; call for hours.

Kids love trains, and at this conveniently located station in the capital region you can take a short train ride to Saratoga Springs, Schenectady, Hudson, or Rhinecliff. The views along the Hudson

---

CITY TOUR

If you are in the Schenectady region, you may want to take a self-guided walking tour of the historic **Stockade District,** which has been described as one of the region's most extensive collections of eighteenth-century architecture. Pick up a tour brochure from the Schenectady Urban Cultural Park visitor center located in the Schenectady Museum. While touring the stockade, visit the **Schenectady County Historical Society** (32 Washington Avenue, Schenectady 12305; (518) 374-0263). Older children with an interest in architecture will enjoy this, and the Stockade area has many interesting shops and eateries. In the Village Square, make sure the kids see "Lawrence the Indian" a statue that memorializes one of the earliest Native American friends of the settlers. **Union College,** on Union Street, is renowned as one of the first architecturally designed campus in America. Adults and children will want to see the sixteen-sided **Nott Memorial** building, a National Historic Landmark and a prime example of high Victorian Gothic architecture on the campus.

River are magnificent any time of year, especially when the boats and ships are chugging up and downriver, but try to schedule a trip for autumn, when the foliage is spectacular. Even if you don't take a train ride, you can watch the trains come and go from the observation area near the tracks, and kids will enjoy getting up close to the tracks, seeing the bustle and color of the train crews, and listening to the whistles and bells. Note that you should time your visit not to coincide with morning and evening rush hours.

Facilities: *Restrooms.*

The Costumer. 1020 Barrett Street, Schenectady 12305; (518) 374-7442. Open year-round, weekdays, from 10 A.M. to 6 P.M.; Saturday 10 A.M. to 5 P.M. Groups and individuals must make arrangements in advance to take a free tour.

The chance to go behind the scenes at this business is a real treat, and school-age children will be delighted with the magnificent costumes and mascots here. They can watch while costumes are manufactured for an array of cartoon-type characters. On display are costumes for Michael Mouse, the Smurfs, and even a character similar to Big Bird. There is a magic shop that holds demonstrations for groups, and the gift shop is filled with all kinds of special tricks, makeup kits, and gadgets.

Facilities: *Restrooms, gift shop.*

Five Rivers Environmental Center. 56 Game Farm Road, Delmar 12054; (518) 475-0291. Located seven miles south of Albany, off Route 443 in Delmar; watch for signs. Open year-round, sunrise to sunset. Interpretive center is open to the public Monday through Saturday, 9 A.M. to 4:30 P.M.; Sunday 1 to 4:30 P.M. Free. Groups are accommodated by advance reservation only.

A unique nature center, Five Rivers offers a wide variety of programs, hikes, and tours for both adults and children. Named after the five large rivers in the general area of the center, this is an excellent place to spend hours exploring the outdoors. A series of self-guided nature trails are specially designed for younger children. Wooden walkways let you explore pond areas, trees, marshes, and woodlands; there are free guide brochures for each walk, which vary in length from an eighth of a mile to two-mile loops. The trails include stops at woodlots, orchards, fields, wildflower meadows, and stream banks, and the brochures include information about animal habits and ecosystems. A butterfly and hummingbird garden is designed to attract wildlife on the wing. Inside the Interpretive Center, kids can see exhibits about local wildlife, including many samples that are touchable, a rare feature in many other museums. Aristotle the owl is a special favorite with kids here, and many events are held in the center all year long. Week-long Family Fun programs run all summer and offer guided walks, special projects, and bird-watching. The center participates in the annual New Year's Day bird count, and visitors are welcome to bring their binoculars and participate. In the winter, activities include maple sugaring, snow tracking, cross-country skiing, snowshoeing (they rent showshoes), and signs of the season; in the fall, there are "wetlands wanders" and nature's harvest workshops; the spring and summer bring animal identification, pond visits, and tree identification classes. When you are in the center, don't forget to ask for copies of nature worksheets and game pages for the kids to use on the trails.

Facilities: *Restrooms, picnic area—both are wheelchair accessible. The site is stroller friendly along most of the trails, and there is wheelchair access both inside and outside the interpretive center; two short trails are wheelchair accessible. There are large-print and braille trail guides available.*

Hoffman's Playland. 608 Loudon Road (Route 9), Latham 12110; (518) 785-3842. Located one mile south of Latham Circle. Open April through September, daily, noon to 10 P.M., but hours may vary seasonally, so call ahead. Free admission to the park, but there is a charge for the rides.

This amusement park has been in business since 1952, and it is a tradition in the Albany area. Hoffman's offers a nice place to escape with kids two years old and up for an afternoon of fun and rides (there are eighteen of them here). The youngest children will enjoy the carousel, boats, bumper cars, Ferris wheel, helicopters, train, small roller coaster, and caterpillar. Older kids will appreciate the Tilt-A-Whirl, Scrambler, and Paratrooper, as well as the large arcade area. There is a miniature golf course adjacent to the site (there is an additional charge for this). This clean, enjoyable park is nicely landscaped and offers a refreshing change from the atmosphere of the mega-amusement parks.

Facilities: *Restrooms, snack bars.*

Hudson River Way. Albany. This magnificent pedestrian walkway opened in August 2002, and extends from Broadway at Maiden Lane over I-787 to the Corning Riverfront Park and amphitheater. It is designed to connect downtown Albany to the shores of the historic Hudson River and to tell the story of Albany through a series of paintings depicting historical artifacts. Created by mural artist Jan Marie Spanard and her talented crew, the paintings adorn the two staircase landings and the thirty lampposts that line both sides of the bridge. The story begins hundreds of millions of years ago when Albany was at the bottom of a prehistoric sea. As you progress over the bridge, the story continues through time, and includes the early Dutch merchants and other scenes of historic importance. There are two large murals on the landings that divide the three flights of the grand staircase. The paintings are done in a permanent liquid stone paint called "keim" that will not fade or peel for decades. Although this isn't a walk for those with very young children, older kids will enjoy walking over the pedestrian bridge to the park. Be aware that river breezes can be quite brisk in the cool weather months.

Facilities: *Restrooms.*

Stratton Air National Guard Base. 1 Air National Guard Road, Scotia 12302; (518) 344-2323. Located at the Schenectady County Airport. Open year-round, Monday through Friday, 7:30 A.M. to 4 P.M. Free. Tour arrangements must be made in advance due to security considerations.

This air base is home to the world-famous Skibirds, the only C-130 aircraft operating on skis in the world. The unit that rescued Dr. Jerri Nielsen from the South Pole when she was stricken with breast cancer came from Stratton. A highlight of a visit here is a chance to get inside one of the aircraft that is on site, but you will also see the firehouse, fire trucks, and even the life-support systems that are used in the event of a plane going down. A slide presentation of Antarctica is shown (this is a military base that supports other bases throughout the world), and the tour includes a question-and-answer session.

Facilities: *Restrooms. Stroller and wheelchair accessible.*

USS *Slater* Destroyer Escort-766. The Snowdock at Broadway & Quay, at the foot of Madison Avenue, Albany 12210. Take exit 3B off Route I-787 South. Open Wednesday through Sunday, 10 A.M. to 4 P.M. Admission.

Step back in time aboard the last destroyer escort warship still in World War II battle configuration. See how the crew lived and carried out its mission of antisubmarine warfare. The armament, combat information, radio rooms, pilot house, galley, mess hall, officer's quarters, and crew's sleeping area are all authentically restored. Older children interested in military history will enjoy this stop.

Facilities: *Restrooms.*

Watervliet Arsenal Museum. Watervliet 12189; (518) 266-5805. Take I-87 to Watervliet exit onto Broadway, Route 32, and follow signs. Open Sunday through Thursday, 10 A.M. to 3 P.M. Free.

The arsenal does not offer tours for security reasons, but the museum is a unique and interesting stop for children over the age of six. The main exhibit traces the history of cannons in the United States and has several fascinating examples on display, including one of George Washington's cannons and several Civil War cannons. There is a re-creation of a nineteenth-century machine shop, which will delight kids interested in gadgets. Photos and a video describe the cannon manufacturing process, and outside, a full-size tank is on display. While this stop is not for everyone, children who are interested in the military and military history will love it.

Facilities: *Restrooms.*

What to Do

BICYCLING

Corning Riverfront Preserve Park. (800) 258-3582. The best section of this park for biking lies along the west bank of the Hudson River, where you pick up the Mohawk-Hudson Bikeway. To get there, take exit 23 off the NYS Thruway; pick up I-787, and get off at exit 4. Follow signs for Colonie Street. This is a delightful park where strollers will enjoy walking along the river and the Bikeway is accessible. To get a map of this forty-one-mile bike trail, call (800) 962-8007.

BOAT CRUISES

Dutch Apple Cruises. 141 Broadway, Albany 12201; (518) 463-0220. River tours daily, April through October. There are two-hour sightseeing cruises or three-hour dinner cruises available on a double-deck tour boat that holds 145 people. The price is reasonable and there are discounts for children, seniors, and groups. You will see old Dutch mansions, tiny hamlets, and ocean-going vessels in the Port of Albany.

ICE-SKATING

Albany County Hockey Training Facility. Albany-Shaker Road, Albany 12210; (518) 452-7396. Open July through May for both figure skating and hockey. Call for schedule. There are both freestyle and public sessions for figure skating. Snack bar on premises.

Empire State Plaza. Outdoor Plaza, Albany 12242; (518) 474-2418. There's outdoor skating here in the winter months, weather permitting.

Swinburne Park Skating Rink. Clinton Avenue below Manning Boulevard, Albany 12210; (518) 438-2406. This is an outdoor skating rink; call before you go for time of sessions. The schedule is weather-dependent here.

PARKS

Central Park. Central Parkway (off State Street—Route 5), Schenectady 12305; (518) 382-5151. Open year-round, dawn to dusk. Free.

This 372-acre city park is a gem, complete with lake, playing fields, swimming pool, tennis courts, duck pond, and playgrounds. Young children enjoy the playground with toddler-size equipment, a train ride, the swimming pond, and the chance to feed the numerous ducks (bring your own bread). Older kids like the boats that can be rented for rides on the pond. All ages can appreciate the exquisite rose gardens, where 4,500 rosebushes bloom (there are over 200 varieties) on a three-acre garden site. Try to visit in June, when the roses are at their peak. During the summer months you may be able to see a concert at the Music Haven Stage in the park.

Facilities: *Restrooms, picnic area, snack bars. Strollers can manage on the pathways, as can wheelchairs.*

Grafton Lakes State Park. Route 2, Grafton 12082; (518) 279-1155. Located twelve miles east of Troy. Open year-round, dawn to dusk. There is a small entrance fee from Memorial Day to Labor Day, and on weekends only through Columbus Day.

This 2,357-acre state park offers a variety of year-round sports and outdoor activities for children of all ages. This is one of the best parks in the Albany area for a day trip, since there is so much to keep the kids busy and parents will enjoy the beautiful lakes and forests. The park contains a range of playgrounds, ball fields, and picnic areas. There are four lakes and the Dunham Reservoir, but swimming is only permitted at Long Pond, which has a lovely sandy beach and rentals of paddleboats, rowboats, and canoes.

Visitors are welcome to bring their own canoes or sailboats to use on any of the lakes. Three of the four lakes are stocked with trout, bass, and pickerel, so be sure to bring fishing poles along; you do need a license to fish here, however. There are over twenty-five miles of groomed trails for hiking, mountain biking, horseback riding, and orienteering in the summer months. Special events for kids at this time of the year include crafts, games, and story time. There is also a miniature golf course. During the winter the trails are used for cross-country skiing, snowshoeing, and snowmobiling. Snowshoes may be rented in the park office, but bring any other equipment. There is also a wheelchair accessible trail in the Long Pond beach area.

Facilities: *Restrooms, picnic areas, lockers and bathhouses at beach area, concession stand (summer only). Strollers and wheelchairs can maneuver in some areas of the park, but not in others. The bathrooms and the Long Pond Beach are wheelchair accessible.*

John Boyd Thacher State Park. Route 157, Voorheesville 12186; (518) 872-1237. Open year-round, 8 A.M. to sunset. Free entrance; parking fee effective first weekend in May through Columbus Day.

Thacher Park is unusual in one respect: it is one of the richest fossil-bearing areas in the world. The park itself is well equipped for a day of fun: there are extensive hiking trails along the escarpment and through beautiful wooded areas. Hikers may also explore sections of the Long Path that runs through Thacher Park. In addition there are five hundred acres of open meadow that are perfect for hiking. The most popular trail is the Indian Ladder Geological Trail, which descends one hundred feet down along the escarpment, and is rich in geological fossils and historical significance. The views along this trail are magnificent. There is an

Olympic-size swimming pool as well as a number of picnic areas and playgrounds. In the winter months, cross-country skiing and snowshoeing are popular here, with several areas suitable for novices and beginners. Snowshoes are available for rental (but bring your own skis), and there are guided snowshoe walks just about every weekend. Call for a schedule of educational programs that are offered at the park throughout the year.

Facilities: *Restrooms, picnic areas, snack bar during summer months, wheelchair accessible.*

Two miles from Thacher State Park on Route 157 is **Thompson's Lake State Park** (518-872-1674), which offers seasonal overnight camping facilities (mid-May through mid-October), and has a sandy beach for swimming on Thompson's Lake. The park is open year-round, 8 A.M. to sunset. This lovely lake is actually an ancient sinkhole formed over one million years ago in fossil-rich Onondaga limestone. Ice fishing is popular here in the winter, and an annual ice fishing contest will be of interest to both adults and children.

Also nearby is the **Emma Treadwell Thacher Nature Center,** 87 Nature Center Way, Voorheesville 12186; (518) 872-0800. Open year-round, Tuesday through Sunday, 9 A.M. to 5 P.M. Closed Monday and holidays. Located near the shore of Thompson's Lake. Inside the Nature Center, kids will find lots to do; they may enjoy exploring a large geological model of the Helderberg Escarpment, watch a working honeybee colony, see an array of natural history exhibits, or participate in exciting natural history programs offered year-round. The Nature Center also offers several miles of trails for hiking, cross-country skiing, and snowshoeing.

Washington Park. Madison Avenue (between State Street and Madison Avenue), Albany 12210; (518) 434-5699. Open year-round, dawn to dusk. Free.

This park has served as a gathering place for the public since the seventeenth century, and it is still one of the most beautiful parks to visit in any city, in any season. The five-acre lake has paddleboats for rent, and the ducks enjoy a handout or two. There are several small play areas throughout the site, some of which include equipment designed for toddlers. The park hosts special events throughout the warm weather months, including the Albany Tulip Festival in April, which takes advantage of the colorful flower plantings throughout the park and features costumed performers. Children will love the horse-drawn cabs that are available for hire, and the rose gardens offer a perfect spot to rest. In the winter, ice-skating is allowed on the lake, and the trails and hills come alive with cross-country skiing and sledding (bring your own equipment). Be sure to plan a stop in Washington Park, especially if you are going to spend the day taking in the other Albany sights; the park is a quiet and restful place for kids to refuel at any time of year.

Facilities: *Restrooms, picnic areas, snack stand. Strollers can manage on some of the paths, but wheelchair access can be a problem in some areas.*

PICK-YOUR-OWN FARMS

Goold Orchards. 1297 Brookview Station Road, Castleton 12033; (518) 732-7317. Head across the Routes 9 and 20 Bridge into Rensselaer County and down Route 9 (follow the Goold Orchards signs) for pick-your-own strawberries in June, or apples and raspberries in September. The farm store and bakery offer homemade cider doughnuts and fresh-pressed cider, an array of fruit pies and cookies, all made fresh on the premises. The store is open year-round for apples and cider. The bakery is open Labor Day through November.

Lansing's Farm Market. 204 Lishakill Road, Colonie 12205; (518) 464-0889. Take the NYS Thruway to exit 24, then pick up Route 5 west to Lishakill Road. Pick your own strawberries here in June. Other goodies on sale in the market include tomatoes, corn, peppers, squash, and all other fruits and vegetables grown on the Lansing farm in season.

Shaker Shed. Junction of Sand Creek Road and Route 155, Colonie 12205; (518) 869-3662. Open Easter through Christmas. Pick your own tomatoes here in late August or enjoy a drink and dessert in the café. The market offers home-grown produce, crafts, candles, and fresh pies. During the spring months there are dozens of plants for sale; at Christmas time, there is a nice selection of wreaths and trees.

SKIING

Maple Ridge. 2725 Mariaville Road, Schenectady 12306; (518) 381-4700. Take I-88 north to exit 25 Rotterdam. Make a left onto Route 7 East, a left onto Route 337, and another left onto Route 159 West; the ski center is three miles ahead on the left. Open December through March, Tuesday through Thursday 3 to 9 P.M.; Friday 3 to 10 P.M.; Saturday 9 A.M. to 10 P.M.; Sunday 9 A.M. to 5 P.M. Call for hours during holidays and school vacations.

For nearly forty years this family-owned-and-operated ski center has offered a warm, friendly atmosphere to both skiers and snowboarders. It is a small center with just eight different runs ranging from beginner to expert. It's a good place for the youngest skiers to learn the basics. The Ski Tykes program is specifically for four- and five-year-olds who have never skied; the Snow Stars program is for six- and seven-year-olds who have never been on skis. There is also a snow-tubing park adjacent to the ski area.

Facilities: *Restrooms, cafeteria, ski school, retail and rental shop.*

THEATER

Capital Repertory Theater. 111 North Pearl Street, Albany 12207; (518) 462-4531 or (518) 445-SHOW. Open year-round. Call for a schedule. Admission. Theater lovers will enjoy the performances here; Capital Rep has been offering first-rate entertainment for nearly twenty-five years. The company employs professional equity actors and designers from New York City. There are usually six productions over the course of the year, which include musicals, comedies, dramas, and family-oriented productions. Several student matinees are also offered in conjunction with the education department.

ESPIA—The Egg. Empire State Plaza, Albany 12242; (518) 473-1061. This marvelous venue includes year-round modern dance, theater, concerts, storytellers, and other musical performances. Visitors may enjoy a virtual cornucopia of entertainment at this half-round building constructed on a pedestal, one of the most architecturally unique theater venues in the world. There are two theaters inside, as well as a wraparound lounge that offers an excellent view of the plaza. Children's programming in the past has included *The Pied Piper, Peter Pan*, and the Sicilian Marionettes.

Pepsi Arena. 51 South Pearl Street, Albany 12207; (518) 487-2000. This sports and entertaiment complex is home to several athletic teams, but it is also where you can see a range of entertainment from Stars on Ice and Cher to Bon Jovi and Sesame Street. There are car shows, regional basketball playoffs, and more. Call for a schedule.

Proctor's Theater. 432 State Street, Schenectady 12305; (518) 346-6204. This theater was completed in 1926 and is furnished in the gilt-and-marble grandeur of the old vaudeville world. The performance season runs from October through May and includes touring productions of Broadway shows. There are also silent films accompanied by Wurlitzer organ music (great fun for older kids) and a complete selection of children's theater programs year-round.

Saratoga County
and Environs

Since the eighteenth century, when natural medicinal springs were discovered in the region, Saratoga has played host to visitors from around the world. Today the county's world-class horse racing, performing arts center, ten museums, charming architecture, fabulous shops, and fine restaurants make it a great choice for a vacation getaway. Over one thousand buildings in the county are listed on the National Register of Historic Places. There are acres of parks and woodland on one side of town, and there's an elegant racetrack with a splendid Victorian grandstand on the other. Saratoga Springs may give the appearance of a small town, but it offers all the culture of a big city with lots of family-friendly activities.

The city's **Children's Museum** should be on the itinerary of all visitors with youngsters between the ages of two and nine. The location of the museum in the downtown area makes it an easy stop to combine with shopping or a visit to Congress Park, where kids can run around. At the lake, parents can sit and watch the ducks while the young ones play along graveled paths. The **Saratoga Performing Arts Center** (SPAC) offers a broad range of entertainment—including jazz, rock, dance, and country—in a unique outdoor setting. While most of the performances are oriented toward adults, if your children enjoy a special type of music or dance, you can purchase lawn tickets that allow you to sit on blankets off to the side where the views of the stage are still fairly decent. In summer, make sure to stop at **Brown's Beach** on Saratoga Lake, a great place to relax with the family; the shallow swim area is perfect for little children. In **Ballston Spa**, seven miles south of Saratoga Springs, kids may be entertained by the National Bottle Museum, which is devoted to the history of the handmade bottle. The permanent collection boasts nearly two thousand bottles, and there's a working glass studio. The nearby **Double M Arena** holds rodeos on Fridays during the summer. Kids can marvel at the bareback riding, barrel racing, bull riding and calf roping, while the rodeo clowns do their best to make everyone laugh. **Saratoga National Historical Park** in Stillwater appeals to older children who have studied the famous "three-pronged attack" of the American Revolution. A battlefield tour begins at the visitors center, where elaborate displays of maps, miniature soldiers, battle arrangements, and slide shows guide the viewer through this turning-point battle in the American Revolution.

The summer season is when Saratoga comes alive with an array of celebrations geared to families. While the city's clear, crisp winter days are perfect for cross-country skiing and ice-skating in the Spa State Park, most travelers prefer the warm-weather months in this part of the world. July brings the Independence Day celebration at Saratoga National Historical Park, an event filled with games and activities for children. The Saratoga County Fair is another July happening with exhibits, food, rides, shows, animals, and live entertainment. The month of August brings Travers Festival Week, a celebration around the race course's midsummer derby, the Travers Stakes.

For further information, contact **Saratoga County Chamber of Commerce,** 28 Clinton Street, Saratoga Springs 12866; (518) 584-3255 or (800) 256-8970; www.saratoga.org.

What to See

MUSEUMS AND HISTORIC SITES

Children's Museum at Saratoga. 69 Caroline Street, Saratoga Springs 12866; (518) 584-5540. Open Labor Day through June, Tuesday through Saturday, 9:30 A.M. to 4:30 P.M.; July through Labor Day, also open on Mondays. Admission fee. Groups welcome by advance reservation.

This unique museum offers children ages one to nine a chance to explore the world, from the local community to the international level. Interactive exhibits allow kids to run a general store, make giant bubbles, and "freeze" their shadows. A tree house, fire truck, science section, movie theater, and two toddler areas are also popular with young visitors. Special events have included art workshops and magic shows. The museum is centrally located in town, so that a visit can be combined with shopping or stops at the Canfield Casino Museum and park.

Facilities: *Restrooms. Wheelchair and stroller accessible.*

National Bottle Museum. 76 Milton Avenue (Route 50), Ballston Spa 12020; (518) 885-7589. Seven miles south of Saratoga Springs on Route 50. Open June through September, daily 10 A.M. to 4 P.M.; October through May, Monday through Friday, 10 A.M. to 4 P.M. Donations appreciated.

This museum focuses on the history of the handmade bottle;

until 1903 glass bottles were handmade, not manufactured. The permanent collection consists of approximately two thousand bottles, but there are also changing exhibits that borrow from collections throughout the nation. Make sure to stop at the working glass studio across the street that is owned by the museum; there are classes in glassblowing and workshops with internationally renowned guest artisans.

Facilities: *Restrooms. Research library available during museum hours.*

National Museum of Dance. 99 South Broadway, Saratoga Springs 12866; (518) 584-2225. Open June through October, Tuesday through Sunday, 10 A.M. to 5 P.M.; November through May, Saturday and Sunday, 10 A.M. to 5 P.M. Admission. Group tours available by advance reservation.

Balletomanes and children who are fascinated by dance will undoubtedly want to spend an hour here. Changing exhibits focus on the history and glamour of dance in America, as told through photos, videos, costumes, and music. The multimedia Hall of the Fame, a permanent exhibit, pays tribute to the founders and shapers of American professional dance, from Fred Astaire and Alvin Ailey to Bill "Bojangles" Robinson and others. There is also a children's wing that is equipped with a stage, wardrobe, and artwork. In July, kids may see performances by students of the New York State Summer School of the Arts program, and modern dance students are in residence during August.

Facilities: *Restrooms, children's gift shop. Strollers are welcome here; wheelchair accessible.*

National Museum of Racing and Hall of Fame. 191 Union Avenue, Saratoga Springs 12866; (518) 584-0400. Open year-round

Monday through Saturday, 10 A.M. to 4 P.M.; Sunday, noon to 4 P.M. In racing season, daily, 9 A.M. to 5 P.M. Admission; children under the age of five are admitted free.

This museum has been updated into one of the most technologically advanced sports museums in the country, and it will entertain any child who has ever shown an interest in horses. The first stop should be the video, *Race America*, which introduces the viewer to the excitement of a day at the races; its noise, music, movement, and color all rolled into one, with lots of visuals and not too much information to confuse younger viewers. In the museum galleries, hands-on exhibits let the viewer participate in such activities as walking through a starting gate, watching a jockey go through a race, and listening to commentaries of famous trainers and jockeys. An elaborate display of costumed mannequins shows nineteenth-century Saratoga at its most elegant, and another shows a reproduction of a famous horse "portrait" painter's studio. Interactive computers in the Hall of Fame let kids call up information on jockeys, horses, and trainers, and the Anatomy Gallery houses a full-size horse skeleton. During the school year there is a discovery room with hands-on activities, including a place to design their own racing silks.

Facilities: *Restrooms with changing tables, gift shop (this is one of the best shops for horse lovers, with gifts for all ages). The museum is stroller friendly, wheelchair accessible, air-conditioned, and a comfortable break from hot Saratoga summers.*

Saratoga Automobile Museum. Spa State Park (off Route 9), Saratoga Springs 12866; (518) 587-1935. Open May through Labor Day, daily 10 A.M. to 5 P.M.; October through April, Tuesday through Sunday, 10 A.M. to 5 P.M. This museum is housed in a restored 1930s Saratoga Water-bottling plant in the park. Dozens of classic cars are on display, including a 1928 sedan once owned by Charles Lindbergh and a 1931 Düsenberg Model J Roadster.

Facilities: *Restrooms, gift shop.*

Saratoga National Historical Park. Route 32, Stillwater 12170; (518) 664-9821. Visitor center open year-round, daily 9 A.M. to 5 P.M. Philip Schulyer House and the Saratoga Monument open Memorial Day through Labor Day, Tuesday through Sunday, 9:30 A.M. to 4 P.M. Battlefield tour drive open April through November, daily, 9 A.M. to 5 P.M., weather permitting. Admission. Group tours available by advance reservation.

Any older child (age ten and up) who has ever studied the famous "three-pronged plan" of the American Revolution or hissed at the memory of Benedict Arnold will enjoy a visit to this park. The battlefield tour begins at the visitors center, where elaborate displays of maps, miniature soldiers, battle arrangements, and an orientation video guide the visitor through this all-important battle of the American Revolution. From the center, you can take a two-hour drive-and-stop battlefield tour, where ten stations offer overlooks and descriptive markers about the days leading up to the battle. The most interesting stops include the monument dedicated to Benedict Arnold's heroics (before he became a traitor) and Schuyler House, which contains memorabilia of General Philip Schuyler and his wife. Younger children enjoy the special events held throughout the summer in the park, which include musketry displays, soldiers' encampments, and old-fashioned craft exhibitions. While the battlefield park is interesting, the tour is a long one, and is not suitable for car-weary children or those who have no interest in revolutionary history.

Facilities: *Restrooms, picnic tables, gift shop.*

Tang Teaching Museum. Skidmore College, 815 North Broadway, Saratoga Springs 12866; (518) 580-8080. Open Tuesday through Sunday, 10 A.M. to 5 P.M. Admission.

In addition to fine art, the Tang has a few peripheral exhibits (including films and performances) in progress and some intriguing auditory treats, including collaborative exhibits with Skidmore's science and history departments. The museum aspires to promote interdisciplinary learning through art for all age levels. There are a variety of educational tours including periodic Family Saturday programs that involve guided tours of displays, as well as activities for children and their parents.

Facilities: *Restrooms and museum shop. Stroller and wheelchair accessible.*

OTHER ATTRACTIONS

Breakfast at Saratoga Racetrack. Union Avenue (Route 9P) in Saratoga Springs. For information in months other than August, write the New York Racing Association, P.O. Box 90, Jamaica 11417; (718) 641-4700. During the month of August, call (518) 584-6200 for information. The track is open from late July to early September only; breakfast is served from 7 A.M. to 9:30 A.M. Free, but there is a charge if you buy breakfast. Group rates and group reservations are available.

Breakfast at Saratoga Racetrack has been a tradition for more than a century, when ladies and gentlemen were brought by elegant carriages to the trackside tables. Today you can still combine breakfast and an exciting look at thoroughbred horses as they work out each morning at the racetrack. Children love to watch the horses gallop around the track. A trackside announcer explains which horses are working out and who is riding them.

Breakfast can be elegant (with champagne for adults), but there also is a selection of simple, traditional fare, or you can bring your own food and sit at a picnic table. Each morning features a starting-gate demonstration that shows how horses are "loaded" into the gate and how they must wait for the bell and the cry of "And they're off!" before they take off around the track. Adults may want to sneak away to one of the free handicapping seminars that explain the mysteries of picking the winner (those under eighteen cannot place a bet). After dining, take a free tour of the paddock area, where the horses live during their stay at the track. Visitors ride through the area on small "people trains" to watch the grooms, owners, trainers, and jockeys as they go about the very busy, and expensive, routine of caring for race-horses.

Facilities: *Restrooms, picnic tables, gift shop. The breakfast area is fine for wheelchairs and strollers, but do not attempt to take them on the paddock tour. Visitors must leave the track area after breakfast ends and before the track reopens for the races.*

Canfield Casino, Congress Park, and the Springs. Congress Park, on Broadway and Circular Street, Saratoga Springs 12866; (518) 584-6920. Open May through October, daily, 10 A.M. to 4 P.M.; closed in January. Hours vary widely from November through April, so call ahead. Admission.

When Saratoga was the "Queen of Spas," the truly elegant would take the waters at the local springs and then walk in Congress Park. In the evenings, the casino would open for gambling and dining, and both the infamous and the famous, like Lillian Russell and Diamond Jim Brady, would attend. Today's visitors can still enjoy the same throwback atmosphere. A walk through the park brings you to hidden pools and fountains surrounded by flowers. My favorites are two puffy-cheeked Tritons nicknamed Spit and Spat, who spew water at each other across a small pool. At the lake, parents can sit and watch the ducks or let the kids play along the graveled paths. Just outside the park, look for the famous Saratoga flower beds, which are planted in the shape of horses and horseshoes. The city has its own watering trucks to ensure that the flowers stay fresh all through the summer. The original red brick casino is now a charming museum that offers vignettes of early Saratoga life, costumes, toys, a gambling room, and various small collections of everything from rocks to Chinese shoes. Across the street from the casino, on Spring Street, is one of the original Saratoga springs, where you can take a cup of natural water for whatever ails you.

Facilities: *Restrooms (for paid visitors only), gift shop. Strollers are perfect for the park, but there is a steep flight of stairs up to the casino museum. The site is not wheelchair accessible.*

Rock Hill Bakehouse Tours. 1338 Route 9, South Glens Falls 12831; (518) 743-1660. Take exit 17-N off the Northway; the bakery is located one-half mile from the exit. Open Monday through Saturday, 7:30 A.M. to 6 P.M. Free.

Rock Hill Bakehouse began producing its critically acclaimed hearth breads in 1988 in the farmhouse of its founders. Made with natural and organic flours and grains, well water and salt, the breads here rise at their own pace, allowing for the full development of both taste and texture. Kids will love this tour, which shows the various different flours used in the chocolate cherry, cinnamon raisin, olive, jalapeño cheddar, pepper parmesan, and dozens of other exotic breads created here. They will have a chance to watch all the steps in the bread-making process: how the dough is mixed, shaped into loaves, put in the oven, cooled, and the finished breads are packed for sale. And the best part, of course, is getting to sample the results at the end!

Facilities: *Restrooms, bakery.*

Rodeo at the Double M Arena. 678 Route 67, Ballston Spa 12020; (518) 885-9543. Take the Northway to exit 12; follow Route 67 west one mile to the arena. Rodeos are held mid-June through Labor Day, every Friday at 8 P.M. Admission.

A visit to a rodeo is exciting for adults and children alike, and this is the oldest professional weekly rodeo in the United States. Cowboys and cowgirls participate in bareback riding, barrel racing, brahma bull riding, and calf roping, just like the Western shows. Rodeo clowns do their best to make you laugh and protect the cowboys by attracting the bulls' attention. Trick riding and roping demonstrations are also given. The action takes place in a lighted, newly renovated outdoor arena, with excellent close-up views from the grandstand.

Facilities: *Restrooms, picnic tables, snack bar. Strollers and wheelchairs can manage here.*

SPAC. 108 Avenue of the Pines, Saratoga Spa State Park, Saratoga Springs 12866; (518) 587-3330 (tickets for performances can also be purchased through major ticket services). Open Mother's Day through early September; hours vary with matinees and evening performances. Discounts for single tickets and packages available.

One of the premier performance centers in America, SPAC offers an amazingly broad range of entertainment in a unique setting. Choose among jazz, rock, folk, dance, opera, country, orchestral, and other music and dance performances throughout the season. While most of the entertainment is suitable only for adults, if your child enjoys a special type of music or dance, then by all means purchase lawn tickets the afternoon of the performances. Covered seats are available, but the lawn seating lets you sit on blankets or chairs under the trees off to the side, or anywhere you like, and the views of the stage are fairly decent. If you like to see every movement of the performance, then bring a pair of binoculars. Even if your child falls asleep, you can still enjoy the performance and baby-sit under the stars at the same time. Some excellent food stands in the park are open during the concerts, but you are not allowed to bring food into the covered seating area.

Facilities: *Restrooms, snack stands, Hall of Springs restaurant. Preconcert dinners, picnics, and outdoor buffets are available by reservation; call (518) 587-8000 for information and reservations. SPAC is fine for strollers, but be aware that if you attend a popular concert, you may have to walk quite a distance from the parking area to the lawn site.*

Saratoga Springs Public Library. 49 Henry Street, Saratoga Springs 12866; (518) 584-7860. Open Monday through Thursday, 9 A.M. to 9 P.M.; Friday, 9 A.M. to 6 P.M.; Saturday, 9 A.M. to 5 P.M., Sunday, noon to 5 P.M. Free.

This library is worth a stop if you want to take a break from sightseeing in the city. They have a huge Children's Room, with seven computers that have Internet access and educational games. There is also an extensive calendar of children's programs featuring puppet shows, videos, storytellers, and musical groups. While the kids are busy, parents can use computers themselves or enjoy reading from the extensive magazine offerings available here.

Facilities: *Restrooms. Stroller and wheelchair accessible.*

What to Do

BOATING, CANOEING, AND KAYAKING

Fish Creek Marina. Saratoga Lake, Saratoga Springs 12866; (518) 587-9788. Open May through September, Thursday through Sunday, from noon until dusk. You can rent canoes, kayaks, or rowboats here. A nice feature is that there is a large pavilion available on the premises for barbecues and campfires. Great sunsets can be seen from this spot on the lake and people come from all over Saratoga to watch the sun go down here!

Point Breeze Marina. Saratoga Lake, Saratoga Springs 12866; (518) 587-3397. Open daily April through November, 9 A.M. to 6 P.M. This is a place to rent several different types of craft including canoes, kayaks, rowboats, pontoon boats, speedboats, and fishing boats. They have it all.

Saratoga Boat Works. Saratoga Lake, Saratoga Springs 12866; (518) 584-BOAT. Open daily most of the year, except December, 7 A.M. to 6 P.M. At the north end of the lake, this full-service marina is a good place to rent a power boat or pontoon boat. If you want to water ski, this is where you can rent the necessary equipment.

HIKING

Bog Meadow Nature Trail. Saratoga Springs 12866; (518) 587-5554. From Broadway, make a right onto Route 29 east. Go through the traffic light at Weibel Avenue; the trail entrance is about five hundred feet farther on the right. Open year-round.

Free. This two-mile nature trail is ideal for those traveling with small children. It is fairly flat and goes through the wetlands just outside the city. You can walk in the warm weather or cross-country ski in the winter months. There is a parking area.

East Side Recreation Field. Lake Avenue, Saratoga Springs 12866; (518) 587-3550. Make a right turn onto Lake Avenue and go about 1.5 miles. The field is on the right side, just after the East Avenue light. Open year-round. Free. This twenty-acre park has an excellent skateboard area that is open daily May through October—a small fee is charged for this activity only. There is also a wading pool for small children as well as tennis courts, playground, basketball courts, and a quarter-mile paved circular track that's great for inline skating and running.

Saratoga Spa State Park. One mile south of town on Route 9, Saratoga Springs 12866; (518) 584-2535. Open year-round. This park is free, although there is a small charge for swimming and the bathhouses. This two-thousand-acre park is a gem: clean, wide-open, full of activities to keep visitors busy. There are several streamside trails for walking that make perfect short hikes for those with children.

ICE-SKATING

Saratoga Spa State Park. South Broadway (Route 9), Saratoga Springs 12866; (518) 584-2535. There is a lovely outdoor rink here in season, weather permitting. Call for hours, which change depending on the weather conditions. Kids may participate in both hockey and figure skating here.

Saratoga Springs Ice Rinks. Weibel Avenue, Saratoga Springs 12866; (518) 583-3462. Open late June to mid-April; call for a schedule, which varies from week to week. There are two rinks here and they accommodate both hockey and figure skating. The Weibel rink is Olympic size, and the Vernon rink is smaller. Both offer family skate sessions, public skates, and hockey sessions.

PICK-YOUR-OWN FARMS

Saratoga County has long been famous for its horses and for its sweet summer cantaloupes (called hand melons) but several farms offer pick-your-own fruits and vegetables as well.

Ariel's Vegetable Farm. 194 Northern Pines Road, Wilton 12831; (518) 584-2189. Five miles north of Saratoga Springs. Open April through September. Call for hours. Here you will find luscious strawberries, asparagus, raspberries, beans, and peas for the picking.

Bowman Orchards. 107 Van Aernam Road, Malta 12020; (518) 885-8888. Open year-round, daily 10 A.M. to 6 P.M. Has orchard fruit available for visitors to pick, as well as a variety of fresh baked goods for sale.

Hand Melon Farm. Route 29 (13 miles east of Saratoga Springs) Greenwich 12834; (518) 692-2376. The melons here are usually ready to be picked from late July through mid-September. They are sweet and resemble cantaloupes. You can also pick your own strawberries here in June, and raspberries in September. The farm stand is open May through September.

Riverview Orchards. 660 Riverview Road, Clifton Park 12065; (518) 371-2174. Call for hours, which vary. They offer pick-your-own apples (there are several varieties), as well as an orchard tour and special autumn events and demonstrations that will delight the kids.

SWIMMING

Brown's Beach. On Saratoga Lake, Saratoga Springs 12866. Take exit 12 off the Northway; make a right and go three miles. At the lake, make a right and go north one more mile; the beach is on the left side of the road. Open Memorial Day weekend through Labor Day, 10 A.M. to 6 P.M.; weekends only until the end of June, then daily. Admission. This 250-foot-long, 25-foot-wide, but only 4-foot-deep beach area has a terrific shallow swimming area that is great for small children. The adjacent marina offers kayak, canoe, and paddleboat rentals. There is a snack bar on the premises.

Peerless Pool. Saratoga Spa State Park; (518) 584-2000. Open late June through Labor Day daily, 10 A.M. to 6 P.M. Admission. This Olympic-sized pool is a great place to cool off after a day of walking around the city. However, the Victoria Pool is a better choice if you have very young children.

Victoria Pool. Saratoga Spa State Park; (518) 584-2000. Open Memorial Day weekend through Labor Day daily, 10 A.M. to 6 P.M. Admission. There is a small children's pool here in addition to a larger swimming pool.

YMCA. 262 Broadway, Saratoga Springs 12866; (518) 583-9622. Open year-round; call for information on public swimming sessions, which change daily. There are family swim times here, which makes for a great rainy-day activity. The pool is twenty-five yards long and five lengths wide; the water temperature is usually around 84 degrees.

THEATER

Home Made Theater. The Spa Little Theater, Saratoga Spa State Park, off Route 9; (518) 587-4427. Open September through April. This theater is open during a calmer time of year in Saratoga Springs. Families will enjoy the full range of children's theater in this venue. Call for a schedule.

Warren County: The Lake George Region and Southern Adirondacks

Travelers will feel the change almost immediately as they cross the county line into Warren—the cooler climate, the aromatic blend of mountain air and hometown atmosphere, the magnificent open spaces of the Adirondack landscape. Ever since the end of the Revolutionary War in 1783, visitors have flocked to Lake George, drawn by its spectacular natural beauty. Still to this day water, wilderness, and fun combine to make the Lake George area a summer paradise for family vacationers. Chock-full of activities kids love—theme parks, arcades, train rides, garnet mining, and miniature golf—this is a place where it's easy to spend quality family time. And if you have never been a fan of winter, Warren County is an excellent place to try your first trek on snowshoes or cross-country skis; miles of trails await you. When the old-fashioned way of sliding in the snow with a toboggan or tube isn't enough, try downhill skiing or snowboarding at Gore Mountain; you can even end the day with a horse-drawn sleigh ride.

No family trip to Warren County is complete without a visit to the **Great Escape/Splashwater Kingdom** in Lake George. Once upon a time, this was a tiny park called Storytown; today it is the largest theme park in New York State with six roller coasters and 125 total rides. The park combines the old and new, the adventurous and the tame, so that everyone enjoys themselves. For an unusual and fun afternoon, don't miss the **Barton Garnet Mines** in North Creek, the oldest continous garnet-mining operation in the world, producing a major portion of the world's industrial garnets. Lake George offers history as well as thrills; **Fort William Henry,** situated magnificently overlooking Lake George, is a huge restored site with interactive displays that bring the Colonial period to life. With the arrival of winter, kids who ski start to imagine piles of deep snow and fun-filled days schussing down the slopes. **Gore Mountain**, the largest state-run ski area in New York, is a ski center that offers a variety of skiing and snowboarding programs for beginners and novices, and all are geared to providing a great mountain experience for young guests.

There are a multitude of seasonal events in Warren County that will enrich your family getaway. In April several maple sugar producers open their establishments to the public. Kids will delight in watching the transition from sap to syrup before enjoying a sumptuous pancake breakfast where they can taste what came out of the trees! July brings the County Youth Fair and Family Fun Days to Warrensburg. Every Thursday night in July and August there are fireworks over Lake George. The third weekend in September is when the colorful Hot Air Balloon Festival is held in Queensbury. Oktoberfest at the Great Escape is a marvelous fall tradition at the amusement park, and the town of Lake George has its own Oktoberfest as well. If you are in the region during the winter, try to coordinate your stay with the Warrensburg Sled Dog Races or the Lake George Winter Carnival in February.

For further information, contact **Warren County Department** of Tourism, 2764 Municipal Center, 1340 State Route 9, Lake George 12845; (800) 365-1050, ext. 2764; www.lakegeorge.com.

What to See

MUSEUMS AND HISTORIC SITES

Fort William Henry. 50 Canada Street (Beach Road at Route 9), Lake George 12845; (518) 668-5471. Open May to mid-October, daily 9 A.M. to 6 P.M. Guided tours every hour on the hour; last tour at 5 P.M. Admission. Group tours by reservation.

Fort William Henry, an important outpost during the tense years of the French and Indian War, was constructed at the urging of Major General William Johnson. In 1757, the fort was overrun by French troops, and the massacres that occurred became the basis for the James Fenimore Cooper novel *The Last of the Mohicans*. Visitors to the fort will see a large restored site complete with innovative history displays that bring the Colonial period to life. In the powder magazine, an underground log house reached by a long brick passageway, there are displays that explain how kegs of gunpowder were stored beneath the earth for safety. The cemetery was the final resting place for more than 2,500 soldiers, and some of the graves are on view; they are shown in a historic context, not a sensational manner. The dungeon is under the main museum, with the remains of the original fireplace and dark, dismal cells, perfect for kids to see, though not so good for the original prisoners. At the Living History Wall, buttons, bullets, and other artifacts found on site are displayed, and a multimedia presentation shows how the artifacts fit into daily Colonial life. Highlights of the Fort William Henry tour are the musket- and cannon-firing demonstrations and the grenadier bomb toss. There is a wonderful interactive kids' program that allows children to join the king's army; after each tour the children are given the chance to dress up and march with the "soldiers" and receive paperwork and a "coin" showing their enlistment into the fort's garrison. There are many costumed guides on site in eighteenth-century dress, and their uniforms are spectacular. The fort itself looks down the length of Lake George, and the view is worth the visit all by itself. During the 2005 season, there will be a celebration of the 250th anniversary of the building of Fort William Henry.

Facilities: *Restrooms, picnic area, gift shop, snack bar. The area is generally good for strollers, but only some parts of the site are wheelchair accessible.*

Hyde Collection Art Museum. 161 Warren Street, Glens Falls 12801; (518) 792-1761. Open year-round, Tuesday through Saturday, 10 A.M. to 5 P.M.; Sunday, noon to 5 P.M. Free admission; charge for guided group tours, which are available by advance reservation.

The Hyde Collection combines the world of fine art and the rich heritage of the Adirondack region. Formerly the home of Louis and Charlotte Hyde, a prominent turn-of-the-century Adirondack industrial family, visitors will enjoy their extraordinary collection of European and American art. The variety of works that cover the walls in this stately Florentine-style villa include paintings by da Vinci, Rubens, Rembrandt, Cezanne, Renoir, Van Gogh, Picasso, Whistler, and Homer. Eight elegant rooms surround a two-story skylighted courtyard studded with sculpture and tropical plants. The Hyde Collection combines the intimacy of this historic house with the sophistication of a larger art museum. Four additional gallery spaces on three floors present a changing schedule of world-class exhibits.

Throughout the school year, the education department offers

ARTfull Afternoons, a program that runs once a week after school for children ages two to twelve. Each week's lesson includes a tour of an exhibit and a hands-on creative art workshop. One Sunday each month families are invited to participate in an art activity at the museum's art studio, which is connected to a temporary exhibition or aspect of the permanent collection. Saturday morning and vacation workshops are held throughout the year, and the summer arts camp for children ages seven through twelve offers both fine arts and theater arts activities for a three-week period during the month of July. This is a wonderful place to introduce children to fine art.

Facilities: *Restrooms, elevator. Stroller and wheelchair accessible.*

Upper Hudson River Railroad. 3 Railroad Place, North Creek 12853; (518) 251-5334. Open Memorial Day weekend through October; call for schedule and departure times, which vary; there are 10 A.M. and 1 P.M. departures daily during July and August. Admission.

Just a short drive from Lake George, this railroad adds an exciting dimension to the Adirondack experience, one that the kids will love. The railroad runs seasonal two-hour round-trip excursions along an 8.5-mile section of the former Adirondack Branch of the Delaware & Hudson Railroad. Visitors board from restored platforms at the North Creek Depot and see breathtaking scenery as the train follows the Hudson River. There is musical entertainment and a "robbery" on just about every ride, which will delight the kids. After arriving at the picturesque Riverside Station, visitors have a chance to explore the museum room, gift shop, and vintage caboose refreshment stand. The railroad line was built at the end of the Civil War by Dr. Thomas Durant of Union Pacific Railroad fame. It terminated at North Creek until World War II, when it was extended to the iron mines in Tahawus to support wartime operations. The D&H continued to operate until 1989, when the mine closed and rail operations ceased. The scenic railroad fulfills the vision of owners John and Jerry Riegel of Delmar, New York, and the company founder, Walter Riegel, whose family has been in railroad construction for decades. The museum at North Creek Depot gives detailed information about the history of the railroad and the Adirondacks; it is open whenever the train is running and is worth a stop.

Facilities: *Restrooms, snack bar, gift shop. Wheelchair accessible.*

OTHER ATTRACTIONS

Barton Garnet Mines. Barton Mines Road (off Route 28, watch for signs), North Creek 12853; (518) 251-2706. Open the last weekend in June through Labor Day, daily, 9:30 A.M. to 5 P.M.; Sunday 11 A.M. to 5 P.M. Open weekends only, Labor Day to Columbus Day. Tours leave on the hour starting at 10 A.M. Admission; children under the age of six admitted free. Group rates available.

These mines represent the oldest continuously running mining operation in the United States and produce a major portion of the world's industrial garnets. The New York State gemstone is deep red in color and has long been popular in jewelry. Visitors are taken on a guided tour of the open-pit mines, where blasting and hand-digging unearth the gems, which are then graded and polished according to the needs of the user. Kids enjoy digging, so a highlight of this site is the chance for visitors to spend time "prospecting" for their own garnets. Prospectors should bring sun hats, sunscreen, and wear sturdy jeans and shoes for comfort. Bring a pillow to sit on if you are serious about digging all afternoon! There are garnet pockets all over the area, and you can purchase the gems that you find. Site guides will answer any questions you have about finding stones. Stop at the mineral shop, which has a great collection of minerals on display and sells an extensive selection of cut and polished gems. On Sundays and Mondays, there are demonstrations of gem cutting and jewelry making, including cabochon cutting, a special way of refining a garnet into a rounded shape.

Facilities: *Restrooms, gift shop. This is an accessible site for strollers and the disabled since the mine floor is firm and flat.*

Boston Candy Kitchen. 21 Elm Street, Glens Falls 12801; (518) 792-1069. Open year-round, Monday through Friday, 7 A.M. to 4 P.M.; Saturday, 7 A.M. to 3 P.M. Free.

This family-run confectionery and luncheonette, founded in 1902, produces homemade ribbon candies and candy canes in flavors that range from peppermint, wintergreen, and lemon to anise, cinnamon, molasses, clove, and orange. Workers color, pull, knead, shape, and cut the candy into brightly colored ribbons and twists. The luncheonette has its original etched-glass soda fountain backing, a fine marble countertop, and old-fashioned stools that spin. This is a nice, homey place to stop for a snack and show the kids how candy canes actually get their stripes!

Facilities: *Restrooms, shop, luncheonette. Wheelchair and stroller accessible.*

The Great Escape/Splashwater Kingdom. Route 9, Lake George 12845; (518) 792-3500. Open Memorial Day weekend through Labor Day, 9:30 A.M. to 6 P.M.; weekends only after Labor Day through October. Admission. Group rates available by advance reservation.

There are over 125 rides, shows and attractions, and a full water park in this amusement park spanning 140 acres. Combining elements from the park's days as Storytown USA, when Mother Goose ruled the roost, and today's fast-paced thrilling roller coasters, the Great Escape is one of the few remaining venues where old and new blend together in delightful harmony, offering something for children of all ages. The park has six roller coasters, including the Comet, a wooden coaster ranked among the ten best in the world. The others are the Boomerang, the Coast to Coaster, the Alpine Bobsled, the Steamin' Demon, the Nightmare Indoor Roller Coaster, and the Canyon Blaster. Families who enjoy a more relaxed time can spend the day here watching shows, taking gentler rides, and eating at the many food pavilions. This "escape" is a nice way for kids to have an adventurous day in a bustling amusement park.

Facilities: *Restrooms, snack stands, restaurants, picnic area, gift shops, arcades. Stroller and wheelchair accessible.*

Magic Forest. Route 9, Lake George 12845; (518) 668-2448. Open late June through Labor Day, daily, 9:30 A.M. to 6 P.M.; Memorial Day weekend through late June, weekends only, 9:30 A.M. to 6 P.M. Admission. Group rates by advance reservation.

This is a mellow, almost old-fashioned attraction that is actually set in a forest, so there is plenty of shade, even on the hottest days. Several entertainment "theme" areas offer attractions and rides as diverse as a small Statue of Liberty to the Santa's Night Before Christmas display and carousel. Younger children will delight in the time spent here as they feed Santa's famous reindeer, pet the baby animals, ride the Magic Forest railroad, and see the magic show. Another treat is watching a horse jump from a low diving platform into a pool. Everything here is geared toward children seven and under. The rides are not too fast or too scary; the colors are bright; and there are lots of places to stop and play make-believe. There are more than two dozen rides (including a new mile-long safari ride) and a fairy-tale trail for the wanderer.

Facilities: *Restrooms, snack stand, shaded picnic areas, gift shop.*

Natural Stone Bridge and Caves. Stone Bridge Road, Pottersville 12860; (518) 494-2283. Open Memorial Day weekend through Columbus Day, 10 A.M. to 6 P.M. Admission; children under the age of five are admitted free.

During the last ice age an east-west fault exposed this ancient rock to the violent waters from retreating glaciers. The resulting stone bridge is the largest natural marble cave entrance in the Northeast. Children will be intrigued by the self-guided tour, which takes visitors to unusual rock formations including the Bridge of God, Artist's Gorge, Echo Cave (yes, there's a real echo), and Cave of the Lost Pool. Two of the caves are lighted for exploration. This unique natural phenomenon is strikingly beautiful and also reveals an extraordinarily rare feature of Adirondack geology.

Facilities: *Restrooms, picnic area, playground, mineral exhibits, gemstone mining, gift shop.*

The Sagamore. 110 Sagamore Road, Bolton Landing 12814; (518) 644-9400 or (800) 358-3585. Take I-87 to exit 22; turn left onto 9N and go ten miles; turn right onto Sagamore Road. Open year-round.

Listed on the National Register of Historic Places, the Sagamore combines nineteenth-century charm with twenty-first-century sophistication for family vacationers. The hotel opened in 1883 and catered for many years to a select, wealthy clientele that flocked to Lake George during the summer months. In 1981 the Sagamore underwent a $72 million restoration. This world-class resort now offers 350 rooms and suites; the main hotel and lakeside lodge buildings are designed especially for families.

The Sagamore, is situated on its own seventy-acre island. A great time to visit is between June and August or during a school holiday like President's Week, spring break, or winter recess. The hotel offers family packages with reduced winter rates and the children's Teepee Club program is in full swing during school holidays. Extended hours allow parents to enjoy a relaxing vacation, because there are plenty of activities on tap for the kids. The well-organized program is directed by a children's entertainment coordinator and includes such fun-filled activities as face painting, kite flying, costume parties, musical chairs, dinosaur hunts, and poolside make-your-own-sundae ice cream socials. Children must be out of diapers to participate, and those under the age of four may attend only if accompanied by a hired baby-sitter (not a sibling). From May to October, there are lake excursions on the *Morgan*, the hotel's own wooden yacht. There is also a Learn to Sail program. During the winter, the grounds have ten miles of trails for cross-country skiing and snowshoeing. A free shuttle service runs to and from Gore Mountain (see Skiing, p.257) for downhill skiers of all ages. If you want to get away with the kids, the Sagamore is an ideal place for everyone to have a great time.

Facilities: *Gift shop, salon and spa, indoor pool, health and fitness clubs, golf course, sailing, indoor and outdoor tennis, table tennis, racquetball, horseback riding, miniature golf, ice-skating, cross-country skiing, snowshoeing, jogging paths, and nature trails. Four restaurants offer a range of dining options. Baby-sitting services can be arranged for guests of the hotel. Most areas in the main building are wheelchair accessible.*

Submerged Heritage Preserve. Information about each site (including directions) is available from the NYS Dept. of Environmental Conservation, Region 5, Route 86, Box 296, Raybrook 12977; (518) 897-1200. This is an unusual site that will intrigue just about anyone interested in shipwrecks. There are actually three shipwrecks in Lake George itself. If you will be in the area and know you want to visit any of the sites, it is best to contact the DEC in advance of your trip. The preserves are protected by law, and damaging them is illegal.

Up Yonda Farm Environmental Education Center. Route 9N, Bolton Landing 12814; (518) 644-9767. Open March through October daily, 8 A.M. to 4 P.M., until 5 P.M. in July and August; November through March, Monday through Friday, 8 A.M. to 4 P.M. Admission. Group tours welcome by advance reservation.

There are seventy-three acres of forest, pond, meadows, and streams here with spectacular views overlooking Lake George. No matter what time of year, kids will enjoy a variety of nature programs on plants, wildlife, and topics of seasonal interest. In March there are maple sugaring demonstrations. Kids will also like the wildlife exhibits, which include a diorama with Adirondack mammals and birds in various habitats and seasons. There are hiking trails, perennial gardens, and a butterfly garden from June to September. During the winter months there is snowshoeing (rentals available).

Yonda was previously owned by Alice and John Scott (who referred to the farm as the place "up yonda"). During the 1980s, they started to search for an organization that would preserve their farm for future generations as an education center and eventually decided on the Warren County Parks and Recreation Department. In 1993, the existing buildings were renovated to create an auditorium and natural history museum. Hiking trails were blazed and a curriculum was created to teach visitors about the wonders of nature. Kids who enjoy nature will particularly enjoy this site.

Facilities: *Restrooms, picnic area. Buildings are stroller and wheelchair accessible.*

Warren County Fish Hatchery. Route 9, Hudson Street, Warrensburg 12885; (518) 623-2877. Take exit 23 off I-87. Open year-round daily, 9 A.M. to 4 P.M. Free. Group tours may be scheduled by advance reservation.

A stop at this hatchery offers kids a chance to view a video presentation on the story of trout, their life cycles and habitats, and then go outside to see trout feeding. This hatchery produces thousands of fish each season that are used to stock trout ponds and streams throughout the county. Since many children have never caught a fish before, this is an interesting place to visit before or after a fishing expedition. I recommend it for kids who love the outdoors; younger children will probably also enjoy watching the Disney fishing cartoon shown here.

Facilities: *Restrooms, picnic area, canoe access, and nature trails; volleyball and basketball area open to the public. Strollers and wheelchairs can manage here.*

Water Slide World. Routes 9 and 9L, Lake George 12845; (518) 668-4407. Take exit 21 off I-87, and go one-half mile south of Lake George Village. Open mid-June through Labor Day daily, 10 A.M. to 6:30 P.M., weather permitting. Admission; there is no refund in the event of inclement weather.

Families with kids who love water and water fun should plan a day at this amusement park. Water Slide World offers dozens of water activities, including New York State's only wave pool, known as Hurricane Harbor, where man-made four-foot waves break over swimmers in a sixteen-thousand-square-foot pool. An enormous series of water slides, up to eleven hundred feet long, allow older swimmers (no toddlers here) to plunge down watery ramps and splash into pools; one of the slides even has a 360-degree loop and a tunnel. (Kids will enjoy the Blue Tornado slide and the Pirate Ship Cove, where Peg Leg watches over the little ones as they slide into the bubble pool.) For an extra charge, kids can ride bumper boats in a confined lake, and parents can relax in hot tubs nearby. Toddlers will really enjoy the Toddler Lagoon with its tiny slides, watery rocking horses, and the all-time favorite, water guns. Throughout the park there are places to rent rafts or buy bathing suits and other sun paraphernalia, so even if you don't come prepared, you and the kids can enjoy the park. Outdoor dry play areas offer volleyball and Ping-Pong for a change of pace. This is an excellent park for a hot day, but younger children must be supervised continuously, especially on a crowded summer day when hundreds of people are splashing and sliding. You can enjoy a quieter time by renting a raft and just floating along on the pools or sunbathing in the many chairs and rest areas that surround the pools.

Facilities: *Restrooms, lockers, shower facilities, restaurant, snack bars with umbrella tables, gift shop (which sells bathing suits and caps).*

What to Do

BEACHES (SWIMMING)

Lake George has been famous for its waterfront for more than three centuries, and although many of the lake's beaches are now privately owned (and so marked), there are still some excellent spots to swim with the kids. Unless otherwise noted, the following beaches are free. They are open daily from Memorial Day weekend through Labor Day, 9 A.M. to 4:30 P.M. Even though this is a resort area, with lots of private beaches, remember that day-trippers fill up the parking lots and the best beach seats very early in the day, so plan accordingly.

The famous **Million-Dollar Beach,** so called because of the

cost of building it and the ritzy clientele it attracted in the resort's
early days, is at the head of Lake George off Beach Road. Park
nearby and walk in, since you are not allowed to park on the pier.
This water playground is part of an extensive system of beaches
that run all along the southern end of Lake George. These public
beaches include **Lake Avenue Beach** (Lake Avenue off Beach
Road) and **Shepard Park** (off Canada Street in Lake George Village). **Lake George Battlefield Park and Public Campground**
(Beach Road, Lake George), directly in back of Million-Dollar
Beach, is a thirty-five-acre park that includes the remains of an
old fort, along with monuments to the men who fought here during the French and Indian Wars and the American Revolution.
The park has restrooms, picnic tables, barbecue pits, and water.

BICYCLING

Warren County Bikeway. Warren County Department of Tourism,
Municipal Center, Lake George 12845; (518) 761-6366. You can
pick up the bikeway at Glenwood Avenue, Route 9, from exit 19
off I-87 (Glens Falls-Queensbury border) and then cycle to the
Lake George Beach State Park.

This section of the Warren County Bikeway is known as the
Glens Falls Feeder Canal Trail. The Warren County area offers a
unique ten-mile trip along this bikeway through mostly flat terrain, complete with lovely mountain and valley views along the
way, ending at the southern tip of Lake George. The one-way trip
takes approximately one and a half to two hours, and follows a
paved and marked pathway, away from traffic. This is an excursion you may want to plan in advance, and a detailed map of the
bikeway is available from the Warren County Department of
Tourism. If you don't bring your own bikes and you plan on riding the full round trip, consider renting a bike at the Fort Mini

Golf Fort William Henry Museum, U.S. 9, Lake George 12845; (518) 668-5471. Bike rentals are available daily from Memorial Day weekend through Labor Day.

BOAT CRUISES

Lake George Steamboat Cruises. Beach Road, Lake George 12845; (518) 668-5777. Open May through October. Tours begin at 9 A.M., but each boat has its own schedule, so call ahead or stop by the headquarters on the pier for up-to-date tour information. On Thursday and Friday at 6:30 P.M. there is a pizza cruise. Admission with children's rates available. Group rates by advance reservation.

This cruise company offers a chance to see Adirondack scenery from a unique vantage point. They run three cruise ships that travel the length of Lake George, on one-hour to four-and-a-half-hour excursions. You can travel from the Lake George pier to Ticonderoga, or just visit the lower end of the lake on the short cruise. I suggest the one-hour cruise on the *Minne-Ha-Ha*, an authentic paddle wheeler with steam-engine pistons visible through a glass-paneled engine room. The ship has a piercing steam whistle and is colorful and noisy as it plows up the lake. A tour guide points out famous homes and historic places, although the kids will be enthralled with watching the paddle wheel and listening to the calliope. This is the oldest boat excursion company in the country and has been offering passengers rides on Lake George since 1817. If you are going to sit out on the deck, it is always windy, and you may want to bring a sun hat and sunscreen; however, there are also enclosed observation areas.

Facilities: *Restrooms, snack bar concession. Stroller and wheelchair accessible. Deck chairs are available.*

CANOEING AND KAYAKING

Adirondack Adventures. Routes 8 & 9, Loon Lake, Chestertown 12817; (518) 251-2802 or (877) 963-RAFT. Open daily; hours vary with the season. If you are interested in planning a kayak, canoe, or raft trip, this outfitter will assist you in getting instruction and equipment, and putting the excursion together for either whitewater or lake touring. They also offer lodging packages for overnight trips with New York State–licensed guides.

Lake George Kayak Company. Sagamore Road, Bolton Landing 12814; (518) 644-5295. Open mid-May through October, daily. Call for hours. This outfitter is a good one to contact if you are new to kayaking; they rent kayaks by the hour, half-day (four hours), or full day (twenty-four hours) on Lake George. Some of their double kayaks open up and you can put a third seat in the middle to accommodate a small child.

FISHING

Warren County's one-hundred-sixty-plus lakes and ponds and one thousand miles of streams and rivers offer some of the finest sport fishing in the country. The area is a good place to introduce children to fishing. The Lake George region boasts nine major game fish: landlocked salmon; lake trout; brown, rainbow, and brook trout; smallmouth and largemouth bass; northern pike; pickerel; sunfish; perch; bluegills; rock bass; and crappies. You must have a fishing license if you are age sixteen or over and one may be obtained at most town and city clerk's offices, as well as most area bait and tackle shops. For further information, contact the New York State DEC Fishing Hotline at (518) 623-3682. The

Warren County establishments listed here also offer fishing licenses, and will supply everything you need for a family outing.

Beach Road Outdoor Supply. 2239 Canada Street, Lake George 12845; (518) 668-4040.

Braley and Noxon Hardware. Main Street, North Creek 12853; (518) 251-2855.

Nemec's Bait and Tackle. 4036 Main Street, Warrensburg 12885; (518) 623-2049.

PARKS AND NATURE TRAILS

Warren County has thousands of acres of public campgrounds and parks, and it would take a lifetime to explore them all. Many of the Lake George–Warren County parks are in wilderness areas, and as such, are not always suitable for the young day hiker or novice. I have selected my favorites among those that appeal to younger children as well as older kids and parents.

Crandall Park International Trail System. Upper Glen Street (Route 9), Glens Falls 12801; (518) 761-3813. Open daily, year-round. Free.

This large outdoor nature complex offers a system of fairly flat nature trails for exploration. There is a fishing pond on the site (bring your own poles), as well as picnic areas, recreation fields, and courts for tennis and basketball. A fitness trail has wooden exercise stations complete with use directions for all levels of fitness. Hikers of all ages and abilities will appreciate the extensive trail areas, which lead through pine forests and cross over brooks and waterfalls. The trails are well marked for the hiker, and they are not challenging, so you can hike with the younger set and still have some energy left over for a cookout!

Facilities: *Restrooms.*

Dynamite Hill Nature Trail. Route 8, Chestertown 12817; (518) 494-2722. Open daily, year-round. Free. This half-mile, marked trail is an ideal stop for those traveling with young children. There are no restrooms or other facilities here.

Lake George REC Park. Route 9N, one quarter mile west of exit 21, Lake George 12845; (518) 668-5771. Open year-round daily, 9 A.M. to 5 P.M. Free. This 364-acre park overlooking Lake George has several marked hiking trails with fairly flat terrain ideal for the youngest hikers.

Facilities: *Restrooms.*

Pack Demonstration Forest. Route 9, just past the junction of Route 9 and Route 28, Warrensburg 12885; (518) 623-9679. Open daily, year-round, dawn to dusk. Free. This 2,500-acre environmental demonstration forest features a well-marked one-mile-long wheelchair-accessible nature trail, as well as ponds, forests, and a small river. Picnic Mountain offers a mild climb and lovely views. Keep in mind that there are no restrooms or other facilities on-site here.

SKIING AND SLEDDING

Dynamite Hill. Route 8, Chestertown 12817; (518) 494-2722. Free. There is one trail here with a rope tow that is perfect for beginner and novice downhill skiers. The area is lighted for night skiing, and there's a warming hut. This is a fairly rustic setup, but it is a great find for those with their own equipment and very young kids starting out in the sport. The price can't be beaten anywhere.

Garnet Hill Ski Center. 13th Lake Road, North River 12856; (518) 251-2444. Take I-87 to exit 23 and follow Route 9 to Route 28 west, twenty-two miles to North River, where you pick up 13th Lake Road and go five miles to the ski center. Open December through March daily, weather permitting, 9 A.M. to 4 P.M.

There are fifty-five kilometers of trails, twenty-five with set track, a warming hut, instruction, rentals, and food. Guided tours and lessons are available, as are night ski tours. There is also an ice-skating rink and there is no additional charge for this, although there is a small fee for skate rentals. The kids' ski program makes learning fun for children age four to thirteen. Younger kids can take a ride in the Pulk, a small sled pulled by adults.

Facilities: *Restrooms, snack bar, rentals.*

Gore Mountain. Peaceful Valley Road, North Creek 12853; (518) 251-2411. Open Thanksgiving until mid-April, daily, 8 A.M. to 4:30 P.M. Ski lift and gondola fees.

Gore Mountain is the largest state-run ski area in New York State and the seventy-nine trails offer skiing for all skill levels, and complete snowmaking capabilities to keep the fun coming all season. Nursery service is available, as are equipment rentals and lessons for all age groups from toddlers upward. There is a Kids' Klub Day of Fun, which includes morning and afternoon lessons, lunch, and all-day supervision. There are also two-hour lessons for children of all skill levels. This is a full-service mountain that offers many options to families, as well as some of the steepest trails in the East.

Facilities: *Restrooms, snack bars, restaurant, rentals, ski shop, nursery.*

Hickory Ski Center. Route 418, three miles west of Warrensburg, 12027; (518) 623-2825. Open December through March, Saturday, Sunday, and holidays, 9 A.M. to 4 P.M. Lift fee.

This is a small, family-oriented ski area with a vertical drop of one thousand two hundred feet; twenty-two slopes and trails are serviced by four lifts. There is snowmaking capability on 75 percent of the terrain. The nice part of this ski center is that it's a homey place with a friendly staff. Lessons are available, as are snacks, but there is no nursery and there are no ski rentals here.

Facilities: *Restrooms, snack bar.*

West Mountain. West Mountain Road, Glens Falls 12801; (518) 793-6606. Open Thanksgiving through March, daily, 9 A.M. to 4 P.M.; night skiing is available on weekdays until 10 P.M. Lift fee.

There are nineteen slopes and trails and five lifts (a triple chair, two double chairs, and two rope tows) at this busy ski center, which is fairly close to the capital district. They offer instructional programs for alpine, telemark, and snowboard enthusiasts. A ski racing program for kids and adults runs all season. Also available for fun times is the Tubing Park with two lifts that will bring you up to the level you are most comfortable with on the slope.

Facilities: *Restrooms, ski school, rentals, cafeteria.*

Dynamite Hill. Route 8, Chestertown 12817; (518) 494-2722. Weather permitting, this area is lighted at night for sledding. Call for hours. There is a warming hut on the hill too. For winter visitors to the area, this makes for a fun Adirondack experience the kids will always remember.

The Berkshires

Dipping your feet in a rushing stream, flying a kite on a spectacular open hillside, skiing down a powder-packed slope, picnicking amid a lush mountain landscape: these are images of family vacations that conjure up powerful memories. Children love rural adventures, but they also require more than such simple pleasures. The Berkshires' mix of breathtaking natural scenery, kid-friendly cultural attractions, and exciting outdoor activities is why so many families visit this part of the world year-round.

A wonderful place to go for a fun family outing is the Berkshire Museum in Pittsfield, one of the nation's finest small museums and one of the few where art, history, and the natural world are displayed together. Both the **Clark Art Institute** in Williamstown and the **Norman Rockwell Museum** in Stockbridge hold family days year-round, while Kidspace at **MASS MoCA** is an art gallery and studio space designed especially for students, teachers, and families. Children enjoy the drive up to **Mt. Greylock,** the highest point in the state of Massachusetts at 3,491 feet. Now a state reservation, the area comprises twelve thousand acres of protected land with spectacular views, alpine forests, and more than forty rare plant species. A worthwhile stop if you are in the Lanes-boro area is the **Par-4 Family Fun Center**, which has go-carts, bumper boats, batting cages, kiddie karts, and miniature golf. After touring the museums, the kids will especially appreciate all the fun activities here.

Agriculture is still a vital part of county life and several Berk-shire farms offer an insider's view of their operations. In Hancock, the six-hundred-acre **Ioka Valley Farm** provides agri-entertainment including a hay maze, hayrides, pedal tractors, and petting zoo. A riding day camp, guided trail riding, and licensed instruction in hunt seat and dressage please horse-loving families visiting **Undermountain Farm** in Lenox. Bicycling through the county's rolling landscape has soared in popularity with the construction of the breathtakingly beautiful eleven-mile bike path, the **Ashuwillticook Rail Trail.** In addition to downhill runs, kids of all ages will enjoy snow tubing and snowshoeing at the area's many fine ski centers: **Brodie, Bousquet, Butternut, Jiminy Peak,** and **Otis Ridge.** Most of these ski areas also offer exciting family activities all summer long, with many special programs and attractions just for kids.

There are many wonderful annual events to add to your stay in the Berkshires. Kids are especially interested in the Kite Work-shop/Fun Fly and sheepshearing at the Hancock Shaker Village in Pittsfield; both weekend events are held in June. The July Berk-shire Arts Festival in Great Barrington features two hundred ju-ried artists, music, and activities for the kids. The Clark Art Institute in Williamstown puts on a Family Day in July with a car-nival, acrobats, magicians, and music; they also have a series of free concerts throughout the summer. Every August is the Berk-shire Botanical Garden's flower show with special children's classes that will appeal to youngsters who love nature. In September, the

annual Great Josh Billing Run-Around, a triathlon from Great Barrington to Lenox, will delight young spectators. October brings
the annual Fall Foliage Festival in North Adams and the Mt. Greylock Ramble.

For further information, contact the **Berkshire Visitors Bureau,** Berkshire Common, Pittsfield, MA 01201; (413) 443-9186
or (866) 444-1815; www.berkshires.org.

What to See

MUSEUMS AND HISTORIC SITES

Berkshire Museum. 39 South Street, Pittsfield, MA 01201; (413)
443-7171, ext. 10. Open year-round, Monday through Saturday,
10 A.M. to 5 P.M.; Sunday noon to 5 P.M. Admission. Group tours
available by advance reservation.

❡ A museum chock-full of art, ancient history, and natural science collections, the Berkshire Museum has plenty of appeal for
families. There are aquariums filled with fresh and saltwater fish,
along with two touch tanks; displays of fossils, gems, minerals;
and a Berkshire Backyard with specimens representing the animals of Berkshire County. A dinosaurs and paleontology gallery
complete with a "Dino-Dig" will appeal to younger children, because they can look for dinosaur bones. A special gallery featuring
miniature dioramas created by Louis Paul Jonas is also a children's
favorite. Don't miss the Egyptian mummy, swathed in linen and
still holding court surrounded by art and artifacts from ancient
civilizations. Older children who enjoy art will like the fine art
galleries, including American and European paintings from the
eighteenth and nineteenth centuries. Of special interest to kids of

all ages is a new exhibit of Alexander Calder's pull toys, along with replicas of several toys for children to play with and enjoy. One weekend each month, the museum hosts a Super Saturday for families, with a theater performance and workshops. The summer schedule features a camp program and an independent film series. There are also several concerts, offering folk music and other original acts.

Facilities: *Restrooms, gift shop with lots of educational toys and fun stuff for kids. Wheelchair and stroller accessible.*

Chesterwood. 4 Williamsville Road, off Route 183, Stockbridge, MA 01262; (413) 298-3579. The site is located off Route 183, 1.5 miles south of the corner of Routes 183 and 102. Turn right on Mohawk Lake Road and follow the signs carefully. Open May through October, daily, 10 A.M. to 5 P.M. Admission; children under the age of six are free.

This lovely site, part of the National Trust for Historic Preservation, was the summer home of Daniel Chester French, the sculptor who created the Lincoln Memorial and the Minute Man statues. Guided tours take you through the studio, residence, and gardens where French spent his summer months. The studio is filled with memorabilia, as well as the tools and plaster casts used to make the Lincoln Memorial. Children will enjoy seeing how sculpture is created, and they can handle some of the tools and reproduction sculptures on display. In the summer, the Sculpture Is Fun program introduces kids to the art form. Outside, there are lovely gardens and walkways and large sculptures. A short woodland trail that was laid out by Mr. French is a pleasant detour for younger walkers who enjoy nature.

Facilities: *Restrooms, museum shop. There are several buildings on the site, and strollers can manage; there is wheelchair accessibility to the studio and barn gallery.*

Clark Art Institute. 225 South Street, Williamstown, MA 01267; (413) 458-2303. Located one-half mile south of the junction of Routes 2 and 7 in the center of town. Open mid-June through Labor Day, daily 10 A.M. to 5 P.M.; early September to mid-June, Tuesday through Sunday, 10 A.M. to 5 P.M. Free admission from November through May; June through October, adult admission charged; children eighteen and under, as well as students with identification, are admitted free year-round.

One of the best collections of fine art in the region, this museum contains an incredible selection of French nineteenth-century paintings and sculpture. The colorful paintings by Renoir, Monet, and Degas are a good way to introduce children to fine art, and special activity sheets are available at the information desk. Many of the paintings are well known, and they all depict realistic scenes and people: earthy peasant women, flowers, dancers, and landscapes. Another exhibit hall displays a large collection of silver from the seventeenth to the twentieth centuries; the candlesticks, ewers, and plates are dazzling. This jewel of a museum is rarely crowded and permits children to get up close to fine art. Throughout the year, the Clark offers a variety of public programs, including school programs, concerts, films, and educational courses. Highlights include free summer concerts, lunchtime gallery talks, and year-round family days presented in conjunction with special exhibitions. There are special gallery talks for children that relate to many different areas of the school curriculum, including history, science, creative writing, and literature.

Facilities: *Restrooms, gift shop, summer café. All galleries and facilities are stroller and wheelchair accessible.*

Eric Carle Museum of Picture Book Art. 125 West Bay Road, Amherst, MA 01002; (413) 658-1100. Open year-round, Tuesday through Saturday, 10 A.M. to 4 P.M.; Sunday, noon to 4 P.M. Admission. Group tours available by advance reservation.

Founded in part by Eric Carle, the renowned author and illustrator of more than seventy childrens' books, including the 1969 classic *The Very Hungry Caterpillar,* this museum is the first one in the country devoted to national and international picture book art. It was built with the aim of celebrating the art we are first exposed to as children. The museum takes children on a colorful journey through the pages of old and new picture book favorites. The museum features three exhibition galleries, a hands-on art studio, a comfortable library for reading and storytelling, and an auditorium for performances, films, and lectures. This is a nice stop for children who are particularly interested in books and their illustrations.

Facilities: *Restrooms, museum shop, café. Wheelchair and stroller accessible.*

Hancock Shaker Village. Route 20 (five miles west of Pittsfield, just west of the junction of routes 20 and 41), Pittsfield, MA 01202; (413) 443-0188 or (800) 817-1137. Open Memorial Day weekend through October, daily 9:30 A.M. to 5:30 P.M. (self-guided visits); November to late May, 10 A.M. to 3 P.M. (guided tours only). Admission (children under the age of eighteen are admitted free). Group tours available by advance reservation.

This original Shaker village and farm is a great site for families, especially those interested in American history. The one-thousand-two-hundred-acre site was home to the Shakers, a communal religious group, from the late eighteenth century through 1959. There are twenty historic buildings, most on site; most are restored to their 1830s appearance, with some structures reflecting early-twentieth-century life.

The Shakers were a religious community that embraced the tenets of communal living, celibacy, and confession of sin. They followed the teachings of Ann Lee and were socially progressive, believing in the equality of men and women. They were also technologically innovative, inventing or improving on many items in daily use, such as the flat broom. Renowned for their crafts and trades, the Shakers saw their daily work as part of their religious life. "Put your hands to work and hearts to God and a blessing will attend you," said Mother Ann Lee.

Points of interest for kids include the famous 1826 round stone barn, which was a model of efficiency and housed fifty-two dairy cattle; neatly tended herb and vegetable gardens that show one hundred different herbs and heirloom plants raised by the Shakers; the schoolhouse with its "schoolteacher" (a costumed staff person in character) giving lessons on penmanship, spelling, and "how to be a good Shaker"; the 1858 reproduction water turbine, which powers equipment in the laundry and machine shop; and the farm, with heritage breeds of livestock including chickens, cattle, sheep, and swine. During the self-guided tour season, a variety of traditional crafts and trades such as woodworking, blacksmithing, oval box making, and textile arts are demonstrated throughout the village. Knowledgeable guides engage children in the process by showing techniques used by the innovative Shakers. Short thematic tours are also offered throughout the day, but you are able to wander through the village at your own pace. In the Discovery Room, children can try their hand at a variety of activities they have seen in the village including learning to spin wool or weave, trying on Shaker clothes, milking "Mary Jane," a life-size replica of a Holstein cow, watching chicks hatch, or playing with nineteenth-century toys.

Facilities: *Restrooms, picnic area, seasonal café, museum store. Not all buildings are accessible by wheelchairs and strollers.*

MASS MoCA. 87 Marshall Street, North Adams, MA 01247; (413) 662-2111. Open June through August, daily, 10 A.M. to

6 P.M.; September through May, Wednesday to Monday, 11 A.M. to 5 P.M. Admission. Group tours by advance reservation.

One of the largest museums in the country with over 300,000 square feet in twenty-six buildings, this is a welcoming place that encourages the dynamic interchange between making and presenting art. The converted factory space works well for the technically complex sculpture and art on display here, much of which requires huge spaces. The site itself fascinates young visitors with its elaborate system of interlocking courtyards, staircases, and passageways. Interestingly, manufacturing began near the site even before the Revolutionary War due to its location at the confluence of two branches of the Hoosic River. Over the past 250 years, the site has had many incarnations: brickyard, saw mill, ironworks, textile factory and electronics manufacturer, and now museum. There are all stages of art production in all its forms, including: rehearsals, sculptural fabrication, developmental workshops, and finished works of art. The enormous sculptures are particularly alluring to children. And don't miss Kidspace, a special gallery where kids can see and create art at their own pace.

Facilities: *Restrooms, gift shop, café, restaurant. Stroller and wheelchair accessible in most areas.*

Norman Rockwell Museum. Route 183, Stockbridge, MA 01262; (413) 298-4100. Open daily, 10 A.M. to 5 P.M. Rockwell's original Stockbridge studio, located on the site, is open May through October, 10 A.M. to 5 P.M. Admission; children eighteen and under are admitted free. Groups tours by advance reservation.

Norman Rockwell was the creator of a special type of American art that celebrated everyday life with all its joys and sorrows, and visitors will appreciate the wealth of art on display here. Set on a picturesque thirty-six-acre estate, the museum holds the world's largest collection of original Rockwell works, with over five hundred paintings, drawings, portraits, and advertising pieces. Highlights include selections from Rockwell's *Saturday Evening Post* covers, the famous "Four Freedoms" collection, and "Stockbridge Main Street at Christmas." As a center devoted to the art of illustration, the museum also exhibits the works of contemporary and past masters in the field. While the youngest children may not be enthralled by the large amount of art on view, children age ten and up will appreciate seeing close-up the pictures they may see in school and on calendars. Outside, visitors can stroll the grounds, take in the views or have a picnic. Special events and workshops are offered throughout the year; call for a schedule.

Facilities: *Restrooms, museum shop. Stroller and wheelchair accessible.*

OTHER ATTRACTIONS

Berkshire Botanical Garden. Routes 102 and 183, Stockbridge, MA 01262; (413) 298-3926. Open May through October daily, 10 A.M. to 5 P.M. Admission; children twelve and under are admitted free.

If you and your children love gardens and flowers, this is a fine place to spend a few hours. The fifteen-acre botanical garden is beautifully landscaped with thousands of species and varieties of annuals, perennials, herbs, shrubs, and trees. Specimens from around the world are represented, but the focus is on plants that thrive in the Berkshires. Plantings include colorful perennial and annual gardens, herb and rock gardens, a pond garden, a children's garden, an ornamental vegetable garden, an arboretum, and a greenhouse. There's also a woodland interpretive trail. Education programs and special events are offered year-round. Events include a plant sale, the Fête des Fleurs (Summer Gala), a flower show, the Stockbridge Summer Arts and Crafts Show, the Harvest Festival, and the Holiday Marketplace. First held in 1934, the October Harvest Festival is the largest and one of the most renowned community gatherings in the Berkshires. A family-oriented event, it features games, rides, food, arts and crafts, live entertaiment, and a giant tag sale.

Facilities: *Restrooms, visitors center, gift shop, picnic area. Wheelchair-accessible pathways serve many areas of the garden.*

Berkshire Community College. 1350 West Street, Pittsfield, MA 01201; (413) 499-4660, ext. 374. Open year-round; call for a schedule.

This community college has a variety of hands-on activities for children throughout the year. The summer workshops for kids are innovative and unusual. There is a circus camp geared to children ages eight to thirteen that teaches circus history and performance skills like walking a tightrope. A robotics workshop appeals to youngsters interested in high-tech games and science. The college even has an aviation-career academy for those ages ten to fourteen, which teaches about the role of aviation in daily life and incorporates day trips to a various aviation facilities; participants also have a chance to fly a plane. The college is continually adding new programs, and they are worth checking out if you will be in the area for a while.

Facilities: *Restrooms. Stroller and wheelchair accessible.*

Berkshire Mountain Llama Hikes. 322 Landers Road, Lee, MA 01238; (413) 243-2224. Open May through October. All hikes are by apointment only and vary in length between one and three hours. Rates are dependent on how many people are in your party and how long you are out on the trail.

Kids love this novel experience—spending time in nature on the back of a llama. Known for their sweet dispositions, wooly coats, and unique personalities, these trusted hiking companions are clever and gentle around children. The hikes are led by experienced guides on well-maintained trails in the forests and hills surrounding a pastoral farm.

Facilities: *Restrooms.*

Berkshire Scenic Railway and Museum. Willow Creek Road at Housatonic Street, Lenox, MA 01240; (413) 637-2210. Located 1.5 miles east of Routes 7 and 20, five miles north of Lee and exit 2 on the Massachusetts Turnpike. Open Memorial Day weekend through October, Saturday, Sunday, and holidays; call for schedule. Admission. Group rates by advance reservation.

This 2.5-hour round trip from Lenox to Stockbridge aboard a train powered by a diesel locomotive from the 1950s (with vintage coaches from the 1920s) will delight everyone in the family. A uniformed conductor narrates the trip, pointing out places of interest. The ride is a fun way to show children the history of railroads in western Massachusetts. There is a museum worth visiting on the premises; admission is included with the price of the rail ride. The Gilded Age exhibition, housed in a vintage 1920s restored Baltimore & Ohio Railroad passenger car, tells the Berkshire story and invites visitors, through photographs and artifacts of the era, to step back in time and imagine themselves as part of the Gilded Age.

Facilities: *Restrooms, gift shop. The museum is stroller and wheelchair accessible.*

Dinosaur Footprints. Route 5, Holyoke, MA; (413) 684-0148. Going north on I-91, take exit 17A and follow Route 141 east to

Holyoke. Turn north on Route 5, then go 2.2 miles. The entrance and parking area are at a small turnout on the right. Open daily dawn to dusk. Free.

The large, meat-eating dinosaur *Eubrontes giganteus*, more than twenty feet in length, lumbered slowly through the mud in this area, leaving great three-toed footprints some fifteen inches long. These footprints and fossils are nearly 200 million years old! Kids are fascinated to see this site, especially those who are captivated by dinosaurs. It's worth a detour, but keep in mind that there are no facilities here.

Ioka Valley Farm. 3475 Route 43, Hancock MA 01237; (413) 738-5915. Open year-round, daily 8 A.M. to 5 P.M. Free. Groups accommodated by advance reservation.

The name Ioka is derived from the Indian word meaning "beautiful," and this farm is certainly picturesque. Although this is a working farm, the owners are also dedicated to entertaining visitors. Kids will have a chance to see all aspects of farm life up close; the animal petting area will particularly delight the youngest visitors. Each season here brings different excitement and special events, including activities like scarecrow making and scavenger hunts. From mid-February to April the maple barn is in full swing, and kids can watch sap flow from the trees and then follow the process until it becomes maple syrup. From mid-June through July is strawberry-picking time. In the fall, there are pumpkins to be picked, free hayrides, and a corn maze to be navigated. December is the time to visit the Christmas tree plantation, where you can cut your own tree and then meet Santa at a pancake breakfast. Ioka is truly a place for all seasons and offers agri-entertainment at its best.

Facilities: *Restrooms, retail store, and gift shop.*

Magic Wings Butterfly Conservancy. 281 Greenfield Road, South Deerfield, MA 01373; (413) 665-2805. Located off I-91 on scenic Routes 5 and 10. Open Memorial Day weekend through Labor Day, daily, 9 A.M. to 6 P.M.; the rest of the year they close at 5 P.M. Admission. Group tours by advance reservation.

Did you know that butterflies taste with their feet as they land on a flower? Did you know almost all butterflies live for approximately two weeks? And like snowflakes, no two butterflies are alike. Children will enjoy this lush tropical butterfly garden inside a four-thousand-square-foot glass conservatory with thousands of native and tropical butterflies fluttering throughout the year. There is a lot to learn about butterfly life cycles, migration, and food sources, and the displays here offer a wealth of fascinating information. There are also outdoor gardens (open seasonally) with iron butterfly sculptures, as well as walking paths among flowers with native butterflies fluttering about. Enjoy the benches, picnic and play areas, and quiet sanctuaries as you explore the grounds. A nature trail at the edge of the woods bordering the conservatory makes for a nice walk. This is a stop that will inspire, educate, and entertain.

Facilities: *Restrooms, gift shop, nature trail. Stroller and wheelchair accessible.*

Par-4 Family Fun Center. 20 Williamstown Road (Route 7), Lanesboro, MA 01237; (413) 499-0051. Located at the base of Mt. Greylock. Open May through October; call for hours. Admission to activities.

This is a good place for the kids to let off some steam after sightseeing or traveling in the car for a long distance. There are go-carts, bumper boats, a miniature golf course, batting cages, and more.

Facilities: *Restrooms, snack bar.*

What to Do

BICYCLING

Ashuwillticook Rail Trail. (413) 442-8928. From the south, take the Mass Pike to exit 2, then Route 20 west to Route 7 north and Route 9 east to Route 8 north. Signs for parking areas are located on Route 8. From the north, take Route 2 to Route 8 south. Open dawn to dusk. Free.

This eleven-mile rail trail, a former railroad corridor, is now a paved ten-foot-wide path that runs parallel to Route 8 through the towns of Cheshire, Lanesborough, and Adams. Phase One, five miles long, begins at the Berkshire Mall in Lanesborough and ends at the Route 8 crossing in Cheshire. Phase Two, six miles long, begins where Phase One ends in Cheshire and extends to the center of Adams. The rail trail passes through the Hoosac River Valley between Mt. Greylock and the Hoosac Mountains. The Native American word *Ashuwillticook* means "the pleasant river between the hills." As its name implies, there are spectacular views here and the area is home to several species of wildlife. This trail provides a safe and easy ride, perfect for a family outing.

HIKING

Bartholomew's Cobble and the Colonel Ashley House. Weatogue Road, Ashley Falls, MA 01222; (413) 229-8600. Take Route 7 south from Great Barrington, then follow Route 7A to Ashley Falls. Take Rannpo Road to Weatogue, which is eleven miles from Great Barrington. The visitor center is open April through November, daily, 8:30 A.M. to 4:30 P.M.; December through March, Wednesday to Saturday, 8:30 A.M. to 4:30 P.M. Trails are open dawn to dusk. Admission.

This is an extremely varied three-hundred-acre natural site that is a delight to hike and explore. Even the youngest visitors will find rocks, eight hundred species of flowering plants, fifty-three species of ferns, numerous species of birds, and other natural objects lovely to look at and experience. A *cobble* is an old English name for an outcropping of rock, and this particular cobble, about 500 million years old, is made of limestone and overlooks the Housatonic Valley. Hike to the top of Hurlburt's Hill and look out over valleys where cows graze and rivers run, or follow the resident naturalist on a guided walk and learn about the natural history of the property. The Ledges Trail takes about a half hour to hike and is a good walk if you are traveling with young children. Another 4.5 miles of trail wind through woods along the river and lead to spectacular viewing areas. At the visitor center, changing displays offer views of local flora and fauna, and trail guides are available. This is also an excellent bird-watching site, so bring along the binoculars and let the kids enjoy nature close up. Many natural history programs are offered throughout the year at this designated National Natural Landmark, but call ahead for a schedule.

Facilities: *Restrooms. Visitor center is wheelchair accessible and easy for strollers to maneuver.*

Mt. Greylock Summit. Visitors center, Rockwell Road, Lanesboro, MA 01237; (413) 499-4262. Open year-round, dawn to dusk. Free.

The highest point in the state of Massachusetts is the peak of Mt. Greylock, at 3,491 feet. Now a state reservation, it comprises twelve thousand acres of protected land offering spectacular views, remote boggy areas, alpine and boreal forests, and more than forty rare plant species. Mt. Greylock has appeared in American literature through the writings of Herman Melville, Nathaniel

Hawthorne, and Henry David Thoreau. Today the mountain offers many activities to visitors, including nature programs for children. The War Memorial Tower and Beacon at the peak is open daily from May through October. You can drive the road all the way to the summit.

Facilities: *Restrooms, gift shop in visitors center.*

Pleasant Valley Wildlife Sanctuary. 472 West Mountain Road, off Route 7, Lenox, MA 01240; (413) 637-0320. Open year-round, Tuesday through Sunday and Monday holidays, dawn to dusk. Open every Monday, July through Columbus Day. Admission.

This Massachusetts Audubon sanctuary covers thirteen hundred acres and contains a wealth of natural settings for animals and plants, plus seven miles of well-marked trails. The short, easy-to-walk trails lead through forests, wildflower meadows, wetlands, and around ponds, and to the summit of Lenox Mountain. Ponds are usually active with beavers, bullfrogs, and the occasional leaping fish. Naturalists are often on hand to answer any

Adjoining the Cobble is the **Colonel Ashley House,** (413) 229-8600. Open Memorial Day weekend through Columbus Day, Saturday, Sunday, and Monday holidays, 1 to 5 P.M. Admission.

Built in 1735, it is the oldest house in Berkshire County and the site of the drafting of the Sheffield Declaration, an early declaration of personal freedom that predated the Declaration of Independence. Older children may enjoy the tour of the homestead, which includes a large tool collection of the last two hundred years, as well as period furnishings and decorative items.

questions. If you are in the area during the summer, you may want to take advantage of the summer day camp, which runs for one- and two-week sessions and includes many outdoor activities. In addition, sanctuary staff conduct a wide array of seasonal public programs, from canoe trips to bat walks. Call in advance to receive a program catalog.

Facilities: *Restrooms. This site is not recommended for strollers or wheelchairs.*

HORSEBACK RIDING

Undermountain Farm. 400 Undermountain Road, Lenox, MA 01240; (413) 637-1008. Located one mile from the center of Lenox. Open year-round.

This picturesque riding facility consists of a collection of beautiful Victorian farm buildings surrounded by one hundred and fifty acres of pasture, forest, and hay fields. A large indoor riding arena, a spacious outdoor arena, and miles of riding trails provide ample terrain for all horse enthusiasts. There are pony rides for young children, and guided trail rides are available for all ages and levels of ability. Lessons may be scheduled as well. During summer vacation there is a weekly day camp for children seven to fifteen years of age.

Facilities: *Restrooms.*

ICE-SKATING

Boys Club of Pittsfield. 16 Melville Street, Pittsfield, MA 01201; (413) 448-8258. This indoor rink is open year-round for public skating, Monday through Friday, 11 A.M. to 2 P.M.; and Saturday and Sunday, 2 to 4 P.M. Admission.

Chapman Rink. On the campus of Williams College, Williamstown, MA 01267; (413) 597-2433. This indoor rink is open year-round, but times for public use vary by season. Make sure to call ahead. Admission.

Vietnam Veterans Skating Rink. South Church Street, North Adams, MA 01247; (413) 662-5112. This indoor rink is open July through March with public skating sessions in the afternoon. Call ahead for hours. Admission.

KAYAKING, CANOEING, AND RAFTING

Crab Apple Whitewater, Inc. Route 2, Charlemont, MA 01339; (413) 625-2288 or (800) 553-RAFT. This family-owned-and-operated outfitter has been in business for over twenty years. They offer a variety of full- and half-day trips on the Deerfield River in rafts or inflatable kayaks. For a fun, easy whitewater rafting trip, ask about going out on the Fife Brook section of the river, which is a ten-mile trip and the perfect outing for families with young children. Calm sections of the trip allow your guide to fill you in on local history and offer an opportunity to take in the beautiful scenery. There is a stop midway through for a hearty riverside picnic lunch.

Wild 'n Wet Sport Rentals. At Reilly's Restaurant, Route 7, Pontoosuc Lake, Pittsfield, MA 01201; (413) 445-5211. Open mid-June through Labor Day. This establishment specializes in renting canoes and paddleboats on Pontoosuc Lake, a lovely place to get out on the water for a relaxed family outing.

Zoar Outdoor. Mohawk Trail, Charlemont, MA 01339; (413) 339-8596 or (800) 532-7483. Located at the west end of the town of

Charlemont. Open May through October. Kayaking or rafting down the Deerfield River is a great way to see the Berkshires and to spend a hot summer day. This is also the place to call if you are interested in taking a canoe or kayak clinic with the kids and learning the finer points of these sports. Clinics range from one to five days for beginner, intermediate, and advanced levels, and are led by certified instructors. In addition to offering classes and renting equipment, they have guided whitewater rafting trips. Whatever you want to do, they will tailor a trip to suit your needs.

PARKS

The Berkshires region extends over hundreds of square miles of villages, parks, and forests, and these areas offer a chance for young visitors to experience the outdoors firsthand. The following state forests offer the most facilities and activities for young children. The park season runs from Memorial Day weekend through Columbus Day, 9 A.M. until dusk. There are day-use charges, and campsites are available by advance reservation for a fee. Each park has picnic tables, grills, and play areas, although they may be crowded on holidays and weekends. Unless otherwise noted, the sites are not wheelchair accessible.

Beartown State Forest. Blue Hill Road, Monterey, MA 01245; (413) 528-0904. Follow Route 17 from Monterey to park entrance. This is a huge 10,500-acre reservation with a full offering of outdoor activities including camping, fishing, walking and hiking trails, and swimming in Benedict Pond. The forest is open in the winter for cross-country skiing when the weather permits.

Mt. Washington State Forest. East Street, Mt. Washington, MA 01223; (413) 528-0330. Take Route 23 to South Egremont and watch for signs to the parking area. This park contains 3,300 acres, including Bash Bish Falls with its spectacular sixty-foot cascade, said to be the home of a witch and her daughter! You can also hike on the numerous well-marked trails, which are converted to cross-country trails in the winter. The main attraction at this park is the falls.

October Mountain State Forest. Woodland Road, Lee, MA 01238; (413) 243-1778. Take Route 20 from Lenox to the entrance of the park. This is the perfect place for an overnight camping trip or a daylong picnic. There are fishing spots and walking trails in the park, which was once a private game preserve; picnic areas are numerous. In winter there are twenty-five miles of cross-country trails.

Pittsfield State Forest. Cascade Street, Pittsfield, MA 00120; (413) 442-8928, ext. 21. From the junction of Routes 20 and 7 in Pittsfield, drive west on West Street; then go north on Churchill Street and west on Cascade Street to park entrance. This park has 9,600 acres filled with hiking and camping facilities as well as an interpretive center. The Tranquility Trail is a three-quarter-mile, paved wheelchair-accessible trail.

Standisfield State Forest. West Street, Sandisfield, MA 01255; (413) 258-4774. York Lake in this park is a popular site for swimming and there is a lifeguard on duty. Visitors can also picnic, hike, and camp at the park. There are several miles of cross-country ski trails in the winter.

Western Gateway Heritage State Park. Furnace Street, North Adams, MA 01247; (413) 663-6312. Located on Route 8, near downtown North Adams. This urban park focuses on the era of railroads. Located in a former railroad yard, various exhibits tell the story of the Hoosier Tunnel, a wonder of engineering. Kids will enjoy the audio-visual history of the park, and there are special events on site throughout the year.

PICK-YOUR-OWN FARMS AND MORE

Farms that welcome visitors are limited in the Berkshires. The following farms welcome guests and offer a chance to see poultry, fruits, vegetables, and maple syrup–making up close. If you are making a long drive to a pick-your-own farm, call ahead to make certain that the harvest is ready.

Blueberry Hill Farm. East Road, Mt. Washington, MA 01223; (413) 528-1479. Open July and August, daily, 9 A.M. to 5 P.M. This lovely farm is open during the summer months for blueberry picking, which makes a nice outing after a hike in nearby Mt. Washington State Forest.

Hopkins Farm Museum. Hopkins Memorial Forest, Northwest Hill Road, Williamstown, MA 01267; (413) 597-2346. Open daily, 11 A.M. to 4 P.M. This farm museum is located on the grounds of a Williams College–owned preserve of two thousand acres. In addition to nature trails, the farm has a collection of old tools on display, and there are seasonal demonstrations of apple cider pressing (September and October) and maple syrup–making (mid-February to April).

Otis Poultry Farm. Route 8, North Otis, MA 01253; (413) 269-4438. Open daily, 9 A.M. to 5 P.M. This farm has been in business since 1904 and kids will love the short tour of the poultry farm.

The farm stand offers a wide selection of gourmet items, honey, maple syrup, freshly baked goods, and, of course, eggs and poultry.

Windy Hill Farm. Route 7, Great Barrington, MA 01230; (413) 298-3217. Located between Stockbridge and Great Barrington; watch for signs. Open September and October, daily, 9 A.M. to 4 P.M. Here you will find twenty-one varieties of pick-your-own apples so that everyone in the family will come away with their favorite type of apple.

SKIING

Bousquet. 101 Dan Fox Drive, Pittsfield, MA 01201; (413) 442-8316. Located one mile from the intersection of Dan Fox Drive and Route 7; follow signs. Open late November through March, daily, 10 A.M. to 4 P.M.; night skiing Monday through Saturday, 5 to 10 P.M. Lift ticket fee.

This is the Berkshires' oldest ski center, dating back to 1932, and the atmosphere is old-time and family-oriented. Bousquet caters particularly to the beginner, novice and intermediate skier, so you can expect to find gentle skiing on many of the fourteen trails and slopes serviced by four lifts. There are ski classes that take all ages, from toddlers on up. In summer, kids can enjoy a splash-down water pool, a miniature golf course, driving range, and go-carts.

Facilities: *Restrooms, snack bar, restaurant, ski shop, nursery (age two and older), equipment rentals, lockers.*

Butternut Basin. Route 23, Great Barrington, MA 01230; (413) 528-2000. Open early November through March, 9 A.M. to 4 P.M. Lift ticket fee.

With its more than twenty-two trails, Butternut is a low-key place to ski and learn. The ski area itself is lovely to look at and offers excellent views of the Massachusetts and New York mountains. A separate beginner's slope is a perfect place for first-time slope sliders to take a tumble or two. A friendly ski lesson program is offered, along with rentals for even the youngest skier or beginner. A full-service nursery tends to kids who prefer not to ski, and the nursery staff has a full-day program guaranteed to keep the kids happy and busy while Mom and Dad are out. Cross-country skiers will find groomed trails, and snowboarders are welcome.

Facilities: *Restrooms, snack bar, restaurant, ski and snowboard shop, nursery, equipment rentals, lockers.*

Jiminy Peak. 37 Corey Road, Hancock, MA 01237; (413) 738-5500. From Route 7, take Route 43 to Brodie Mountain Road and follow signs. Open late November through March, Saturday, Sunday, and holidays, 8:30 A.M. to 10:30 P.M.; Monday through Friday, 9 A.M. to 10:30 P.M. Lift ticket fee.

This is a demanding mountain for skiers and snowboarders, and it's recommended only for adults and children who are comfortable on the slopes. The mountain offers over forty trails and slopes serviced by six high-speed chairlifts. There are complete rentals, and snowboard and ski lessons on site, with extensive ski classes geared to all ages and abilities, but new, younger skiers may feel a bit overwhelmed at all the action on this large, busy slope. For parents who want to ski the advanced terrain, note that a fine supervised play area is open daily and charges by the hour; children must be at least two years of age and toilet-trained. The Children's Learning Center offers daylong (9:30 A.M. to 3:30 P.M.) ski and snowboard programs that include lessons and lunch for children between the ages of four and twelve. Summer visitors enjoy the Alpine Slide, a coaster on wheels that wends its way down the slopes, and the miniature golf course.

Facilities: *Restrooms, snack bar, restaurant, ski shop, nursery, equipment rentals, lockers. This ski center includes a complete resort/condominium complex and offers special overnight rates to those traveling with children.*

Kennedy Park. Route 7, Lenox, MA 01240; (413) 637-3010. The access point for this park is behind the Lenox House Restaurant, just north of the village of Lenox on Route 7. Open daily, dawn to dusk. Free.

The over forty miles of old carriage roads and bridle paths here are great for cross-country skiing. The roads wind in and out of what was once the site of a grand old hotel. Each trail is well marked with colorful blazes of paint, and the white novice trail is especially nice to try if the kids are new on skis. There are no facilities here, and you must have your own equipment.

Notchview Reservation. Route 9, Windsor, MA 01270; (413) 684-0148. Located northeast of Pittsfield. Open daily 8 A.M. to 4:30 P.M. Admission.

This three-thousand-acre preserve has twenty-five kilometers of marked and maintained trails. The reservation's visitors center provides trail maps; several of them are suitable for young children and beginner skiers.

Facilities: *Restrooms, visitors center.*

Otis Ridge. Route 23, Otis, MA 01253; (413) 269-4444. Open late November through March, daily, 9 A.M. to 4 P.M. Lift ticket fee.

A tiny hill in comparison to other Berkshire behemoth mountains, Otis Ridge has eleven slopes and trails, and five lifts. However, I can't think of a nicer place to take kids who want to learn to ski without pressure from large classes or advanced instructors. The whole setup here considers careful ski instruction as the best way to manage younger skiers, and there is little of the competition found at larger slopes. Note that children must be at least four years old for group lessons. Only eight hundred lift tickets a day are sold here, so the trails never become too crowded. A ski camp is offered for kids age eight to sixteen, and complete learn-to-ski packages are available for day or weekend use. There is no child care available here, but the price of the lift tickets is very reasonable, and this is one of the best places in the Berkshires for beginning skiers.

Facilities: *Restrooms, cafeteria, ski shop, ski school, equipment rentals, lockers.*

Stone Hill Loop. Clark Art Institute, 225 South Street, Williamstown, MA 01267. Access from the west parking lot of the museum. Open daily, dawn to dusk. Free.

This cross-country "loop" circles Stone Hill with its lovely vistas of the nearby mountains. The neighborhood-type ski trail is perfect for a family outing.

SWIMMING

There are numerous places to swim in the Berkshires, from swimming holes to state forest preserves to private pools, but the following places offer some of the best kid-friendly water fun. Don't forget to check the state parks listings here for other swimming areas. Unless otherwise noted, each site charges an admission fee, and there are lifeguards on duty.

Green River. One mile west of Great Barrington, off Route 23. This is river swimming at its best, a beautiful site to sunbathe and swim. There are no lifeguards, however. You will see cars parked along the roadside on hot summer days. This is not a place for very young children.

Onota Lake. Onota Boulevard, Pittsfield, MA 01201. Open Memorial Day weekend through Labor Day, daily, noon to 8 P.M. The lake is supervised all day by lifeguards, and it's a nice place for a family outing.

Sands Springs Pool and Spa. Sand Springs Road, Williamstown, MA 01267; (413) 458-5205. Located off Route 7; call for directions. Open Memorial Day weekend through Labor Day, daily, 11 A.M. to 7 P.M. This is one of the oldest continuously running spas in the country, and it still soothes both adults and kids with its heated mineral waters. Facilities include a fifty-by-seventy-five-foot pool fed by natural mineral springs, along with a heated toddler pool with fountain, and oversized hot tubs fed by natural mineral springs.

Windsor Lake. Kemp Avenue, via East Main Street, North Adams, MA 01247. Open Memorial Day weekend through Labor Day, daily, 10 A.M. to 6 P.M. This lovely lake has a large swimming area and may be crowded on weekends, but there are always lifeguards on duty.

THEATER

Theater in the Berkshires is a summer event with professional entertainment, and children are particularly enchanted with many of the productions. Everything from comedy to Shakespeare is on tap, and it's a sure bet that if you are near a major town, you will be able to find a theater group in residence during July and August. The following theaters have all offered children's programming in the past, but schedules change each year, so call for an up-to-date program and schedule.

Barrington Stage Company. P.O. Box 946, Great Barrington, MA 01230; (413) 528-8806. From June through August enjoy award-winning musicals, comedies, and dramas in an air-conditioned state-of-the-art theater. They offer children's productions like *The Wizard of Oz,* and a three-week Kids Act program for those young people interested in the performing arts. There are reduced ticket rates for children and students.

Berkshire Theater Festival. East Main Street, Stockbridge, MA 01262; (413) 298-5536. This theater festival was founded in the nineteenth century and has been going strong ever since. In the past, stars such as Katharine Hepburn, James Cagney, and Montgomery Clift (he started here as a twelve-year-old actor) have appeared here. The wide variety of programs includes a children's theater, Theater Under the Tent, and a series of plays written by children. I recommend this theater for older children who are fascinated by the theatrical arts.

Jacob's Pillow Dance Festival. 358 George Carter Road, Becket, MA 01223; (413) 243-0745. Located on Route 20, eight miles east of the Lee Interchange on the Massachusetts Turnpike; watch for signs. Performances are scheduled from late June through late August, but call for a brochure. Admission. Group rates by advance reservation.

This is one of the best dance festivals in the country, and I recommend it for children interested in dance of any kind. A few performances each summer appeal to older children, as well as younger children who can sit through an entire performance. In the past, spectators have enjoyed the colorful costumes and vibrant music of the Magic of Creole troupe; Pilobolus, with its acrobatic and silly-shaped dances; and the Hubbard Street Dance Company, complete with tap, jazz, and ballet's fancy footwork. If you don't think the kids can sit through an entire show, watch a free performance of a work in progress, held a couple of hours before each scheduled main event at the Inside/Out Stage, or take the time to watch the dancers at work in the studios, some of which are open to the public.

Shakespeare & Company. 70 Kemble Street, Lenox, MA 01240; (413) 637-1199 or (413) 637-3353. There are two air-conditioned theaters presenting a variety of works by the Bard. Some of the plays will be enjoyed by older children. These productions are a wonderful way to introduce young people to Shakespeare.

Williamstown Theater Festival. Route 2, Williamstown, MA 01267; (413) 597-3399. This nationally renowned festival presents over two hundred performances every summer (mid-June through August), with some of them moving to Off-Broadway, and occasionally to Broadway. Offerings range from classics to modern plays, which are performed in two theaters. Ask for a schedule of their free outdoor theater performances and special program for youngsters called the Greylock Theater Project. A great way to spend a summer evening is watching one of their outdoor productions under the stars. Besides, the younger ones can fall asleep on the lawn when they get tired, and you can still enjoy the show.

Index